# LUTHER'S
# THREE TREATISES

# LUTHER'S THREE TREATISES

AN OPEN LETTER TO THE CHRISTIAN NOBILITY,
THE BABYLONIAN CAPTIVITY OF THE CHURCH
& THE FREEDOM OF THE CHRISTIAN

## MARTIN LUTHER

*Translated by C.M. Jacobs, A.T.W. Steinhaeuser,
and W.A. Lambert
with an Introduction by Steven Wedgeworth*

Published by Canon Press
P.O. Box 8729, Moscow, Idaho 83843
800.488.2034 | www.canonpress.com

Martin Luther, *Luther's Three Treatises: An Open Letter to the Christian Nobility, The Babylonian Captivity of the Church, and The Freedom of the Christian*
Translators: C.M. Jacobs (*Letter to the Christian Nobility*), A.T.W. Steinhaeuser (*Babylonian Captivity*), and W.A. Lambert (*Freedom of the Christian*)
Introduction by Steven Wedgeworth.

This Christian Heritage Series first edition copyright ©2021.
First published in 1520.

Cover design by James Engerbretson
Cover illustration by Forrest Dickison
Interior design by Valerie Anne Bost and James Engerbretson

Printed in the United States of America.

All rights reserved. No part of this publication may be reproduced, stored in a retrieval system, or transmitted in any form by any means, electronic, mechanical, photocopy, recording, or otherwise, without prior permission of the author, except as provided by USA copyright law.

21 22 23 24 25 26 27 28    10 9 8 7 6 5 4 3 2 1

# CONTENTS

Introduction *by Steven Wedgeworth* . . . . . . . . . . . . . . . . . . . . . . .i

## AN OPEN LETTER TO THE CHRISTIAN NOBILITY

Luther's Introduction . . . . . . . . . . . . . . . . . . . . . . . . . . . . . . . 3
I. The Three Walls of the Romanists . . . . . . . . . . . . . . . . . . . . . 7
II. Abuses to be Discussed in Councils . . . . . . . . . . . . . . . . . . . 20
III. Proposals for Reform . . . . . . . . . . . . . . . . . . . . . . . . . . . . 36

## THE BABYLONIAN CAPTIVITY OF THE CHURCH

Luther's Introduction . . . . . . . . . . . . . . . . . . . . . . . . . . . . . . 95
The Sacrament of the Bread . . . . . . . . . . . . . . . . . . . . . . . . . 103
The Sacrament of Baptism . . . . . . . . . . . . . . . . . . . . . . . . . . 142
The Sacrament of Penance . . . . . . . . . . . . . . . . . . . . . . . . . . 168
The Sacrament of Confirmation . . . . . . . . . . . . . . . . . . . . . . 179

The Sacrament of Marriage . . . . . . . . . . . . . . . . . . . . . . . . . . . 181

The Sacrament of Ordination. . . . . . . . . . . . . . . . . . . . . . . . . 196

The Sacrament of Extreme Unction. . . . . . . . . . . . . . . . . . . . 207

## ON THE FREEDOM OF THE CHRISTIAN

Letter to Pope Leo X . . . . . . . . . . . . . . . . . . . . . . . . . . . . . . . . 219

The Freedom of a Christian . . . . . . . . . . . . . . . . . . . . . . . . . . 230

# INTRODUCTION
*by Steven Wedgeworth*

Martin Luther is justly celebrated as the father of the Protestant Reformation, and laymen in Reformed and Evangelical churches are familiar with his general life story. His posting of the 95 Theses and heroic stance at the Diet of Worms are identity-forming narratives for even the broadest of evangelical traditions. And yet, for this same broad evangelical tradition, nearly all of Luther's books go unread. Even members of Reformed churches tend to read only *The Bondage of the Will*, being scared off from going any further by the later dogmatic controversies that separated Calvinists from Lutherans. When compared to the books by Calvin or the Puritans which line our shelves, Luther can hardly be found! It is therefore with eagerness and gratitude that I can introduce to you a small correction to this unfortunate state of affairs, a new edition of his famous "Three Treatises." This trilogy, made up of Luther's *Letter to the Christian Nobility*, *The Babylonian Captivity of the Church*, and *The Freedom of the Christian*, contains the heart of the Reformation. The themes and arguments found in these treatises are not the peculiar marks of one denominational tradition but are indeed the common possession of all magisterial Protestants.

These treatises were written in short succession, respectively in August, October, and November of 1520. This energetic season represents the crescendo of Luther's protest. He had published the 95 Theses three years earlier and immediately followed that with his *Sermon on Indulgence and Grace*. But in 1517, Luther still expected to receive a fair hearing from the Pope and perhaps even to win over the leadership of the Church and see his reforms implemented by them. The events of 1518 and 1519 would prove otherwise. In April of 1518, Luther participated in the *Heidelberg Disputation* on the authority of the pope. In October of that same year, he was summoned to Augsburg to be questioned by Cardinal Cajetan. It was there that Luther was forced to acknowledge that the current law of the church stood against his own position and was thus compelled to directly challenge the church with a direct appeal to the teaching of the Scriptures. Cajetan instructed Luther that there was no more room for dialogue. He simply had to recant. This Luther could not do, and so he continued to teach and promote his understanding of both salvation by grace alone and the role of the Scriptures as the only ultimate authority in faith and practice. He went on to debate John Eck in the 1519 Leipzig disputation, causing Pope Leo X to issue his bull *Exsurge Domine*, threatening Luther with excommunication. The Diet of Worms was still two years away. This was the setting in which Luther penned the three treatises.[1]

The themes of the three treatises can be summed up along the following lines: *Letter to the Christian Nobility* lays out Luther's doctrine of the priesthood of all believers, *The Babylonian Captivity of the Church* rejects the sacramental system of Roman Catholicism, particularly their doctrine of the sacrifice of the Mass, and *The Freedom of the Christian* proclaims the doctrine of justification by faith alone and its implications for the life of the Christian. Such a description only

---

1. For the history of this period, see Roland Bainton, *Here I Stand* (Abingdon Press: 1978), 71-141 and Heiko Oberman, *Luther: Man Between God and the Devil* (Yale University Press: 1989), 190-201, 356-358.

scratches the surface, however, as the themes of universal priesthood and justification by faith alone are mutually intertwined and appear in all three treatises. Many other important arguments are made in these three treatises, and the later developments of the Reformation can already be detected in an early form.

To say a bit more, the *Letter to the Christian Nobility* articulates Luther's view of a united Christian social polity. Contrary to the Roman Catholic notion of the two estates, divided between the spiritual clergy and the temporal laity (including all civic powers), Luther argues that all Christians are of the "spiritual estate." The difference is only a matter of office. Baptism consecrates all Christians to the true priesthood (p. 6),[2] and therefore all Christians have some claim to the maintenance of the church. This means that Christian magistrates can indeed make rules inspired by their faith, but even more, for Luther, these Christian magistrates can oversee the reformation of the church should the clergy fail to do so. This may surprise modern readers. We too-often assume that Luther was an early advocate of the separation of church and state. But as becomes clear in the *Letter to the Christian Nobility*, Luther's definition of "church" is more expansive. It includes princes, as well as pastors and bishops. If representing and governing a Christian community, the "state," for Luther, is itself a part of the "church." His main concern is rather to protect the church from the domination of certain clergy, particularly the bishop of Rome. Thus, Luther's own doctrine of "the two kingdoms" allows for a dramatic unity between church and state, as both bear the Christian name and both are called to be faithful to that name.

In the course of this argument, Luther also articulates a variant of *sola Scriptura*, the principle that the Scriptures function as the only unchangeable standard and that they can be faithfully interpreted even by the laity. Luther writes, "it is a wickedly invented fable, and

---

2. All references and quotes in this introduction are from this edition.

they cannot produce a letter in defense of it, that the interpretation of Scripture or the confirmation of its interpretation belongs to the pope alone. They have themselves usurped this power, and although they allege that this power was given to Peter when the keys were given to him, it is plain enough that the keys were not given to Peter alone, but to the whole community" (13). With such a statement, Luther highlights the Scriptural principle as well as the argument that the whole people of God, rather than a priestly caste, have a claim to the government of the church. This argument led to further reforms within the church, but it also led to more wide-ranging educational reforms across Europe, furthering the movement begun earlier by the Christian humanists of the Renaissance. Luther's theology greatly encouraged the growth of lay scholarship, and both Lutheran and Calvinistic countries would contribute to the proliferation of classical Christian schools and universities.

Some selections of the *Letter* may prove tedious reading. Luther lays out extensive and specific observations on the matters in need of reform. Some of these involve aspects of clerical discipline of 16th century life which are obsolete. But Luther also offers important and often controversial thoughts on Christian marriage, economics, educational curriculum, and even how it came to be that Germans governed the "Roman Empire." Readers will certainly want to prioritize the first section of the *Letter*, but there is much of interest for specialized studies throughout. Luther concludes this first treatise with a call for a council of the whole church, called not by the pope or the bishops but rather by the emperor on behalf of the whole Christian people.

*The Babylonian Captivity of the Church* is certainly the most explosive of the treatises. Luther argues that five of the seven sacraments of the day were no sacraments at all, and he dramatically redefines the meaning of the remaining two. Baptism, Luther states, is not a good work done by the person being baptized, nor is it a political claim over the baptized by the clergy. It is rather a word of promise from

God, a sign of the gospel itself. The Lord's Supper is not a sacrifice made by the priests to God but is, again, an offering of the promise of God's gracious covenant to the people. Both baptism and the Lord's Supper are only to be received by faith. This treatise entirely undermined the Roman Catholic understanding of salvation, and it rocked the church. When the celebrated humanist Erasmus read it, he said, "The breach is irreparable."[3]

It should be noted that Luther's doctrine of the "real presence" of Christ in the Supper is not the same as that of the Reformed, including Calvin. Even as he criticizes Rome's attempt to make transubstantiation binding dogma, Luther allows individuals to hold that view as their own private opinion. He prefers the view that both Christ's body and blood *and* bread and wine are present in the elements of the Supper. And yet, when Luther explains his larger theory of how the Supper works as a sign of the covenant and how it can only communicate saving grace as it is received by faith, Reformed readers will find themselves in complete agreement. The Supper, Luther argues, is a sign of a promise, much like the rainbow was a sign of God's promise to Noah and circumcision was a sign of God's promise to Abraham (125, 129-130). Here then is Luther's conclusion:

> We learn from this that in every promise of God two things are presented to us—the word and the sign—so that we are to understand the word to be the testament, but the sign to be the sacrament. Thus in the mass, the word of Christ is the testament, and the bread and wine are the sacrament. And as there is greater power in the word than in the sign, so there is greater power in the testament than in the sacrament, for a man can have and use the word, or testament, apart from the sign, or sacrament. "Believe," says Augustine, "and thou hast eaten." But what does

---

3. Bainton, 129.

one believe save the word of promise? Therefore I can hold mass every day, yea, every hour, for I can set the words of Christ before me, and with them refresh and strengthen my faith, as often as I choose. That is a truly spiritual eating and drinking. (130)

The third treatise, *The Freedom of the Christian*, is the most triumphant. At points, Luther is lyrical, even ecstatic, as he proclaims the benefits of justification by faith alone. Since acceptance by God is entirely a free gift, the Christian is *free from* the burden of the law and is *free to* do good works in the proper spirit. "A Christian man is a perfectly free lord of all, subject to none. A Christian man is a perfectly dutiful servant of all, subject to all" (237). This succinct formula safeguards Luther's theology from both legalism and antinomianism.

While Luther had repeatedly stated that the papacy was antichrist in his first two treatises, he begins this third one with a direct appeal to Leo X himself. Surprisingly, Luther calls him "most blessed father" (227) and showers praises upon him. Luther says that Leo is a "Daniel in Babylon." He has never thought evil of Leo's "person" (228). It is instead the "Roman Curia" and "See" that are to be blamed (229). Leo is a good man surrounded by wicked men who are using his name to promote their evil purposes. The wrath of God is being poured out upon this churchly apparatus, Luther says, but perhaps Leo will yet be persuaded by his argument. The following treatise, Luther says, is but his gift to the blessed Father.

Is such an argument truly to be accepted at face value? Probably not. There are hints of irony throughout, and Luther makes no effort to restate his theological position in a way that might still fit within the Roman Catholic system. It is possible that Luther is trying to cut through all of the church politics and make a direct evangelistic appeal to Leo. But it could also be the case that Luther, having now received Leo's bull threatening excommunication, was resigned to the reality of a definite split between the papacy and himself. Luther's kind tone here is less an attempt to persuade Leo than it is a content proclamation of the gospel as a sort of victory speech. The arguments have all run their course, at least with the papacy. Or perhaps Luther's true audience is the larger one of Christian Europe. He isn't so much speaking to Leo as he is to those Catholics (and other future readers) who have yet to fully make up their minds. Either way, the end result is the same—all that remains at this point is to preach Christ and Him crucified.

The three treatises are short reads, with even the longest still coming short of a hundred pages. It would not be unfair to refer to them as pamphlets. But they are surely the weightiest pamphlets in Christian history. With this new edition, their power continues to resound.

# AN OPEN LETTER TO THE CHRISTIAN NOBILITY

OF THE GERMAN NATION
CONCERNING THE REFORM
OF THE CHRISTIAN ESTATE

*Translated by C.M. Jacobs*

# LUTHER'S INTRODUCTION

To the esteemed and Reverend Master Nicholas Von Amsdorf, Licentiate of Holy Scripture and Canon at Wittenberg, my special and kind friend; Doctor Martin Luther.

The grace and peace of God be with thee, esteemed and reverend dear sir and friend.

The time to keep silence has passed and the time to speak is come, as saith Ecclesiastes (3:7). I have followed out our intention and brought together some matters touching the reform of the Christian Estate, to be laid before the Christian Nobility of the German Nation, in the hope that God may deign to help His Church through the efforts of the laity, since the clergy, to whom this task more properly belongs, have grown quite indifferent. I am sending the whole thing to your Reverence, that you may pass judgment on it and, if necessary, improve it.

I know full well that I shall not escape the charge of presumption in that I, a despised monk, venture to address such high and great estates on matters of such moment, and to give advice to people of such high intelligence. I shall offer no apologies, no matter who may chide me. Perchance I owe my God and the world another piece of folly, and I have now made up my mind honestly to pay that debt, if I can do so, and for once to become court-jester; if I fail, I still have one advantage—no one need buy me a cap or cut me my comb. It is a question which one will put the bells on the other. I must fulfill the proverb, "Whatever the world does, a monk must be in it, even if he has to be painted in." More than once a fool has spoken wisely, and wise men often have been arrant fools, as Paul says, "If any one will be wise, let him become a fool" (1 Cor. 3:18). Moreover since I am not only a fool, but also a sworn doctor of Holy Scripture, I am glad for the chance to fulfill my doctor's oath in this fool's way.

I pray you, make my excuses to the moderately intelligent, for I know not how to earn the grace and favor of the immoderately intelligent, though I have often sought to do so with great pains. Henceforth I neither desire nor regard their favor. God help us to seek not our own glory, but His alone! Amen.

Wittenberg, in the house of the Augustinians, on the Eve of St. John the Baptist (June 23rd), in the year fifteen hundred and twenty.

To His Most Illustrious and Mighty Imperial Majesty, and to the Christian Nobility of the German Nation, Doctor Martin Luther.

Grace and power from God, Most Illustrious Majesty, and most gracious and dear Lords.

It is not out of sheer frowardness or rashness that I, a single, poor man, have undertaken to address your worships. The distress and oppression which weigh down all the Estates of Christendom, especially of Germany, and which move not me alone, but everyone to cry out time and again, and to pray for help, have forced me even now to cry aloud that God may inspire someone with His Spirit to lend this suffering nation a helping hand. Ofttimes the councils have made some pretense at reformation, but their attempts have been cleverly hindered by the guile of certain men and things have gone from bad to worse. I now intend, by the help of God, to throw some light upon the wiles and wickedness of these men, to the end that when they are known, they may not henceforth be so hurtful and so great a hindrance. God has given us a noble youth to be our head and thereby has awakened great hopes of good in many hearts; wherefore it is meet that we should do our part and profitably use this time of grace.

In this whole matter the first and most important thing is that we take earnest heed not to enter on it trusting in great might or in human reason, even though all power in the world were ours; for God cannot and will not suffer a good work to be begun with trust in our own power or reason. Such works He crushes ruthlessly to earth, as it is written in the 33rd Psalm, "There is no king saved by the multitude of an host: a mighty man is not delivered by much strength" (v. 16). On this account, I fear, it came to pass of old that the good Emperors Frederick I and II, and many other German emperors were shamefully oppressed and trodden underfoot by the popes, although all the world feared them. It may be that they relied on their own might more than on God, and therefore they had to fall. In our own times, too, what was it that raised the bloodthirsty Pope Julius II to such heights? Nothing else, I fear, except that France, the Germans, and Venice relied upon themselves. The children of Benjamin slew 42,000 Israelites because the latter relied on their own strength.

That it may not so fare with us and our noble young Emperor Charles, we must be sure that in this matter we are dealing not with men, but with the princes of Hell, who can fill the world with war and bloodshed, but whom war and bloodshed do not overcome. We must go at this work despairing of physical force and humbly trusting God; we must seek God's help with earnest prayer, and fix our minds on nothing else than the misery and distress of suffering Christendom, without regard to the deserts of evil men. Otherwise we may start the game with great prospect of success, but when we get well into it the evil spirits will stir up such confusion that the whole world will swim in blood, and yet nothing will come of it. Let us act wisely, therefore, and in the fear of God. The more force we use, the greater our disaster if we do not act humbly and in God's fear. The popes and the Romans have hitherto been able, by the devil's help, to set kings at odds with one another, and they may well be able to do it again, if we proceed by our own might and cunning, without God's help.

# I. THE THREE WALLS OF THE ROMANISTS

The Romanists, with great adroitness, have built three walls about them, behind which they have hitherto defended themselves in such wise that no one has been able to reform them; and this has been the cause of terrible corruption throughout all Christendom.

First, when pressed by the temporal power, they have made decrees and said that the temporal power has no jurisdiction over them, but, on the other hand, that the spiritual is above the temporal power. Second, when the attempt is made to reprove them out of the Scriptures, they raise the objection that the interpretation of the Scriptures belongs to no one except the pope. Third, if threatened with a council, they answer with the fable that no one can call a council but the pope.

In this wise they have slyly stolen from us our three rods,[1] that they may go unpunished, and have ensconced themselves within the safe stronghold of these three walls, that they may practice all the knavery and wickedness which we now see. Even when they have been compelled to hold a council they have weakened its power in advance by previously binding the princes with an oath to let them

---

1. The three rods for the punishment of an evil pope.

remain as they are. Moreover, they have given the pope full authority over all the decisions of the council, so that it is all one whether there are many councils or no councils—except that they deceive us with puppet-shows and sham-battles. So terribly do they fear for their skin in a really free council! And they have intimidated kings and princes by making them believe it would be an offense against God not to obey them in all these knavish, crafty deceptions. Now God help us, and give us one of the trumpets with which the walls of Jericho were overthrown (Josh. 6:20), that we may blow down these walls of straw and paper, and may set free the Christian rods or the punishment of sin, bringing to light the craft and deceit of the devil, to the end that through punishment we may reform ourselves, and once more attain God's favor.

Against the first wall we will direct our first attack. It is pure invention that pope, bishops, priests and monks are to be called the "spiritual estate"; princes, lords, artisans, and farmers the temporal estate. That is indeed a fine bit of lying and hypocrisy. Yet no one should be frightened by it, and for this reason—namely, that all Christians are truly of the "spiritual estate," and there is among them no difference at all but that of office, as Paul says in 1 Corinthians 12. We are all one body, yet every member has its own work, whereby it serves every other, all because we have one baptism, one Gospel, one faith, and are all alike Christians (1 Cor. 12:12ff), for baptism, Gospel and faith alone make us "spiritual" and a Christian people.

But that a pope or a bishop anoints, confers tonsures, ordains, consecrates, or prescribes dress unlike that of the laity—this may make hypocrites and graven images,[2] but it never makes a Christian or "spiritual" man. Through baptism all of us are consecrated to the priesthood, as St. Peter says in 1 Peter 2, "Ye are a royal priesthood, a priestly kingdom," (1 Pet. 2:9) and the book of Revelation says, "Thou

---

2. Blockheads.

hast made us by thy blood to be priests and kings" (Rev. 5:10). For if we had no higher consecration than pope or bishop gives, the consecration by pope or bishop would never make a priest, nor might anyone either say Mass or preach a sermon or give absolution. Therefore when the bishop consecrates, it is the same thing as if he, in the place and stead of the whole congregation, all of whom have like power, were to take one out of their number and charge him to use this power for the others; just as though ten brothers, all king's sons and equal heirs, were to choose one of themselves to rule the inheritance or them all—they would all be kings and equal in power, though one of them would be charged with the duty of ruling.

To make it still clearer. If a little group of pious Christian laymen were taken captive and set down in a wilderness, and had among them no priest consecrated by a bishop, and if there in the wilderness they were to agree in choosing one of themselves, married or unmarried, and were to charge him with the office of baptizing, saying Mass, absolving and preaching, such a man would be as truly a priest as though all bishops and popes had consecrated him. That is why in cases of necessity anyone can baptize and give absolution, which would be impossible unless we were all priests. This great grace and power of baptism and of the Christian Estate they have well-nigh destroyed and caused us to forget through the canon law.[3] It was in the manner aforesaid that Christians in olden days chose from their number bishops and priests, who were afterwards confirmed by other bishops, without all the show which now obtains. It was thus that Saints Augustine, Ambrose, and Cyprian became bishops.

Since, then, the temporal authorities are baptized with same baptism and have the same faith and Gospel as we, we must grant that

---

3. The canon law, called by Luther throughout this treatise and elsewhere, the "spiritual law," is a general name for the decrees of councils ("canons" in the strict sense) and decisions of the popes ("decretals," "constitutions," etc.), promulgated by authority of the popes, and collected in the so-called *Corpus juris canonici*.

they are priests and bishops, and count their office one which has a proper and a useful place in the Christian community. For whoever comes out of the water of baptism can boast that he is already consecrated priest, bishop and pope, though it is not seemly that every one should exercise the office. Nay, just because we are all in like manner priests, no one must put himself forward and undertake, without our consent and election, to do what is in the power of all of us. For what is common to all, no one dare take upon himself without the will and the command of the community, and should it happen that one chosen for such an office were deposed for malfeasance, he would then be just what he was before he held office. Therefore a priest in Christendom is nothing else than an office-holder. While he is in office, he has precedence; holder when deposed, he is a peasant or a townsman like the rest. Beyond all doubt, then, a priest is no longer a priest when he is deposed. But now they have invented indelible characters,[4] and prate that a deposed priest is nevertheless something different from a mere layman. They even dream that a priest can never become a layman, or be anything else than a priest. All this is mere talk and man-made law.

From all this it follows that there is really no difference between laymen and priests, princes and bishops, "spirituals" and "temporals," as they call them, except that of office and work, but not of "estate"; or they are all of the same estate[5]—true priests, bishops and popes—

---

4. The *character indelebilis*, or "indelible mark," received authoritative statement in the bull Exultate Deo (1439). Eugenius IV, summing up the Decrees of the Council of Florence, says: "Among these sacraments there are three—baptism, confirmation, and orders—which indelibly impress upon the soul a character, i.e., a certain spiritual mark which distinguishes them from the rest" (Mirbt, *Quellen*, 2d ed., No. 150).

5. Medieval Christians divided people into three estates—the clergy, the nobility, and the commoners. Luther here is denying a spiritual distinction between the clergy and the laity.

though they are not all engaged in the same work, just as all priests and monks have not the same work. This is the teaching of St. Paul in Romans 12 (Rom. 12:4ff) and 1 Corinthians 12 (1 Cor. 12:12ff), and of St. Peter (1 Pet. 2:9), as I have said above, namely, that we are all one body of Christ, the Head, all members one of another. Christ has not two different bodies, one "temporal," the other "spiritual." He is one Head, and He has one body.

Therefore, just as those who are now called "spiritual"—priests, bishops or popes—are neither different from other Christians nor superior to them, except that they are charged with the administration of the Word of God and the sacraments, which is their work and office, so it is with the temporal authorities—they bear sword and rod with which to punish the evil and to protect the good (Rom. 13:4). A cobbler, a smith, a farmer—each has the work and office of his trade, and yet they are all alike consecrated priests and bishops, and every one by means of his own work or office must benefit and serve every other, that in this way many kinds of work may be done for the bodily and spiritual welfare of the community, even as all the members of the body serve one another.

See now how Christian is the decree which says that the temporal power is not above the "spiritual estate" and may not punish it.[6] That is as much as to say that the hand shall lend no aid when the eye is suffering. Is it not unnatural, not to say unchristian, that one member should not help another and prevent its destruction? Verily, the more honorable the member, the more should the others help. I say then, since the temporal power is ordained of God to punish evil-doers and to protect them that do well (Rom. 13), it should therefore be left free to perform its office without hindrance

---

6. The sharp distinction which the Roman Church drew between clergy and laity found practical application in the contention that the clergy should be exempt from the jurisdiction of the civil courts.

through the whole body of Christendom without respect of persons, whether it affect pope, bishops, priests, monks, nuns, or anybody else. For if the mere act that the temporal power has a smaller place among the Christian offices than has the office of preachers or confessors, or of the clergy, then the tailors, cobblers, masons, carpenters, pot-boys, tapsters, farmers, and all the secular tradesmen, should also be prevented from providing pope, bishops, priests, and monks with shoes, clothing, houses, meat, and drink, and from paying them tribute. But if these laymen are allowed to do their work unhindered, what do the Roman scribes mean by their laws with which they withdraw themselves from the jurisdiction of the temporal Christian power, only so that they may be free to do evil and to fulfill what St. Peter has said: "There shall be false teachers among you, and through covetousness shall they with feigned words make merchandise of you" (2 Pet. 2:1ff).

On this account the Christian temporal power should exercise its office without let or hindrance, regardless whether it be pope, bishop, or priest whom it affects; whoever is guilty, let him suffer. All that the canon law has said to the contrary is sheer invention of Roman presumption. For thus saith St. Paul to all Christians, "Let every soul (I take that to mean the pope's soul also) be subject unto the higher powers; for they bear not the sword in vain, but are the ministers of God for the punishment of evil-doers, and for the praise of them that do well" (Rom. 13:1, 4). St. Peter also says, "Submit yourselves unto every ordinance of man for the Lord's sake, for so is the will of God" (1 Pet. 2:13, 15). He has also prophesied that such men shall come as will despise the temporal authorities (1 Pet. 2:10), and this has come to pass through the canon law.

So then, I think this first paper-wall is overthrown, since the temporal power has become a member of the body of Christendom, and is of the "spiritual estate," though its work is of a temporal nature. Therefore its work should extend freely and without hindrance to all the members of the whole body; it should punish and use force whenever guilt deserves or necessity demands, without regard to pope, bishops and priests—let them hurl threats and bans as much as they will.

This is why guilty priests, if they are surrendered to the temporal law, are first deprived of their priestly dignities, which would not be right unless the temporal sword had previously had authority over them by divine right. Again, it is intolerable that in the canon law so much importance is attached to the freedom, life, and property of the clergy, as though the laity were not also as spiritual and as good Christians as they, or did not belong to the Church. Why are your life and limb, your property and honor so free, and mine not? <u>We are all alike Christians, and have baptism, faith, Spirit, and all things alike</u>. If a priest is killed, the land is laid under interdict[7]—why not when a peasant is killed? Whence comes this great distinction between those who are equally Christians? Only from human laws and inventions!

Moreover, it can be no good spirit who has invented such exceptions and granted to sin such license and impunity. For if we are bound to strive against the works and words of the evil spirit, and to drive him out in whatever way we can, as Christ commands and His apostles, ought we, then, to suffer it in silence when the pope or his underlings are bent on devilish words and works? Ought we for the sake of men to allow the suppression of divine commandments and truths which we have sworn in baptism to support with life and limb? Of a truth we should then have to answer for all the souls that would thereby be abandoned and led astray.

It must therefore have been the very prince of devils who said what is written in the canon law: "If the pope were so scandalously bad as

---

7. The interdict is the prohibition of the administration of the sacraments and of the other rites of the Church within the territory upon which the interdict is laid.

to lead souls in crowds to the devil, yet he could not be deposed."⁸ On this accursed and devilish foundation they build at Rome, and think that we should let all the world go to the devil, rather than resist their knavery. If the act that one man is set over others were sufficient reason why he should escape punishment, then no Christian could punish another, since Christ commands that every man shall esteem himself the lowliest and the least (Matt. 18:4).

Where sin is, there is no escape from punishment, as St. Gregory also writes that we are indeed all equal, but guilt puts us in subjection one to another. Now we see how they whom God and the apostles have made subject to the temporal sword deal with Christendom, depriving it of its liberty by their own wickedness, without warrant of Scripture. It is to be feared that this is a game of antichrist or a sign that he is close at hand.⁹

The second wall is still more flimsy and worthless. They wish to be the only masters of the Holy Scriptures even though in all their lives they learn nothing from them. They assume for themselves sole authority, and with insolent juggling of words they would persuade us that the pope, whether he be a bad man or a good man, cannot err in matters of faith; and yet they cannot prove a single letter of it. Hence it comes that so many heretical and unchristian, nay, even unnatural ordinances have a place in the canon law, of which, however, there is no present need to speak. For since they think that the Holy Spirit never leaves them, be they never so unlearned and wicked, they make bold to decree whatever they will. And if it were true, where would be the need or use of the Holy Scriptures? Let us burn them, and be satisfied with the unlearned lords at Rome, who are possessed of the Holy Spirit—although He can possess only

---

8. Decretum of Gratian, *Dist. XL*, c.6.
9. Calling the Pope the antichrist actually has a long history among medieval Reformers, and was not unique to Luther and Protestants.

pious hearts! Unless I had read it myself, I could not have believed that the devil would make such clumsy pretensions at Rome, and find a following.

But not to fight them with mere words, we will quote the Scriptures. St. Paul says in 1 Corinthians 14: "If to anyone something better is revealed, though he be sitting and listening to another in God's Word, then the first, who is speaking, shall hold his peace and give place" (1 Cor. 14:30). What would be the use of this commandment, if we were only to believe him who does the talking or who has the highest seat? Christ also says in John 6 that all Christians shall be taught of God (v. 45). Thus it may well happen that the pope and his followers are wicked men, and no true Christians, not taught of God, not having true understanding. On the other hand, an ordinary man may have true understanding. Why then should we not follow him? Has not the pope erred many times? Who would help Christendom when the pope errs, if we were not to believe another, who had the Scriptures on his side, more than the pope?

Therefore it is a wickedly invented fable, and they cannot produce a letter in defense of it, that the interpretation of Scripture or the confirmation of its interpretation belongs to the pope alone. They have themselves usurped this power, and although they allege that this power was given to Peter when the keys were given to him, it is plain enough that the keys were not given to Peter alone, but to the whole community. Moreover, the keys were not ordained for doctrine or government, but only for the binding and loosing of sin (John 20:22ff), and whatever further power of the keys they arrogate to themselves is mere invention. But Christ's word to Peter, "I have prayed for thee that thy faith fail not" (Luke 22:32) cannot be applied to the pope, since the majority of the popes have been without faith, as they must themselves confess. Besides, it is not only for Peter that Christ prayed, but also for all apostles and Christians, as He says in John 17, "Father, I pray for those whom Thou hast given Me, and not for these only, but for all who believe on Me through their word" (John 17:9, 20). Is not this clear enough?

Only think of it yourself! They must confess that there are pious Christians among us, who have the true faith, Spirit, understanding, word and mind of Christ. Why then should we reject their word and understanding and follow the pope, who has neither faith nor Spirit? That would be to deny the whole faith and the Christian Church. Moreover, it is not the pope alone who is always in the right, if the article of the Creed is correct: "I believe one holy Christian Church"; otherwise the prayer must run: "I believe in the pope at Rome," and so reduce the Christian Church to one man—which would be nothing else than a devilish and hellish error.

Besides, if we are all priests, as was said above, and all have one faith, one Gospel, one sacrament, why should we not also have the power to test and judge what is correct or incorrect in matters of faith? What becomes of the words of Paul in 1 Corinthians 2: "He that is spiritual judgeth all things, yet he himself is judged of no man," (1 Cor. 2:15) and 2 Corinthians 4: "We have all the same Spirit of faith" (2 Cor. 4:13)? Why, then, should not we perceive what squares with faith and what does not, as well as does an unbelieving pope?

All these and many other texts should make us bold and free, and we should not allow the Spirit of liberty, as Paul calls Him (2 Cor. 3:17), to be frightened off by the fabrications of the popes, but we ought to go boldly forward to test all that they do or leave undone, according to our interpretation of the Scriptures, which rests on faith, and compel them to follow not their own interpretation, but the one that is better. In the olden days Abraham had to listen to his Sarah, although she was in more complete subjection to him than we are to anyone on earth (Gen. 21:12). Balaam's ass, also, was wiser than the prophet himself (Num. 22:28). If God then spoke by an ass against a prophet, why should He not be able even now to speak by a righteous man against the pope? In like manner St. Paul rebukes St. Peter as a man in error (Gal. 2:11ff). Therefore it behooves every Christian to espouse the cause of the faith, to understand and defend it, and to rebuke all errors.

The third wall falls of itself when the first two are down. For when the pope acts contrary to the Pope and Scriptures, it is our duty to stand by the Scriptures, to reprove him, and to constrain him, according to the word of Christ in Matthew 18: "If thy brother sin against thee, go and tell it him between thee and him alone; if he hear thee not, then take with thee one or two more; if he hear them not, tell it to the Church; if he hear not the Church, consider him a heathen" (Matt. 18:15). Here every member is commanded to care for every other. How much rather should we do this when the member that does evil is a ruling member, and by his evil-doing is the cause of much harm and offense to the rest! But if I am to accuse him before the Church, I must bring the Church together.

They have no basis in Scripture or their contention that it belongs to the pope alone to call a council or confirm its actions, for this is based merely upon their own laws, which are valid only insofar as they are not injurious to Christendom or contrary to the laws of God. When the pope deserves punishment, such laws go out of force, since it is injurious to Christendom not to punish him by means of a council.

Thus we read in Acts 15 that it was not St. Peter who called the apostolic council, but the apostles and elders (Acts 15:6). If, then, that right had belonged to St. Peter alone, the council would not have been a Christian council, but a mere heretical gathering. Even the council of Nicaea—the most famous of all—was neither called nor confirmed by the bishop of Rome, but by the Emperor Constantine, and many other emperors after him did the like, yet these councils were the most Christian of all. But if the pope alone had the right to call councils, then all these councils must have been heretical. Moreover, if I consider the councils which the pope has created, I find that they have done nothing of special importance.

Therefore, when necessity demands, and the pope is an offense to Christendom, the first man who is able should, as a faithful member of the whole body, do what he can to bring about a truly free council. No one can do this so well as the temporal authorities, especially since now they also are fellow-Christians, fellow-priests, "fellow-spirituals," fellow-lords over all things, and whenever it is needful or profitable, they should give free course to the office and work in which God has put them above every man. Would it not be an unnatural thing if a fire broke out in a city, and everybody were to stand by and let it burn on and on and consume everything that could burn, for the sole reason that nobody had the authority of the burgomaster, or because, perhaps, the fire broke out in the burgomaster's house? In such case is it not the duty of every citizen to arouse and call the rest? How much more should this be done in the spiritual city of Christ, if a fire of offense breaks out, whether in the papal government, or anywhere else? In the same way, if the enemy attacks a city, he who first rouses the others deserves honor and thanks; why then should he not deserve honor who makes known the presence of the enemy from Hell, and awakens the Christians, and calls them together?

But all their boasts of an authority which dare not be opposed amount to nothing after all. No one in Christendom has authority to do injury, or to forbid the resisting of injury. There is no authority in the Church save for edification. Therefore, if the pope were to use his authority to prevent the calling of a free council, and thus became a hindrance to the edification of the Church, we should have regard neither for him nor for his authority, and if he were to hurl his bans and thunderbolts, we should despise his conduct as that of a madman, and relying on God, hurl back the ban on him, and coerce him as best we could. For this presumptuous authority of his is nothing; he has no such authority, and he is quickly overthrown by a text of Scripture, for Paul says to the Corinthians, "God has given us authority not for the destruction, but for the edification of Christendom" (2 Cor. 10:8). Who is ready to overleap this text? It is only the power of the devil and of antichrist which resists the things that serve for the edification of Christendom; it is therefore in no wise to be obeyed, but is to be opposed with life and goods and all our strength.

Even though a miracle were to be done in the pope's behalf against the temporal powers, or though someone were to be stricken with a plague—which they boast has sometimes happened—it should be considered only the work of the devil, because of the weakness of our faith in God. Christ Himself prophesied in Matthew 24: "There shall come in my name false christs and false prophets, and do signs and wonders, so as to deceive even the elect" (Matt. 24:24) and Paul says in 2 Thessalonians 2 that antichrist shall, through the power of Satan, be mighty in lying wonders (2 Thes. 2:9). Let us, therefore, hold fast to this: no Christian authority can do anything against Christ, as St. Paul says, "We can do nothing against Christ, but for Christ" (2 Cor. 13:8). Whatever does aught against Christ is the power of antichrist and of the devil, even though it were to rain and hail wonders and plagues. Wonders and plagues prove nothing, especially in these last evil times, for which all the Scriptures prophesy false wonders (2 Thes. 2:9ff). Therefore we must cling with firm faith to the words of God, and then the devil will cease from wonders.

Thus I hope that the false, lying terror with which the Romans have this long time made our conscience timid and stupid has been allayed. They, like all of us, are subject to the temporal sword; they have no power to interpret the Scriptures by mere authority, without learning; they have no authority to prevent a council or, in sheer wantonness to pledge it, bind it, or take away its liberty; but if they do this, they are in truth the communion of antichrist and of the devil, and have nothing at all of Christ except the name.

# II. ABUSES TO BE DISCUSSED IN COUNCILS

We shall now look at the matters which should be discussed in the councils, and with which popes, cardinals, bishops and all the scholars ought properly to be occupied day and night if they loved Christ and His Church. But if they neglect this duty, then let the laity and the temporal authorities see to it, regardless of bans and thunders, for an unjust ban is better than ten just releases, and an unjust release worse than ten just bans. Let us, therefore, awake, dear Germans, and fear God rather than men (Acts 5:29), that we may not share the fate of all the poor souls who are so lamentably lost through the shameful and devilish rule of the Romans, in which the devil daily takes a larger and larger place—if, indeed, it were possible that such a hellish rule could grow worse, a thing I can neither conceive nor believe.

1. It is a horrible and frightful thing that the ruler of Christendom, who boasts himself vicar of Christ and successor of St. Peter, lives in such worldly splendor that in this regard no king nor emperor can equal or approach him, and that he who claims the title of "most holy" and "most spiritual" is more worldly than the world itself. He wears a triple crown, when the greatest kings wear but a single crown; if that is like the poverty of Christ and of St. Peter, then it is a new kind of

likeness. When a word is said against it, they cry out "Heresy!" but that is because they do not wish to hear how unchristian and ungodly such a practice is. I think, however, that if the pope were with tears to pray to God, he would have to lay aside these crowns, for our God can suffer no pride, and his office is nothing else than this—daily to weep and pray for Christendom, and to set an example of all humility.

However that may be, this splendor of his is an offense, and the pope is bound on his soul's salvation to lay it aside, because St. Paul says, "Abstain from all outward shows, which give offense" (1 Thes. 5:21) and in Romans 12, "We should provide good, not only in the sight of God, but also in the sight of all men" (v. 17). An ordinary bishop's crown would be enough for the pope; he should be greater than others in wisdom and holiness, and leave the crown of pride to antichrist, as did his predecessors several centuries ago. They say he is a lord of the world; that is a lie, for Christ, whose vicar and officer he boasts himself to be, said before Pilate, "My kingdom is not of this world" (John 17:36) and no vicar's rule can go beyond his lord's. Moreover he is not the vicar of the glorified, but of the crucified Christ, as Paul says, "I was willing to know nothing among you save Christ, and Him only as the Crucified" (1 Cor. 2:2); and in Philippians 2, "So think of yourselves as ye see in Christ, who emptied Himself and took upon Him the appearance of a servant" (Phil. 2:5); and again in 1 Corinthians 1, "We preach Christ, the Crucified" (1 Cor. 1:23). Now they make the pope a vicar of the glorified Christ in Heaven, and some of them have allowed the devil to rule them so completely that they have maintained that the pope is above the angels in Heaven and has authority over them. These are indeed the very works of the very antichrist.

2. What is the use in Christendom of those people who are called the cardinals? I shall tell you. Italy and Germany have many rich monasteries, foundations, benefices, and livings. No better way has been discovered to bring all these to Rome than by creating cardinals

and giving them the bishoprics, monasteries and prelacies, and so overthrowing the worship of God. For this reason we now see Italy a very wilderness—monasteries in ruins, bishoprics devoured, the prelacies and the revenues of all the churches drawn to Rome, cities decayed, land and people laid waste, because there is no more worship or preaching. Why? The cardinals must have the income. No Turk could have so devastated Italy and suppressed the worship of God.

Now that Italy is sucked dry, they come into Germany, and begin oh, so gently. But let us beware, for Germany will soon become like Italy. Already we have some cardinals; what the Romans seek by that the "drunken Germans" are not to understand until we have not a bishopric, a monastery, a living, a benefice, a heller or a pfennig left.[10] antichrist must take the treasures of the earth, as it was prophesied (Dan. 11:39, 43). So it goes on. They skim the cream of the bishoprics, monasteries, and benefices, and because they do not yet venture to turn them all to shameful use, as they have done in Italy, they only practice for the present the sacred trickery of coupling together ten or twenty prelacies and taking a yearly portion from each of them, so as to make a tidy sum after all. The priory of Würzburg yields a thousand gulden;[11] that of Bamberg, something; Mainz, Trier and the others, something more; and so from one to ten thousand gulden might be got together, in order that a cardinal might live at Rome like a rich king: 'After they are used to this, we will create thirty or forty cardinals in a day, and give to one Mount St. Michael at Bamberg[12] and the bishopric of Würzburg to boot, hang on to these a few rich livings, until churches and cities are waste, and after that we will say, "We are Christ's vicars and shepherds of Christ's sheep; the mad, drunken Germans must put up with it."'

---

10. The heller and pfennig were German coins.
11. Another German coin.
12. A monastery.

I advise, however, that the number of the cardinals be reduced, or that the pope be made to keep them at his own expense. Twelve of them would be more than enough, and each of them might have an income of a thousand gulden a year. How comes it that we Germans must put up with such robbery and such extortion of our property, at the hands of the pope? If the kingdom of France has prevented it, why do we Germans let them make such fools and apes of us? It would all be more bearable if in this way they only stole our property, but they lay waste the churches and rob Christ's sheep of their pious shepherds, and destroy the worship and the Word of God. Even if there were not a single cardinal, the Church would not go under. As it is they do nothing for the good of Christendom; they only wrangle about the incomes of bishoprics and prelacies, and that any robber could do.

3. If ninety-nine parts of the papal court were done away and only the hundredth part allowed to remain, it would still be large enough to give decisions in matters of faith. Now, however, there is such a swarm of vermin yonder in Rome, all boasting that they are "papal," that there was nothing like it in Babylon. There are more than three thousand papal secretaries alone, who will count the other offices, when they are so many that they scarcely can be counted? And they all lie in wait for the prebends and benefices of Germany as wolves lie in wait for the sheep. I believe that Germany now gives much more to the pope at Rome than it gave in former times to the emperors. Indeed, some estimate that every year more than three hundred thousand gulden find their way from Germany to Rome, quite uselessly and fruitlessly; we get nothing for it but scorn and contempt. And yet we wonder that princes, nobles, cities, endowments, land, and people are impoverished! We should rather wonder that we still have anything to eat!

Since we here come to the heart of the matter, we will pause a little, and let it be seen that the Germans are not quite such gross fools as not to note or understand the sharp practices of the Romans. I do not now complain that at Rome God's command and Christian law are despised, for such is the state of Christendom, and particularly of Rome, that we may not now complain of such high matters. Nor do I complain that natural or temporal law and reason count for nothing. The case is worse even than that. I complain that they do not keep their own self-devised canon law, though it is, to be sure, mere tyranny, avarice and temporal splendor, rather than law. Let us see!

In former times German emperors and princes permitted the pope to receive the annates from all the benefices of the German nation, i.e., the half of the first year's revenues from each benefice.[13] This permission was given, however, in order that by means of these large sums of money, the pope might accumulate a treasure for fighting against the Turks and infidels in defense of Christendom, so that the burden of the war might not rest too heavily upon the nobility, but that the clergy also should contribute something toward it. This single-hearted devotion of the German nation the popes have so used, that they who have received this money for more than a hundred years have now made of it a binding tax and tribute, and have not only accumulated no treasure, but have used the money to endow many orders and offices at Rome, and to provide these offices with salaries as though the annates were a fixed rent.

When they pretend that they are about to fight against the Turks, they send out emissaries to gather money. Ofttimes they issue an indulgence on this same pretext of fighting the Turks, for they think the mad Germans are forever to remain utter and arrant fools, give them money without end, and satisfy their unspeakable greed, though we clearly see that not a heller of the annates or of the indulgence-money or of all the rest is used against the Turks, but all of it goes into the bottomless bag. They lie and deceive, make laws and make agreements

---

13. Annates was a payment from a church to the authorities.

with us, and they do not intend to keep any of them. All this must be counted the work of Christ and St. Peter!

Now, in this matter the German nation, bishops and princes, should consider that they too are Christians, and should protect the people, whom they are set to rule and guard in things temporal and spiritual, against these ravening wolves who in sheep's clothing pretend to be shepherds and rulers, and since the annates are so shamefully abused and the stipulated conditions are not fulfilled, they should not permit their land and people to be so sadly robbed and ruined against all justice, but by a law of the emperor or of the whole nation, they should either keep the annates at home or else abolish them again. For since the Romans do not keep the terms of the agreement, they have no right to the annates. Therefore the bishops and princes are bound to punish or prevent such thievery and robbery, as the law requires.

In this they should aid the pope and support him, or he is perchance too weak to prevent such an abuse all by himself, or if he were to undertake to defend and maintain this practice, they ought resist him and fight against him as against a wolf and a tyrant, for he has no authority to do or to defend evil. Moreover, if it were ever desired to accumulate such a treasure against the Turks, we ought in the future to have sense enough to see that the German nation would be a better custodian for it than the pope, for the German nation has people enough for the fighting, if only the money is forthcoming. It is with the annates as it has been with many another Roman pretense.

Again, the year has been so divided between the pope and the ruling bishops and canons, that the pope has six months in the year—every other month—in which to bestow the benefices which all vacate in his months. In this way almost all the benefices are absorbed by Rome, especially the very best livings and dignities, and when once they fall into the hands of Rome, they never come out of them again, though a vacancy may never again occur in the pope's month. Thus the canons are cheated. This is a genuine robbery, which intends to let nothing escape. Therefore it is high time that the "papal months" be altogether abolished, and that everything which they have brought to Rome be taken back again. For the princes and nobles should take measures that the stolen goods be returned, the thieves punished, and those who have abused privilege be deprived of privilege. If it is binding and valid when the pope on the day after his election makes in his chancery rules and laws whereby our foundations and livings are robbed—a thing which he has no right to do—then it should be still more valid if the Emperor Charles[14] on the day after his coronation were to make rules and laws that not another benefice or living in all Germany shall be allowed to come into the hands of Rome by means of the "papal months," and that the livings which have already fallen into its hands shall be released, and redeemed from the Roman robbers, for he has this right by virtue of his office and his sword.

But now the Roman See of avarice and robbery has not been able to await the time when all the benefices, one after another, would by the "papal months" come into its power, but hastens, with insatiable appetite, to get possession of them all as speedily as possible, and so besides the annates and the "months" it has hit upon a device by which benefices and livings all to Rome in three ways:

First, if anyone who holds a free living dies at Rome or on the way to Rome, his living must forever belong to the Roman—I should rather say the robbing—See, and yet they will not be called robbers, though they are guilty of such robbery as no one has ever heard or read about.

Second, in case any one who belongs to the household of the pope or of the cardinals holds or takes over a benefice, or in case one who already holds a benefice afterwards enters the "household" of the

---

14. Charles V ruled over the Holy Roman Empire from 1519 to 1556, and he would eventually preside over the Diet of Worms at which Luther made his defense. At this point there was a possibility that he would support the Reformation, but he chose to support the more traditional religion.

pope or of a cardinal. But who can count the "household" of the pope and of the cardinals, when the pope, if he only goes on a pleasure-ride, takes with him three or four thousand mule-riders, eclipsing all emperors and kings? Christ and St. Peter went on foot in order that their vicars might have the more pomp and splendor. Now avarice has cleverly thought out another scheme, and brings it to pass that even here many have the name of "papal servant," just as though they were in Rome, all in order that in every place the mere rascally little word "papal servant" may bring all benefices to Rome and tie them fast there forever. Are not these vexatious and devilish inventions? Let us beware! Soon Mainz, Magdeburg, and Halberstadt will gently pass into the hands of Rome, and the cardinalate will be paid for dearly enough. 'Afterwards we will make all the German bishops cardinals so that there will be nothing left outside.'

Third, when a contest has started at Rome over a benefice. This I hold to be almost the commonest and widest road for bringing livings to Rome. For when there is no contest at home, unnumbered knaves will be found at Rome to dig up contests out of the earth and assail livings at their will. Thus many a good priest has to lose his living, or settle the contest for a time by the payment of a sum of money. Such a living rightly or wrongly contested must also belong forever to the Roman See. It would be no wonder if God were to rain from Heaven fire and brimstone and to sink Rome in the abyss, as He did Sodom and Gomorrah of old (Gen. 19:24). Why should there be a pope in Christendom, if his power is used or nothing else than such archknavery, and if he protects and practices it? O noble Princes and Lords, how long will ye leave your lands and people naked to these ravening wolves!

Since even these practices were not enough, and Avarice grew impatient at the long time it took to get hold of all the bishoprics, therefore my Lord Avarice devised the fiction that the bishoprics should be nominally abroad, but that their land and soil should be at Rome, and no bishop can be confirmed unless with a great sum of money he buy the pallium,[15] and bind himself with terrible oaths to be the pope's servant. This is the reason that no bishop ventures to act against the pope. That, too, is what the Romans were seeking when they imposed the oath, and thus the very richest bishoprics have fallen into debt and ruin. Mainz pays, as I hear, 20,000 gulden. These be your Romans! To be sure they decreed of old in the canon law that the pallium should be bestowed gratis, the number of papal servants diminished, the contests lessened, the chapters[16] and bishops allowed their liberty. But this did not bring in money, and so they turned over a new leaf, and all authority was taken from the bishops and chapters; they are made ciphers,[17] and have no office nor authority nor work, but everything is ruled by the archknaves at Rome; soon they will have in hand even the office of sexton[18] and bell-ringer in all the churches. All contests are brought to Rome, and by authority of the pope everyone does as he likes.

What happened this very year? The Bishop of Strasbourg wished to govern his chapter properly and to institute reforms in worship, and with this end in view made certain godly and Christian regulations. But my dear Lord Pope and the Holy Roman See, at the instigation of the priests, overthrew and altogether condemned this holy and spiritual ordinance. This is called "feeding the sheep of Christ" (John 20:15-17)! Thus priests are to be encouraged against their own bishop, and their disobedience to divine law is to be protected! Antichrist himself, I hope, will not dare to put God to such open shame! There you have your pope after your own heart! Why did he do this? Ah! If one church were reformed, it would be a dangerous departure; Rome's

---

15. The pallium is a woolen shoulder-cape which is the emblem of the archbishop's office, and which must be secured from Rome.
16. A group of clergy that advised a bishop.
17. Zeroes: they mean nothing anymore.
18. Someone who took care of a church.

turn too might come! Therefore it were better that no priest should be left at peace with another, that kings and princes should be set at odds, as has been the custom heretofore, and the world filled with the blood of Christians, only so the concord of Christians should not trouble the Holy Roman See with a reformation.

So far we have been getting an idea of how they deal with livings which become vacant. But for tender-hearted Avarice the vacancies are too few, and so he brings his foresight to bear upon the benefices which are still occupied by their incumbents, so that they must be unfilled, even though they are not unfilled. And this he does in many ways, as follows:

First, he lies in wait for fat prebends[19] or bishoprics which are held by an old or a sick man, or by one with an alleged disability. To such an incumbent, without his desire or consent, the Holy See gives a coadjutor, i.e., an "assistant," or the coadjutor's benefit, because he is a "papal servant," or has paid for the position, or has earned it by some other ignoble service to Rome. In this case the rights of the chapter or the rights of him who has the bestowal of the living must be surrendered, and the whole thing all into the hands of Rome.

Second, there is a little word "commend," by which the pope entrusts the keeping of a rich, fat monastery or church to a cardinal or to another of his people, just as though I were to give you a hundred gulden to keep. This is not called the giving or bestowing of the monastery nor even its destruction, or the abolition of the worship of God, but only "giving it into keeping"; not that he to whom it is entrusted is to care for it, or build it up, but he is to drive out the incumbent, to receive the goods and revenues, and to install some apostate, renegade monk who accepts five or six gulden a year and sits in the church all day selling pictures and images to the pilgrims, so that henceforth neither prayers nor Masses are said there. If this

---

19. The revenue of a church.

were to be called destroying monasteries and abolishing the worship of God, then the pope would have to be called a destroyer of Christendom and an abolisher of God's worship, because this is his constant practice. That would be a hard saying at Rome, and so we must call it a commend or a "command to take charge" of the monastery. The pope can every year make commends out of one or more of these monasteries, a single one of which may have an income of more than six thousand gulden. This is the way the Romans increase the worship of God and preserve the monasteries. The Germans also are beginning to find it out.

Third, there are some benefices which they call *incompatibilia*, and which, according to the ordinances of the canon law, cannot be held by one man at the same time, as for instance, two parishes, two bishoprics and the like. In these cases the Holy Roman See of avarice evades the canon law by making "glosses," called *unio* and *incorporatio*, i.e., by "incorporating" many *incompatibilia*, so that each becomes a part of every other and all of them together are looked upon as though they were one living. They are then no longer "incompatible," and the holy canon law is satisfied, in that it is no longer binding, except upon those who do not buy these "glosses" from the pope or his *datarius*. The *unio*, i.e., "uniting," is of the same nature. The pope binds many such benefices together like a bundle of sticks, and by virtue of this bond they are all regarded as one benefice. So there is at Rome one harlot who holds, for himself alone, twenty-two parishes, seven priories and forty-four canonries besides—all by the help of that masterly "gloss," which holds that this is not illegal. What cardinals and other prelates have, everyone may imagine for himself. In this way the Germans are to have their purses eased and their itch cured.

Another of the "glosses" is the *administratio*, i.e., a man may have beside his bishopric, an abbacy or a dignity, and possess all the property which goes with it, only he has no other title than that of "administrator." For at Rome it is sufficient that words are changed and not the things they stand for; as though I were to teach that a bawdy-house keeper should have the name of "burgomaster's wife," and yet continue to ply her trade. This kind of Roman rule St. Peter foretold when he said, in 2 Peter 2: "There shall come false teachers, who in covetousness, with feigned words, shall make merchandise of you, to get their gains" (v. 3).

Again, dear Roman Avarice has invented the custom of selling and bestowing livings to such advantage that the seller or disposer retains reversionary rights upon them: to wit, if the incumbent dies, the benefice freely reverts to him who previously sold, bestowed or surrendered it. In this way they have made livings hereditary property, so that henceforth no one can come into possession of them, except the man to whom the seller is willing to dispose of them, or to whom he bequeaths his rights at death. Besides, there are many who transfer to others the mere title to a benefice from which those who get the title derive not a heller of income. It is now an old custom, too, to give another man a benefice and to reserve a certain part out of the annual revenue. In olden times this was simony.[20] Of these things there are so many more that they cannot all be counted. They treat livings more shamefully than the heathen beneath the cross treated the garments of Christ (Matt. 27:35).

Yet all that has hitherto been said is ancient history and an everyday occurrence at Rome. Avarice has devised one thing more, which may, I hope, be his last morsel, and choke him. The pope has a noble little device called *pectoralis reservatio*, i.e., his "mental reservation," and *proprius motus*, i.e., the "arbitrary will of his authority." It goes like this. When one man has gotten a benefice at Rome, and the appointment has been regularly signed and sealed, according to custom, and

---

20. Simony was the practice of selling bishoprics, named after Simon Magus who tried to buy the Holy Spirit from Peter (Acts 8:9-25).

there comes another who brings money or has laid the pope under obligation in some other way, of which we will not speak, and desires of the pope the same benefice, then the pope takes it from the first man and gives it to the second. If it is said that this is unjust, then the Most Holy Father must make some excuse, that he may not be reproved for doing such open violence to the law, and says that in his mind and heart he had reserved that benefice to himself and his own plenary disposal, although he had never before in his whole life either thought or heard of it. Thus he has now found a little "gloss" by which he can, in his own person, lie and deceive, and make a fool and an ape of anybody—all this he does brazenly and openly, and yet he wishes to be the head of Christendom, though with his open lies he lets the Evil Spirit rule him.

This arbitrary will and lying "reservation" of the pope creates in Rome a state of affairs which is unspeakable. There is buying, selling, bartering, trading, trafficking, lying, deceiving, robbing, stealing, luxury, harlotry, knavery, and every sort of contempt of God, and even the rule of antichrist could not be more scandalous. Venice, Antwerp, Cairo are nothing compared to this fair which is held at Rome and the business which is done there, except that in those other places they still observe right and reason. At Rome everything goes as the devil wills, and out of this ocean like virtue flows into all the world. Is it a wonder that such people fear a reformation and a free council, and prefer to set all kings and princes at enmity rather than have them unite and bring about a council? Who could bear to have such knavery exposed if it were his own?

Finally, for all this noble commerce the pope has built a warehouse, namely, the house of the *datarius*, in Rome. Thither all must come who deal after this fashion in benefices and livings. From him they must buy their "glosses" and get the power to practice such archknavery. In former times Rome was generous, and then justice had either to be bought or else suppressed with money, but now she has become exorbitant, and no one dare be a knave unless with a great sum he has first bought the right. If that is not a brothel above all the brothels one can imagine, then I do not know what brothel means.

If you have money in this house, then you can come by all the things I have said; and not only these, but all sorts of usury are here made honest, and the possession of all property acquired by theft or robbery is legalized. Here vows are dissolved; here monks are granted liberty to leave their orders; here marriage is on sale to the clergy; here bastards can become legitimate; here all dishonor and shame can come to honor; all ill-repute and stigma of evil are here knighted and ennobled; here is permitted the marriage which is within the forbidden degrees or has some other defect. Oh! What a taxing and a robbing rules there! It looks as though all the laws of the Church were made for one purpose only—to be nothing but so many money-snares, from which a man must extricate himself if he would be a Christian. Yea, here the devil becomes a saint, and a god to boot. What Heaven and earth cannot, that this house can do! They call them *compositiones*! "Compositions" indeed! rather "confusions"! Oh, what a modest tax is the Rhine-toll, compared with the tribute taken by this holy house!

Let no one accuse me of exaggeration! It is all so open that even at Rome they must confess the evil to be greater and more terrible than anyone can say. I have not yet stirred up the hell-broth of personal vices, nor do I intend to do so. I speak of things which are common talk, and yet I have not words to tell them all. The bishops, the priests, and, above all, the doctors in the universities who draw their salaries for this purpose should have done their duty and with common consent have written and cried out against these things; but they have done the very opposite.

There remains one last word, and I must say that too. Since boundless avarice has not been satisfied with all these treasures, which three great kings might well think sufficient, he now begins to transfer this trade and sell it to Fugger of Augsburg,[21] so that the lending and trading and buying of bishoprics and benefices, and the driving of bargains in spiritual goods has now come to the right place, and spiritual and temporal goods have become one business. And now I would fain hear of a mind so lofty that it could imagine what this Roman avarice might yet be able to do and has not already done, unless Fugger were to transfer or sell this combination of two lines of business to somebody else. I believe we have reached the limit.

As for what they have stolen in all lands and still steal and extort, by means of indulgences, bulls, letters of confession, "butter-letters"[22] and other *confessionalia*—all this I consider mere patchwork, and like casting a single devil more into Hell. Not that they bring in little, for a mighty king could well support himself on their returns, but they are not to be compared with the streams of treasure above mentioned. I shall also say nothing at present of how this indulgence money has been applied. Another time I shall inquire about that, for Campoflore and Belvidere and certain other places probably know something about it.

Since, then, such devilish rule is not only open robbery and deceit, and the tyranny of the gates of Hell, but also ruins Christendom in body and soul, it is our duty to use all diligence in protecting Christendom against such misery and destruction. If we would fight the Turks, let us make a beginning here, where they are at their worst. If we justly hang thieves and behead robbers, why should we let Roman avarice go free? For he is the greatest thief and robber that has come or can come into the world, and all in the holy name of Christ and of St. Peter! Who can longer endure it or keep silence? Almost

---

21. The Fuggers of Augsburg were a family of bankers, who had their tentacles in practically all the major events of Europe, including the indulgences which Luther protested against.
22. Certificates granting their possessor permission to eat milk, eggs, butter and cheese on fast days.

everything he owns has been gotten by theft and robbery; that is the truth, and all history shows it. The pope never got by purchase such great properties that from his offices alone he can raise about a million ducats, not to mention the mines of treasure named above and the income of his lands. Nor did it come to him by inheritance from Christ or from St. Peter; no one ever loaned it or gave it to him; it has not become his by virtue of immemorial use and enjoyment. Tell me, then, whence he can have it? Learn from this what they have in mind when they send out legates to collect money or use against the Turks.

# III. PROPOSALS FOR REFORM

Now, although I am too small a man to make propositions which might effect a reform in this dreadful state of things, nevertheless I may as well sing my fool's song to the end, and say, so far as I am able, what could and should be done by the temporal authorities or by a general council.

1. Every prince, nobleman and city should boldly forbid their subjects to pay the annates to Rome and should abolish them entirely, for the pope has broken the compact, and made the annates a robbery, to the injury and shame of the whole German nation. He gives them to his friends, sells them for large amounts of money, and uses them to endow offices. He has thus lost his right to them, and deserves punishment. It is therefore the duty of the temporal authorities to protect the innocent and prevent injustice, as Paul teaches in Romans 13, and St. Peter in 1 Peter 2:14, and even the canon law in (*Filiis vel nepotibus*, case 16, question 7). Thus it has come about that men are saying to the pope and his followers, *Tu ora*, "Thou shalt pray"; to the emperor and his followers, *Tu protege*, "Thou shalt guard"; to the common man, *Tu labora*, "Thou shalt work." Not, however, as though everyone were not to pray, guard, and work, for the man who is diligent in his calling is praying, guarding, and working in all that he does, but everyone should have his own especial task.

2. Since the pope with his Roman practices—his commends, adjutories, reservations, *gratiae expectativae*,[23] papal months, incorporations, unions, *pallia*,[24] rules in chancery,[25] and such like knavery—usurps all the German foundations without authority and right, and gives and sells them to foreigners at Rome, who do nothing in German lands to earn them; and since he thereby robs the ordinaries[26] of their rights, makes the bishops mere ciphers and figure-heads, and acts against his own canon law, against nature and against reason, until it has finally gone so far that out of sheer avarice the livings and benefices are sold to gross, ignorant asses and knaves at Rome, while pious and learned folk have no profit of their wisdom and merit, so that the poor people of the German nation have to go without good and learned prelates and thus go to ruin:

Therefore, the Christian nobility should set itself against the pope as against a common enemy and destroyer of Christendom, and should do this for the salvation of the poor souls who must go to ruin through his tyranny. They should ordain, order, and decree that henceforth no benefice shall be drawn into the hands of Rome, and that hereafter no appointment shall be obtained there in any manner whatsoever, but that the benefices shall be brought out and kept out from under this tyrannical authority; and they should restore to the ordinaries the right and office of ordering these benefices in the German nation as best they may. And if a harlot were to come from Rome, he should receive a strict command either to keep his distance, or else to jump into the Rhine or the nearest river, and take the Roman ban, with its seals and letters, to a cold bath. They would then take note at Rome that the Germans are not always mad and drunken, but that they have really become Christians,

23. Promises to bestow on certain persons livings not yet vacant.
24. Wooden shoulder-capes bestowed on bishops as a sign of their office.
25. Rules for the transaction of papal business.
26. The local church authorities.

and intend to permit no longer the mockery and scorn of the holy name of Christ, under which all this knavery and destruction of souls goes on, but have more regard to God and His glory than to the authority of men.

3. An imperial law should be issued, that no bishop's cloak and no confirmation of any dignity whatsoever shall henceforth be secured from Rome, but that the Church ordinance of the most holy and most famous Council of Nicaea shall be restored, in which it is decreed that a bishop shall be confirmed by the two nearest bishops or by the archbishop. If the pope will break the statutes of this and of all other councils, what is the use of holding councils; or who has given him the authority thus to despise and break the rules of councils?

If he has this power then we should depose all bishops, archbishops and primates and make them mere parish-priests, so that the pope alone may be over them, as he now is. He leaves to bishops, archbishops and primates no regular authority or office, usurps everything for himself, and lets them keep only the name and empty title. It has gone so far that by his "exemptions" the monasteries, the abbots and the prelates are withdrawn from the regular authority of the bishops, so that there is no longer any order in Christendom. From this must follow what has followed—relaxation of discipline and license to do evil everywhere—so that I verily fear the pope can be called the "man of sin" (2 Thes. 2:3). There is in Christendom no discipline, no rule, no order; and who is to blame except the pope? This usurped authority of his he applies strictly to all the prelates, and takes away their rods, and he is generous to all subjects, giving them or selling them their liberty.

Nevertheless, for fear he may complain that he is robbed of his authority, it should be decreed that when the primates or archbishops are unable to settle a case, or when a controversy arises among themselves, such a case must be laid before the pope, but not every little matter. Thus it was done in olden times, and thus the famous Council of Nicaea decreed. If a case can be settled without the pope, then his Holiness should not be troubled with such minor matters, but give himself to that prayer, meditation, and care for all Christendom, of which he boasts. This is what the apostles did. They said, "It is not meet that we should leave the Word of God and serve tables, but we will keep to preaching and prayer and set others over the work" (Acts 6:2). But now Rome stands on nothing else than the despising of the Gospel and of prayer, and for the serving of "tables," i.e., of temporal affairs, and the rule of the apostles and of the pope agree as Christ agrees with Lucifer, Heaven with Hell, night with day; yet he is called "Vicar of Christ and Successor of the apostles."

4. It should be decreed that no temporal matter shall be taken to Rome, but that all such cases shall be left to the temporal authorities, as the Romans themselves decree in that canon law of theirs, which they do not keep. For it should be the duty of the pope, as the man most learned in the Scriptures and most holy, not in name only, but in truth, to administer affairs which concern the faith and holy life of Christians, to hold the primates and archbishops to these things, and to help them in dealing with and caring for these matters. So St. Paul teaches in 1 Corinthians 6, and takes the Corinthians severely to task or their concern with worldly things (v. 7). For it works intolerable injury to all lands that such cases are tried at Rome. It increases the costs, and moreover the judges do not know the manners, laws and customs of the various countries, so that they often do violence to the acts and base their decisions on their own laws and opinions, and thus injustice is inevitably done the contestants.

Moreover, the outrageous extortion practiced by the officials must be forbidden in all the dioceses, courts, so that they may attend to nothing else than matters of faith and good morals, and leave to the temporal judges the things that concern money, property, life, and honor. The temporal authorities, therefore, should not permit sentences of ban or exile when faith or right life is not concerned.

Spiritual authorities should have rule over spiritual goods, as reason teaches, but spiritual goods are not money, nor anything pertaining to the body, but they are faith and good works.

Nevertheless it might be granted that cases which concern benefices or livings should be tried before bishops, archbishops, and primates. Therefore, in order to decide contests and contentions, it might be possible for the Primate of Germany to maintain a general consistory, with auditors and chancellors, which should have control over the *signaturae gratiae* and *signaturae justitiae*,[27] that are now controlled at Rome, and which should be the final court of appeal for German cases. The officers of this consistory must not, however, be paid, as at Rome, by chance presents and gifts, and thereby acquire the habit of selling justice and injustice, which they now have to do at Rome because the pope gives them no remuneration, but allows them to fatten themselves on presents. For at Rome no one cares what is right or not right, but only what is money or not money. This court might, however, be paid out of the annates, or some other way might easily be devised by those who are more intelligent and who have more experience in these matters than I. All I wish to do is to arouse and set to thinking those who have the ability and the inclination to help the German nation become once more free and Christian after the wretched, heathenish, and unchristian rule of the pope.

5. No more reservations should be valid, and no more benefices should be seized by Rome, even if the incumbent dies, or there is a contest, or the incumbent is a "servant" of a cardinal or of the pope, and it should be strictly forbidden and prevented that any "harlot" should institute a contest over any benefice, so as to cite pious priests to Rome, harass them and drive them into lawsuits. If,

---

27. Bureaus through which the pope regulated those matters of administration which belonged to his own special prerogative.

in consequence of this prohibition, there should come from Rome a ban or an ecclesiastical censure, it should be disregarded, just as though a thief were to lay a man under the ban because he would not let him steal. Indeed they should be severely punished because they so blasphemously misuse the ban and the name of God to support their robbery, and with falsely devised threats would drive us to endure and to praise such blasphemy of God's name and such abuse of Christian authority, and thus to become, in the sight of God, partakers in their rascality; it is our duty before God to resist it, or St. Paul in Romans 1 reproves as guilty of death not only "those who do such things," but also those who consent to such things and allow them to be done (v. 32). Most unbearable of all is the lying *reservatio pectoralis* ("mental reservation") whereby Christendom is so scandalously and openly put to shame and scorn because its head deals in open lies, and out of love for the accursed money shamelessly deceives and fools everybody.

6. The *casus reservati*, the "reserved cases," should also be abolished, for not only are they the means of extorting much money from the people, but by means of them the ravening tyrants ensnare and confuse many poor consciences, to the intolerable injury of their faith in God. This is especially true of the ridiculous and childish cases about which they make so much ado in the Bull *Coena Domini*, and which are not worth calling daily sins, still less cases so grave that the pope may not remit them by any indulgence; as for example, hindering a pilgrim on his way to Rome, furnishing weapons to the Turks, or tampering with papal letters. With such gross, crazy, clumsy things do they make fools of us! Sodom and Gomorrah and all the sins which are committed and can be committed against the commandments of God are not reserved cases, but sins against what God has never commanded and what they have themselves devised, these must be reserved cases, solely that no one be hindered in bringing money to Rome, in order that safe from the Turks they may live in luxury and

keep the world under their tyranny with their wanton, useless bulls and breves.[28]

All priests ought rightly to know, or else there should be a public ordinance to that effect, that no secret sin of which a man has not been publicly accused is a reserved case, and that every priest has the power to remit all sorts of sins, however they may be called, so long as they are secret; moreover that no abbot, bishop or pope has the power to reserve any such case to himself. If they attempt it, their reservation does not hold and is not valid, and they should be reproved as men who without authority interfere in God's judgment and without cause ensnare and burden poor, ignorant consciences. But if great public sins are committed, especially sins against God's commandments, then there is indeed a reason for reserved cases, but even then there should not be too many of them, and they should not be reserved arbitrarily and without cause; for Christ has set in His Church not tyrants, but shepherds, as saith St. Peter (1 Pet. 5:3).

7. The Roman See should also do away with the offices, and diminish the swarm of vermin at Rome, so that the pope's household can be supported by the pope's own purse. The pope should not allow his court to surpass in pomp and extravagance the courts of all kings, seeing that such a condition not only has never been serviceable to the cause of Christian faith, but the courtiers have been kept thereby from study and prayer, until they are scarce able to speak about the faith at all. This they proved quite plainly at the last Roman Council,[29] in which, amongst many other childish and frivolous things, they decreed that the soul of man is immortal and that every priest must say his prayers once a month on pain of losing his benefice. How shall matters which concern faith and the Church be decided by people so hardened and blinded by great avarice, wealth, and worldly splendor,

---

28. Bulls and breves are both papal decrees.
29. Lateran V.

that they have only now decreed that the soul is immortal? It is no small shame to all Christians that at Rome they deal so disgracefully with the faith. If they had less wealth and pomp, they could pray and study better, and so become worthy and able to deal with matters of faith, as was the case in olden times when they were bishops, and did not presume to be kings over all kings.

8. The hard and terrible oaths should be abolished, which the bishops are wrongfully compelled to render to the pope, and by which they are bound like servants, as that worthless and unlearned chapter, *Significasti* (*Decretal. Greg.* I.6.4), arbitrarily and most stupidly decrees. It is not enough that they burden us in body, soul, and property with their many mad laws, by which faith is weakened and Christendom ruined, but they seize upon the person and office and work of the bishops, and now upon the investiture[30] also, which was in olden times the right of the German emperors, and in France and other kingdoms still belongs to the kings. On this point they had great wars and disputes with the emperors until at last, with impudent authority, they took the right and have kept it until now, just as though the Germans, above all the Christians on earth, had to be the puppets of the pope and the Roman See and do and suffer what no one else will do and suffer. Since then this is sheer violence and robbery, hindering the regular authority of the bishops and injuring poor souls, therefore the emperor and his nobles are in duty bound to prevent and punish such tyranny.

9. The pope should have no authority over the emperor, except that he anoints and crowns him at the altar, just as a bishop anoints and crowns a king, and we should not henceforth yield to that devilish pride which compels the emperor to kiss the pope's feet or sit at his feet, or, as they claim, hold his stirrup or the bridle of his mule when

---

30. The right to consecrate bishops, which was famously disputed by the Emperor Henry IV and Pope Gregory VII.

he mounts for a ride; still less should he do homage and swear faithful allegiance to the pope, as the popes have shamelessly ventured to demand as if they possessed that right. The chapter *Solite* (*Decretal. Greg.* I.33.6), in which the papal authority is raised above the imperial authority, is not worth a heller, nor are any of those who rest upon it or fear it; for it does nothing else than force the holy words of God out of their true meaning, and wrest them to human dreams, as I have showed in a Latin treatise.

Such extravagant, over-presumptuous, and more than wicked doings of the pope have been devised by the devil, in order that under their cover he may in time bring in antichrist, and raise the pope above God, as many are already doing and have done. It is not proper for the pope to exalt himself above the temporal authorities, save only in spiritual offices such as preaching and absolving. In other things he is to be subject, as Paul and Peter teach, in Romans 13:1, and 1 Peter 2:13ff, and as I have said above.

He is not vicar of Christ in Heaven, but of Christ as He walked on earth (Phil. 2:7). For Christ in Heaven, in the form of a ruler, needs no vicar, but He sits and sees, does, and knows all things, and has all power. But He needs a vicar in the form of a servant, in which He walked on earth, toiling, preaching, suffering, and dying. Now they turn it around, take from Christ the Heavenly form of ruler and give it to the pope, leaving the form of a servant to perish utterly. He might almost be the "Counter-christ" whom the Scriptures call antichrist, for all his nature, work, and doings are against Christ, for the destruction of Christ's nature and work.

It is also ridiculous and childish that the pope, with such perverted and deluded reasoning, boasts in his decretal *Pastoralis* that he is rightful heir to the Empire, in case of a vacancy. Who has given him this right? Did Christ, when He said, "The princes of the Gentiles are lords, but ye shall not be so" (Luke 22:25ff)? Did St. Peter will it to him? It vexes me that we must read and learn such shameless, gross, crazy lies in the canon law, and must even hold them for Christian doctrine, when they are devilish lies. Of the same sort is also that unheard-of lie about the "Donation of Constantine."[31] It must have been some special plague of God that so many people of understanding have let themselves be talked into accepting such lies as these, which are so manifest and clumsy that I should think any drunken peasant could lie more adroitly and skillfully. How can a man rule an empire and at the same time continue to preach, pray, study, and care for the poor? Yet these are the duties which properly and peculiarly belong to the pope, and they were imposed by Christ in such earnest that He even forbade His disciples to take with them cloak or money (Matt. 10:10), since these duties can scarcely be performed by one who has to rule even a single household. Yet the pope would rule an empire and continue to be pope! This is a device of the knaves who would like, under the pope's name, to be lords of the world, and by means of the pope and the name of Christ, to restore the Roman Empire to its former state.

10. The pope should restrain himself, take his fingers out of the pie, and claim no title to the Kingdom of Naples and Sicily. He has exactly as much right to that kingdom as I have, and yet he wishes to be its overlord. It is plunder got by violence, like almost all his other possessions. The emperor, therefore, should not grant him this fief, and if it has been granted, he should no longer give his consent to it, and should point him instead to the Bible and the prayer-books, so that he may preach and pray, and leave to temporal lords the ruling of lands and peoples, especially when no one has given them to him.

The same opinion should hold as regards Bologna, Imola, Vicenza, Ravenna, and all the territories in the Mark of Ancona, in

---

31. A forgery in which the first Christian Emperor Constantine gave Rome to Pope Sylvester. Lorenzo Valla proved it was a forgery in 1440 through careful analysis of the language.

Romagna, and in other Italian lands, which the pope has taken by force and possesses without right. Moreover, he has meddled in these things against all the commands of Christ and of St. Paul. For thus saith St. Paul, "No one entangleth himself with worldly affairs, whose business it is to wait upon the divine knighthood"(2 Tim. 2:3). Now the pope should be the head and front of this knighthood, yet he meddles in worldly affairs more than any emperor or king. Why then he must be helped out of them and allowed to attend to his knighthood! Christ also, whose vicar he boasts himself to be, was never willing to have aught to do with temporal rule; indeed, to one who asked of him a decision respecting his brother. He said, "Who made Me a judge over you?" (Luke 12:14). But the pope rushes in unbidden, and boldly takes hold of everything as though he were a god, until he no longer knows what Christ is, whose vicar he pretends to be.

11. The kissing of the pope's feet should take place no more. It is an unchristian, nay, an antichristian thing for a poor sinful man to let his feet be kissed by one who is a hundred times better than himself. If it is done in honor of his authority, why does not the pope do the same to others in honor of their holiness? Compare the two—Christ and the pope! Christ washed His disciples' feet and dried them (John 13:1ff), and the disciples never washed His feet; the pope, as though he were higher than Christ, turns things around and, as a great favor, allows people to kiss his feet, though he ought properly to use all his power to prevent it, if anyone wished to do it; like Paul and Barnabas, who would not let the people of Lystra pay them divine honor, but said, "We are men like you" (Acts 14:11-16). But our sycophants have gone so far as to make for us an idol, and now no one fears God so much as he fears the pope, no one pays Him such ceremonious honor. That they can endure! What they cannot endure is that a hair's-breadth should be taken away from the proud estate of the pope. Now if they were Christians, and held God's honor above their own, the

pope would never be happy while he knew that God's honor was despised and his own exalted, and he would let no man pay him honor until he saw that God's honor was again exalted and was greater than his own.

(It is another piece of the same scandalous pride that the pope is not satisfied to ride or to be driven in a vehicle, but although he is strong and in good health, he has himself borne by men, with unheard-of splendor, like an idol. How, pray, does such satanic pride agree with the example of Christ, who went on foot, as did all His disciples? Where has there ever been a worldly monarch who went about in such worldly glory as he who wishes to be the head of all those who are to despise and flee worldly glory, i.e., of Christians? Not that this in itself should give us very much concern, but we should rightly fear the wrath of God, if we flatter this kind of pride and do not show our indignation. It is enough that the pope should rant and play the fool in this wise, but that we should approve it and tolerate it—this is too much.

For what Christian heart can or ought to take pleasure in seeing that when the pope wishes to receive the communion, he sits quiet, like a gracious lord, and has the sacrament passed to him on a golden rod by a bowing cardinal on bended knee? As though the holy sacrament were not worthy that a pope, a poor stinking sinner, should rise to show God honor, when all other Christians, who are much more holy than the Most Holy Father, the pope, receive it with all reverence! Would it be a wonder if God were to send a plague upon us all because we suffer such dishonor to be done Him by our prelates, and approve it, and by our silence or our flattery make ourselves partakers of such damnable pride?

It is the same way when he carries the sacrament in procession. He must be carried, but the sacrament is set before him, like a can of wine on the table. In short, at Rome Christ counts for nothing, the pope counts for everything; and yet they would compel us with threats to approve, and praise and honor such antichristian sins, though this is against God and against all Christian doctrine. Now God help a free council to teach the pope that he too is a man, and is not more than God, as he presumes to be.)

12. Pilgrimages to Rome should either be abolished, or else no one should be allowed to make such a pilgrimage out of curiosity or because of a pious impulse, unless it is first recognized by his parish-priest, his town authorities or his overlord, that he has good and sufficient reason for it. I say this not because pilgrimages are bad, but because they are at this time ill-advised. For men see at Rome no good example, but only that which offends; and they have themselves made the proverb, "The nearer Rome, the worse Christians." Men bring back with them contempt for God and His commandments. It is said: "The first time one goes to Rome he seeks a rascal, the second time he finds him, the third time he brings him home with him." Now, however, they have become so clever that they make the three journeys at once, and they have verily brought back from Rome such pretty things that it were better never to have seen or known Rome.

Even if this reason did not exist, there is still another and a better: to wit, that by these pilgrimages men are led away into a false conceit and a misunderstanding of the divine commandments, or they think that this going on pilgrimage is a precious, good work, and this is not true. It is a very small good work, oftentimes an evil, delusive work, for God has not commanded it. But He has commanded that a man shall care for his wife and children, and look after such other duties as belong to the married state, and besides this, to serve and help his neighbor. Now it comes to pass that a man makes a pilgrimage to Rome when no one has commanded him to do so, spends fifty or a hundred gulden, more or less, and leaves his wife and child, or at least his neighbor, at home to suffer want. Yet the foolish fellow thinks to gloss over such disobedience and contempt of the divine commandments with his self-willed pilgriming, when it is really only curiosity or devilish delusion which leads him to it. The popes have helped this along with their false, feigned, foolish, "golden years," by which the people are excited, stirred up, torn away from God's commandments, and drawn toward their own deluded undertakings. Thus they have accomplished the very thing they should have forbidden, but it has brought in money and strengthened false authority, therefore it has had to continue, though it is against God and the salvation of souls.

In order to destroy in simple Christians this false, seductive faith, and to restore a true understanding of good works, all pilgrimages should be given up; for there is in them nothing good—no commandment, no obedience—but, on the contrary, numberless occasions for sin and for the despising of God's commandments. Hence come the many beggars, who by this pilgriming carry on endless knaveries and learn the habit of begging when they are not in want. Hence, too, come vagabondage, and many other ills which I shall not now recount.

If anyone now wishes to go on pilgrimage or take a pilgrim's vow, he should first show his reasons to his parish-priest or to his lord. If it turns out that he wishes to do it for the sake of the good work, the priest or lord should boldly tread the vow and good work underfoot, as though it were a lure of the devil, and show him how to apply the money and labor necessary for the pilgrimage to the keeping of God's commandments and to works a thousandfold better, namely, by spending it on his own family or on his poor neighbors. But if he wishes to make the pilgrimage out of curiosity, to see new lands and cities, he may be allowed to do as he likes. If, however, he has made the vow while ill, then such vows ought to be forbidden and canceled, and the commandments of God exalted, and he ought to be shown that he should henceforth be satisfied with the vow he made in baptism to keep the commandments of God. And yet, in order to quiet his conscience, he may be allowed this once to perform his foolish vow. No one wants to walk in the straight and common path of God's commandments; everyone makes himself new roads and new vows, as though he had fulfilled all the commandments of God.

13. Next we come to that great crowd who vow much and keep little. Be not angry, dear Lords! Truly, I mean it well. It is the truth, and bitter-sweet, and it is this—the building of mendicant-houses[32] should no more be permitted. God help us, there are already far too many of them! Would to God they were all done away, or at least given over to two or three orders! Wandering about the land has never brought any good, and never will bring any good. It is my advice, therefore, to put together ten of these houses, or as many as may be necessary, and out of them all to make one house, which will be well provided and need no more begging. It is much more important to consider what the common people need for their salvation, than what St. Francis, St. Dominic, St. Augustine, or any other man has decreed; especially since things have not turned out as they expected.

The mendicants should also be relieved of preaching and hearing confession, except when they are called to this work by the express desire of bishops, parishes, congregations or the temporal authorities. Out of their preaching and shriving there has come nothing but hatred and envy between priests and monks, and great offense and hindrance to the common people. For this reason it should properly and deservedly cease, because it can well be dispensed with. It looks suspiciously as though it were not for nothing that the Holy Roman See has increased this army, so that the priests and bishops, tired of its tyranny, might not some time become too strong for it and begin a reformation which would not be to the liking of his Holiness.

---

32. The houses, or monasteries, of the mendicant or "begging" orders—the "friars." The members of these orders were sworn to support themselves on the alms of the faithful.

## III. PROPOSALS FOR REFORM

At the same time the manifold divisions and differences within one and the same order should be abolished. These divisions have at times arisen for small reason and maintained themselves for still smaller, combatting one another with unspeakable hatred and envy. Nevertheless the Christian faith, which can well exist without any of these distinctions, is lost by both sides, and a good Christian life is valued and sought after only in outward laws, works and forms, and this results only in the devising of hypocrisy and the destruction of souls, as everyone may see with his own eyes.

The pope must also be forbidden to found and confirm any more of these orders; nay, he must be commanded to abolish some of them and reduce their number, since the faith of Christ, which is alone the highest good and which exists without any orders, is in no small danger, because these many different works and forms easily mislead men into living for them instead of giving heed to the faith. Unless there are in the monasteries wise prelates, who preach and who concern themselves with faith more than with the rules of the orders, the order cannot but harm and delude simple souls who think only of works.

In our days, however, the prelates who have had faith and who founded the orders have almost all passed away. Just as in olden days among the children of Israel, when the fathers, who knew God's works and wonders, had passed away, the children, from ignorance of God's works and of faith, immediately became idolatrous and set up their own human works; so now, alas! these orders have lost the understanding of God's works and of faith, and only torture themselves pitifully, with labor and sorrow, in their own rules, laws, and customs, and withal never come to a right understanding of a good spiritual life, as the apostle declared when he said, in 2 Timothy 3: "They have the appearance of a spiritual life, yet there is nothing back of it; they are ever and ever learning, but they never come to a knowledge of what a true spiritual life is" (vv. 5, 7) There should be no monastery unless there were a spiritual prelate, learned in the Christian faith, to rule it, for no other kind of prelate can rule without injury and ruin, and the holier and better he appears to be in his outward works and life, the more injury and ruin he causes.

To my way of thinking it would be a necessary measure, especially in these perilous times of ours, that all foundations and monasteries should be re-established as they were at the first, in the days of the apostles and for a long time afterwards, when they were all open to every man, and every man might remain in them as long as he pleased. For what were the foundations and monasteries except Christian schools in which the Scriptures and Christian living were taught, and people were trained to rule and to preach? So we read that St. Agnes went to school, and we still see the same practice in some of the nunneries, like that at Quedlinburg and others elsewhere. And in truth all monasteries and convents ought to be so free that God is served in them with free will and not with forced avarice. Afterward, however, they hedged them about with vows and turned them into a lifelong prison, so that these vows are thought to be of more account than the vows of baptism. What sort of fruit this has borne, we see, hear, read, and learn more and more every day.

I suppose this advice of mine will be regarded as the height of foolishness; but I am not concerned about that just now. I advise what I think best; let him reject it who will! I see how the vows are kept, especially the vow of chastity, which has become so universal through these monasteries and yet is not commanded by Christ; on the contrary, it is given to very few to keep it, as He himself says (Matt. 19:11ff), and St. Paul (1 Cor. 7:7; Col. 2:20). I would have all men to be helped, and not have Christian souls caught in human, self-devised customs and laws.

14. We also see how the priesthood has fallen, and how many a poor priest is overburdened with wife and child, and his conscience troubled, yet no one does anything to help him though he might

easily be helped. Though pope and bishops may let things go as they go, and let them go to ruin if they will, I will save my conscience and open my mouth freely, whether it vex pope, bishops or anyone else. Wherefore I say that according to the institution of Christ and the apostles every city should have a priest or bishop, as St. Paul clearly says in Titus 1:6; and this priest should not be compelled to live without a wedded wife, but should be permitted to have one, as St. Paul says in 1 Timothy 3, and Titus 1, "A bishop should be a man who is blameless, and the husband of but one wedded wife, whose children are obedient and virtuous," etc. (1 Tim. 3:2; Tit. 1:6). For with St. Paul a bishop and a priest are one and the same thing, as witness also St. Jerome. But of bishops as they now are, the Scriptures know nothing; they have been appointed by the ordinance of the Christian Church, that one of them may rule over many priests.

So then we clearly learn from the apostle that it should be the custom for every town to choose out of the congregation a learned and pious citizen, entrust to him the office of the ministry, and support him at the expense of the community, leaving him free choice to marry or not. He should have with him several priests or deacons, who might also be married or not, as they chose, to help him rule the people of the community by means of preaching and the sacraments, as is still the practice in the Greek Church. At a later time, when there were so many persecutions and controversies with heretics, there were many holy fathers who of their own accord abstained from matrimony, to the end that they might the better devote themselves to study and be prepared at any time for death or for controversy. Then the Roman See interfered, out of sheer wantonness, and made a universal commandment forbidding priests to marry.[33] This was done at the bidding of the devil, as St. Paul declares in 1 Timothy 4, "There shall

---

33. The first absolute prohibition of marriage to the clergy is contained in a decree of Pope Siricius and dated 385.

come teachers who bring doctrines of devils, and forbid to marry." From this has arisen so much untold misery, occasion was given for the withdrawal of the Greek Church, and division, sin, shame and scandal were increased without end—which is the result of everything the devil does.

What, then, shall we do about it? My advice is that matrimony be again made free, and that every one be let free choice to marry or not to marry. In that case, however, there must be a very different government and administration of Church property, the whole canon law must go to pieces and not many benefices find their way to Rome. I fear that greed has been a cause of this wretched unchaste chastity, and as a result of greed every man has wished to become a priest and everyone wants his son to study for the priesthood, not with the idea of living in chastity, for that could be done outside the priesthood, but of being supported in temporal things without care or labor, contrary to the command of God in Genesis 3, "In the sweat of thy face shat thou eat thy bread" (v. 19). They have construed this to mean that their labor was to pray and say Mass.

I am not referring here to popes, bishops, canons, and monks. God has not instituted these offices. They have taken burdens on themselves; let them bear them. I would speak only of the ministry which God has instituted and which is to rule a congregation by means of preaching and sacraments, whose incumbents are to live and be at home among the people. Such ministers should be granted liberty by a Christian council to marry, for the avoidance of temptation and sin. For since God has not bound them, no one else ought to bind them or can bind them, even though he were an angel from Heaven (Gal. 1:8), still less if he be only a pope, and everything that the canon law decrees to the contrary is mere fable and idle talk.

Furthermore, I advise that henceforth neither at his consecration to the priesthood nor at any other time shall any one under any circumstances promise the bishop to live in celibacy, but shall declare to the bishop that he has no authority to demand such a vow, and that to demand it is the devil's own tyranny.

But if anyone is compelled to say or wishes to say, as do some, "so far as human frailty permits," let everyone frankly interpret these words negatively, to mean "I do not promise chastity." For human frailty does not permit a chaste life, but only angelic power and celestial might (2 Pet. 2:11). Thus he should keep his conscience free from all vows.

On the question whether those who are not yet married should marry or remain unmarried, I do not care to give advice either way. I leave that to common Christian order and to everyone's better judgment. But as regards the wretched multitude who now sit in shame and heaviness of conscience because their wives are called "priests' harlots" and their children "priests' children" I will not withhold my faithful counsel nor deprive them of the comfort which is their due. I say this boldly by my jester's right. You will find many a pious priest against whom no one has anything to say except that he is weak and has come to shame with a woman, though both parties may be minded with all their heart to live always together in wedded love and troth, if only they could do it with a clear conscience, even though they might have to bear public shame. Two such persons are certainly married before God. And I say that where they are thus minded, and so come to live together, they should boldly save their consciences; let him take and keep her as his wedded wife, and live honestly with her as her husband, caring nothing whether the pope will have it so or not, whether it be against canon law or human law. The salvation of your soul is of more importance than tyrannical, arbitrary, wicked laws, which are not necessary for salvation and are not commanded by God. You should do like the children of Israel, who stole from the Egyptians the hire they had earned (Exod. 12:35ff), or like a servant who steals from his wicked master the wages he has earned. In like manner steal thou from the pope thy wife and child! Let the man who has faith enough to venture this, boldly follow me; I shall not lead him astray. Though I have not the authority of a pope, I have the authority of a Christian to advise and help my neighbor against sins and temptations; and that not without cause and reason.

First, not every priest can do without a woman, not only on account of the weakness of the flesh, but much more because of the necessities of the household. If he, then, may have a woman, and the pope grants him that, and yet may not have her in marriage—what is that but leaving a man and a woman alone and forbidding them to fall? It is as though one were to put fire and straw together and command that it shall neither smoke nor burn.

Second, the pope has as little power to command this, as he has to forbid eating, drinking, the natural movement of the bowels or growing fat. No one, therefore, is bound to keep it, but the pope is responsible for all the sins which are committed against this ordinance, for all the souls which are lost thereby, for all the consciences which are thereby confused and tortured; and therefore he has long deserved that some one should drive him out of the world, so many wretched souls has he strangled with this devil's snare, though I hope that there are many to whom God has been more gracious at their last hour than the pope has been in their life. Nothing good has ever come out of the papacy and its laws, nor ever will.

Third, although the law of the pope is against it, nevertheless, when the estate of matrimony has been entered against the pope's law, then his law is at an end, and is no longer valid, for the commandment of God, which decrees that no one shall put man and wife asunder (Matt. 19:6) takes precedence of the law of the pope, and the commandments of God must not be broken and neglected for the sake of the pope's commandment, though many mad jurists, in the papal interest, have devised "impediments" and have prevented, destroyed and confused the estate of matrimony, until by their means God's commandment has been altogether destroyed. To make a long story short, there are not in the whole "spiritual" law of the pope two lines which could be instructive to a pious Christian, and there are, alas! so many mistaken and dangerous laws that the best thing would be to make a bonfire of it.

But if you say that this would give offense, and the pope must first grant dispensation, I reply that whatever offense is in it, is the fault of the Roman See, which has established such laws without right and against God; before God and the Scriptures it is no offense. Moreover, if the pope can grant dispensations from his avaricious and tyrannical laws for money's sake, then every Christian can grant dispensations from them—for the sake of God and the salvation of souls. For Christ has set us free from all human laws, especially when they are opposed to God and the salvation of souls, as St. Paul teaches in Galatians 5:1 and 1 Corinthians 9:4ff.

15. Nor must I forget the poor convents! The evil spirit, who by human laws now confuses all estates in life, and has made them unbearable, has taken possession of in certain abbots, abbesses, and prelates also, and causes them so to govern their brethren and sisters as to send them the more speedily to Hell, and make them lead a wretched life even here, for such is the lot of all the devil's martyrs. That is to say, they have reserved to themselves in confession, all, or at least some, of the mortal sins which are secret, so that no brother, on his obedience and on pain of the ban, can absolve another from these sins. Now we do not always find angels everywhere, but we find also flesh and blood, which suffers all bannings and threatenings rather than confess secret sins to the prelates and the appointed confessors. Thus they go to the sacrament with such consciences that they become "irregular" and all sorts of other terrible things. O blind shepherds! O mad prelates! O ravening wolves!

To this I say: if a sin is public or notorious, then it is proper that the prelate alone should punish it, and of these sins only and no others he may make exceptions, and reserve them to himself; over secret sins he has no authority, even though they were the worst sins that are or ever can be found, and if the prelate makes exceptions of these sins, he is a tyrant, for he has no such right and is interfering in the judgment of God.

And so I advise these children, brethren and sisters: If your superiors are unwilling to grant you permission to confess your secret sins to whomever you wish, then take them to whatever brother or sister you will and confess them, receive absolution, and then go and do whatever you wish and ought to do; only believe firmly that you are absolved, and nothing more is needed. And do not allow yourself to be troubled by ban, "irregularity," or any of the other things they threaten; these things are valid only in the case of public or notorious sins which one is unwilling to confess; they do not affect you at all. Why do you try by your threatenings, O blind prelate, to prevent secret sins? Let go what you cannot publicly prove, so that God's judgment and grace may also have its work in your subjects! He did not give them so entirely into your hands as to let them go entirely out of His own! Nay, what you have under your rule is but the smaller part. Let your statutes be statutes, but do not exalt them to Heaven, to the judgment seat of God.

16. It were also necessary to abolish all anniversary, mortuary and "soul" Masses, or at least to diminish their number, since we plainly see that they have become nothing but a mockery, by which God is deeply angered, and that their only purpose is money-getting, gorging, and drunkenness. What kind of pleasure should God have in such a miserable gabbling of wretched vigils and Masses, which is neither reading nor praying, and even when prayed, they are performed not for God's sake and out of willing love, but for money's sake and because they are a binding duty. Now it is not possible that any work not done out of willing love can please God or obtain anything from Him. And so it is altogether Christian to abolish, or at least diminish, everything which we see growing into an abuse, and which angers rather than

reconciles God. It would please me more—nay, it would be more acceptable to God and far better—that a foundation, church or monastery should put all its anniversary Masses and vigils together, and on one day, with hearty sincerity, devotion and faith, hold a true vigil and Mass for all its benefactors, rather than hold them by the thousand every year, for each benefactor a special Mass, without this devotion and faith. O dear Christians! God cares not for much praying, but for true praying! Nay, He condemns the many and long prayers, and says in Matthew 6, they will only earn more punishment thereby (Matt. 67:7; 23:14). But avarice, which cannot trust God, brings such things to pass, fearing that otherwise it must die of hunger!

17. Certain penalties or punishments of the canon law should also be abolished, especially the interdict, which is, beyond all doubt, an invention of the evil spirit. Is it not a devil's work to try to atone for one sin with many greater sins? And yet, to put God's Word and worship to silence, or to do away with them, is a greater sin than strangling twenty popes at once, and far greater than killing a priest or keeping back some church property. This is another of the tender virtues taught in the "spiritual law." For one of the reasons why this law is called "spiritual" is because it comes from the spirit; not, however, from the Holy Spirit, but from the evil spirit.

The ban is to be used in no case except where the Scriptures prescribe its use, i.e., against those who do not hold the true faith, or who live in open sin; it is not to be used for the sake of temporal possessions. But now it is the other way around. Everyone believes and lives as he pleases, most of all those who use the ban to plunder and defame other people, and all the bans are now laid only on account of temporal possessions, or which we have no one to thank but the holy "spiritual lawlessness." Of this I have previously said more in my Discourse.

The other punishments and penalties—suspension, irregularity, aggravation, re-aggravation, deposition, lightnings, thunderings, cursings, damnings and the rest of these devices—should be buried ten fathoms deep in the earth, so that there should be neither name nor memory of them left on earth. The evil spirit, who has been let loose by the "spiritual law" has brought this terrible plague and misery into the Heavenly kingdom of the holy Church, and has accomplished by it nothing else than the destruction and hindrance of souls, so that the word of Christ may well be applied to them: "Woe unto you scribes! Ye have taken upon you the authority to teach, and ye shut up the kingdom of Heaven against men. Ye go not in yourselves, and ye suffer not them that are entering" (Matt. 23:13).

18. All festivals[34] should be abolished, and Sunday alone retained. If it were desired, however, to retain the festivals of Our Lady and of the greater saints, they should be transferred to Sunday, or observed only by a morning Mass, after which all the rest of the day should be a working-day. The reason is this: the feast-days are now abused by drinking, gaming, idleness and all manner of sins, so that on the holy days we anger God more than on other days, and have altogether turned things around; the holy days are not holy and the working days are holy, and not only is no service done to God and His saints by the many holy days, but rather great dishonor. There are, indeed, some mad prelates who think they are doing a good work if they make a festival in honor of St. Ottilia or St. Barbara or some other saint, according to the promptings of their blind devotion, but they would be doing a far better work if they honored the saint by turning a saint's-day into a working day.

Over and above the spiritual injury, the common man receives two material injuries from this practice, i.e., he neglects his work and he spends more than at other times; nay, he also weakens his body and unfits it for work. We see this every day, yet no one thinks to make it better. We ought not to consider whether or not the pope

---

34. Saints' days.

has instituted the feasts, and whether we must have dispensation and permission to omit them. If a thing is opposed to God, and harmful to man in body and soul, any community, council or government has not only the right to abolish it and put a stop to it, without the will or knowledge of pope or bishop, but they are bound on their souls' salvation to prevent it, even against the will of pope and bishop, though these ought to be themselves the first to forbid it.

Above all, we ought utterly to abolish the consecration days, since they have become nothing else than taverns, airs, and gaming places,[35] and serve only to the increase of God's dishonor and to the damnation of souls. All the pretense about the custom having had a good beginning and being a good work is of no avail. Did not God Himself set aside His own law, which He had given from Heaven, when it was perverted and abused? And does He not still daily overturn what He has appointed and destroy what He has made, because of such perversion and abuse? As it is written of Him in Psalm 18, "With the perverted Thou wilt show Thyself perverse" (v. 27).

19. The grades or degrees within which marriage is forbidden should be changed, as, for instance, the sponsorships and the third and fourth degrees, and if the pope can grant dispensation in these matters or money and for the sake of his shameful traffic, then every parish priest may give the same dispensations gratis and for the salvation of souls. Yea, would to God that all the things which we must buy at Rome to free ourselves from that money-snare, the canon law—such things as indulgences, letters of indulgence, "butter-letters," "Mass-letters," and all the rest of the *confessionalia* and knaveries for sale at Rome, with which the poor folk are deceived and robbed of their money—would to God, I say, that any priest could, without payment, do and omit all these things! For if the pope has the authority to sell his snares for money and his spiritual

---

35. The anniversary celebration of the consecration of a church.

nets (I should say laws), surely any priest has much more authority to rend his nets and for God's sake to tread them under foot. But if he has not this right, neither has the pope the right to sell them at his shameful fair.

This is the place to say too that the fasts should be matters of liberty, and all sorts of food made free, as the Gospel makes them (Matt. 15:11). For at Rome they themselves laugh at the fasts, making us foreigners eat the oil with which they would not grease their shoes, and afterwards selling us liberty to eat butter and all sorts of other things; yet the holy apostle says that in all these things we already have liberty through the Gospel (1 Cor. 10:25ff). But they have caught us with their canon law and stolen our rights from us, so that we may have to buy them back with money. Thus they have made our consciences so timid and shy that it is no longer easy to preach about this liberty because the common people take such great offense, thinking it a greater sin to eat butter than to lie, to swear, or even to live unchastely. Nevertheless, what men have decreed, that is the work of man; put it where you will, nothing good ever comes out of it.

20. The forest chapels and rustic churches must be utterly destroyed—those, namely, to which the recent pilgrimages have been directed—Wilsnack, Sternberg, Trier, the Grimmenthal, and now Regensburg, and a goodly number of others. Oh, what a terrible and heavy account will the bishops have to render, who permit this devilish deceit and receive its profits! They should be the first to forbid it, and yet they think it a divine and holy thing, and do not see that it is the devil's doing, to strengthen avarice, to create a false, feigned faith, to weaken the parish churches, to multiply taverns and harlotry, to waste money and labor, and to lead the poor folk by the nose. If they had only read the Scriptures to as good purpose as they have read their damnable canon law, they would know well how to deal with this matter.

That miracles are done at these places does not help things, for the evil spirit can do miracles, as Christ has told us in Matthew 24:24. If they took the matter seriously and forbade this sort of thing, the miracles would quickly come to an end; on the other hand, if the thing were of God their prohibition would not hinder it (Acts 5:39). And if there were no other evidence that it is not of God, this would be enough—that people run to these places in excited crowds, as though they had lost their reason, like herds of cattle; for this cannot possibly be of God. Moreover, God has commanded nothing of all this; there is neither obedience nor merit in it; the bishops, therefore, should boldly step in and keep the folk away. For what is not commanded—and is concerned for self rather than for the commands of God—that is surely the devil himself. Then, too, the parish churches receive injury, because they are held in smaller honor. In short, these things are signs of great unbelief among the people; if they truly believed, they would have all that they need in their own churches, for to them they are commanded to go.

But what shall I say? Everyone plans only how he may establish and maintain such a place of pilgrimage in his diocese and is not at all concerned to have the people believe and live aright; the rulers are like the people; one blind man leads another (Matt. 13:14). Nay, where pilgrimages are not successful, they begin to canonize saints, not in honor of the saints—for they are sufficiently honored without canonization—but in order to draw crowds and bring in money. Pope and bishop help along; it rains indulgences; there is always money enough for that. But for what God has commanded no one provides; no one runs after these things; there is no money for them. Alas, that we should be so blind! We not only give the devil his own way in his tricks, but we even strengthen him in his wantonness and increase his pranks. I would that the dear saints were left in peace, and the poor folk not led astray! What spirit has given the pope the authority to canonize the saints? Who tells him whether they are saints or not? Are there not already sins enough on earth, that we too must tempt God, interfere in His judgment and set up the dear saints as lures for money?

Therefore I advise that the saints be left to canonize themselves. Yea, it is God alone who should canonize them. And let every man stay in his own parish, where he finds more than in all the shrines of pilgrimage, even though all the shrines were one. Here we find baptism, the sacrament, preaching, and our neighbor, and these are greater things than all the saints in Heaven, for it is by God's Word and sacrament that they have all been made saints. So long as we despise such great things God is just in the wrathful judgment by which He appoints the devil to lead us hither and thither, to establish pilgrimages, to found churches and chapels, to secure the canonization of saints, and to do other such fool's works, by which we depart from true faith into new, false misbelief. This is what he did in olden times to the people of Israel, when he led them away from the temple at Jerusalem to countless other places, though he did it in the name of God and under the plausible guise of holiness, though all the prophets preached against it and were persecuted for so doing. But now no one preaches against it, perhaps for fear that pope, priests, and monks would persecute him also. In this way St. Antoninus of Florence and certain others must now be made saints and canonized, that their holiness, which would otherwise have served only for the glory of God and as a good example, may serve to bring in fame and money.

Although the canonizing of saints may have been good in olden times, it is not good now; just as many other things were good in olden times and are now scandalous and injurious, such as feast-days, church-treasures, and church-adornment. For it is evident that through the canonizing of saints neither God's glory nor the improvement of Christians is sought, but only money and glory, in that one church wants to be something more and have something more

## III. PROPOSALS FOR REFORM

than others, and would be sorry if another had the same thing and its advantage were common property. So entirely, in these last, evil days have spiritual goods been misused and applied to the gaining of temporal goods, that everything, even God Himself, has been forced into the service of avarice. And even these special advantages lead only to dissensions, divisions, and pride, in that the churches, differing from one another, hold each other in contempt, and exalt themselves one above another, though all the gifts which God bestows are the common and equal property of all churches and should only serve the cause of unity. The pope, too, is glad of the present state of affairs; he would be sorry if all Christians were equal and were at one.

This is the place to speak of the church licenses, bulls, and other things which the pope sells at his laying-place in Rome. We should either abolish them or disregard them, or at least make them the common property of all churches. For if he sells or gives away licenses and privileges, indulgences, graces, advantages, faculties to Wittenberg, to Halle, to Venice and, above all, to his own Rome, why does he not give these things to all churches alike? Is he not bound to do for all Christians, gratis and for God's sake, everything that he can, and even to shed his blood for them? Tell me, then, why he gives or sells to one church and not to another? Or must the accursed money make, in the eyes of His Holiness, so great a difference among Christians, who all have the same baptism, Word, faith, Christ, God, and all things (Eph. 4:4ff)? Are we to be blind while we have eyes to see, fools while we have our reason, that they expect us to worship such greed, knavery and humbug? He is a shepherd—yes, so long as you have money, and no longer! And yet they are not ashamed of their knavery, leading us hither and yon with their bulls! Their one concern is the accursed money, and nothing else!

My advice is this: if such fool's work cannot be abolished, then every pious Christian man should open his eyes, and not be misled by the hypocritical Roman bulls and seals, stay at home in his own church and be content with his baptism, his Gospel, his faith, his Christ, and with God, who is everywhere the same, and let the pope remain a blind leader of the blind. Neither angel nor pope can give you as much as God gives you in your parish-church. Nay, the pope leads you away from the gifts of God, which you have without pay, to his gifts, which you must buy, and he gives you lead for gold, hide for meat, the string for the purse, wax for honey, words for goods, the letter for the Spirit. You see this before your very eyes, but you are unwilling to notice it. If you are to ride to Heaven on his wax and parchment, your chariot will soon go to pieces, and you will fall into Hell, not in God's name!

Let this be your fixed rule: what you must buy from the pope is neither good nor of God; for what is from God, to wit, the Gospel and the works of God, is not only given without money, but the whole world is punished and damned because it has not been willing to receive it as a free gift. We have deserved of God that we should be so deceived, because we have despised His holy Word and the grace of baptism, as St. Paul says: "God shall send a strong delusion upon all those who have not received the truth to their salvation, to the end that they may believe and follow after lies and knavery," (2 Thes. 2:11) which serves them right.

21. One of our greatest necessities is the abolition of all begging throughout Christendom. Among Christians no one ought to go begging! It would also be easy to make a law, if only we had the courage and the serious intention, to the effect that every city should provide for its own poor, and admit no foreign beggars by whatever name they might be called, whether pilgrims or mendicant monks. Every city could support its own poor, and if it were too small, the people in the surrounding villages also should be exhorted to contribute, since in any case they have to feed so many vagabonds and knaves in the guise of mendicants. In this way, too, it could be known who were really poor and who not.

There would have to be an overseer or warden who knew all the poor and informed the city council or the priests what they needed, or some other better arrangement might be made. In my judgment there is no other business in which so much knavery and deceit are practiced as in begging, and yet it could all be easily abolished. Moreover, this free and universal begging hurts the common people. I have considered that each of the five or six mendicant orders visits the same place more than six or seven times every year; besides these there are the common beggars, the "stationaries" and the palmers, so that it has been reckoned that every town is laid under tribute about sixty times a year, not counting what is given to the government in taxes, imposts and assessments, what is stolen by the Roman See with its wares, and what is uselessly consumed. Thus it seems to me one of God's greatest miracles that we can continue to support ourselves.

To be sure, some think that in this way the poor would not be so well provided for and that not so many great stone houses and monasteries would be built. This I can well believe. Nor is it necessary. He who wishes to be poor should not be rich, and if he wishes to be rich, let him put his hand to the plow and seek his riches in the earth! It is enough if the poor are decently cared for, so that they do not die of hunger or of cold. It is not fitting that one man should live in idleness on another's labor, or be rich and live comfortably at the cost of another's discomfort, according to the present perverted custom; for St. Paul says, "If a man will not work, neither shall he eat" (2 Thes. 3:10). God has not decreed that any man shall live from another's goods save only the priests, who rule and preach, and these because of their spiritual labor, as Paul says in 1 Corinthians 9:14, and Christ also says to the apostles, "Every laborer is worthy of his hire" (Luke 10:7).

22. It is also to be feared that the many Masses which are endowed in the foundations and monasteries are not only of little use,

but greatly arouse the wrath of God. It would therefore be profitable not to endow any more, but rather to abolish many that are already endowed, since we see that they are regarded only as sacrifices and good works, though they are really sacraments, just like baptism and penance, which profit only those who receive them, and no others. But now the custom has crept in that Masses are said for the living and the dead, and all hopes are built upon them; for this reason so many of them have been founded and the present state of affairs has come about.

My proposal is perhaps too novel and daring, especially for those who fear that through the discontinuance of these Masses their trade and livelihood may be destroyed, and so I must refrain from saying more about it until we have come back to a correct understanding of what the Mass is and what it is good for. These many years, alas, it has been made a trade practiced for a temporal livelihood, so that I would henceforth advise a man to become a shepherd or to seek some other trade rather than become a priest or a monk, unless he first knows well what it is to celebrate Mass. I am not speaking, however, of the old foundations and cathedrals, which were doubtless established in order that the children of the nobility (since, according to the customs of the German nation not all of them can become heirs or rulers), might be provided for in these foundations, and there be free to serve God, to study, to become scholars and to make scholars. But I am speaking of the new foundations, which have been established only for the saying of prayers and Masses; for after their example, even the old foundations have been burdened with like prayers and Masses, so that they are of little or no profit, though it is also of God's grace that they too come at last, as they deserve, to the dregs, i.e., to the wailing of organs and of choral singers, and to dead, cold Masses, by which the incomes of the worldly endowments are gotten and spent. Such things pope, bishops, and doctors should examine and proscribe, but now it is they who are most given to them. They let everything pass, if only it brings in money; one blind man is always leading another. This is the work of avarice and of the spiritual law.

Again, no one person should be allowed any longer to hold more than one canonry or prebend. He must be content with a modest position, that someone else may also have something. This would do away with the excuses of those who say that they must hold more than one such office to "maintain a proper station." A "proper station" might be so broadly interpreted that a whole land would not be enough to maintain it! Moreover avarice and veiled distrust of God assuredly go with it, so that what is alleged to be the need of "a proper station" is often nothing else than avarice and distrust.

23. Sodalities,[36] indulgences, letters of indulgence, "butter-letters," Mass-letters,[37] dispensations, and everything else of the sort, are to be drowned and destroyed. There is nothing good in them. If the pope has the power to grant you dispensation to eat butter and to absent yourself from Mass, then he ought also be able to leave this power to the priests, from whom, indeed, he has no right to take it. I speak especially of those fraternities in which indulgences, Masses and good works are portioned out. Dear friend, in your baptism you entered into a fraternity with Christ, all the angels, saints and Christians on earth. Hold to this fraternity and live up to its demands, and you have fraternities enough. The others—let them glitter as they will—are but as counters compared with guldens.[38] But if there were a fraternity which contributed money to feed the poor or to help somebody in some other way, such a one would be good, and would have its indulgence and its merit in Heaven. Now, however, they have become excuses or gluttony and drunkenness.

---

36. Associations in which the members are obligated to the recite certain prayers and to attend Masses.
37. Letters that allowed one to not attend Mass.
38. Like mere gambling tokens compared to real money.

Above all, we should drive out of German lands the papal legates with their "faculties," which they sell us for large sums of money, though that is sheer knavery. For example, in return for money they legalize unjust gains, dissolve oaths, vows, and agreements, break and teach men to break the faith and fealty which they have pledged to one another, and they say the pope has the authority to do this. It is the evil spirit who bids them say this. Thus they sell us a doctrine of devils, and take money for teaching us sin and leading us to Hell.

If there were no other evil wiles to prove the pope the true antichrist, yet this one thing were enough to prove it. Hearest thou this, pope, not most holy, but most sinful? O that God from Heaven would soon destroy thy throne and sink it in the abyss of Hell! Who hath given thee authority to exalt thyself above thy God, to break and to loose His commandments, and to teach Christians, especially the German nation, praised in all history for its nobility, its constancy and fidelity, to be inconstant, perjurers, traitors, profligates, faithless? God hath commanded to keep oath and faith even with an enemy, and thou undertakest to loose this His commandment, and ordainest in thine heretical, antichristian decretals that thou hast His power. Thus through thy throat and through thy pen the wicked Satan doth lie as he hath never lied before. Thou dost force and wrest the Scriptures to thy fancy. O Christ, my Lord, look down, let the day of Thy judgment break, and destroy the devil's nest at Rome! Here sitteth the man of whom St. Paul hath said that he shall exalt himself above Thee, sit in Thy Church and set himself up as God (2 Thes. 2:3ff)—the man of sin and the son of perdition! What else is the papal power than only the teaching and increasing of sin and evil, the leading of souls to damnation under Thy name and guise?

In olden times the children of Israel had to keep the oath which they had unwittingly been deceived into giving to their enemies, the Gibeonites (Josh. 9:19ff), and King Zedekiah was miserably lost, with all his people, because he broke this oath to the King of Babylon

## III. PROPOSALS FOR REFORM

(2 Kings 24:20; 25:4ff). Even among us, a hundred years ago, that fine king of Hungary and Poland, Wladislav, was slain by the Turk, with so many noble people, because he allowed himself to be deceived by the papal legate and cardinal, and broke the good and advantageous treaty which he had sworn with the Turk. The pious Emperor Sigismund had no good fortune after the Council of Constance, when he allowed the knaves to break the safe-conduct which had been given to John Hus and Jerome and all the trouble between us and the Bohemians was the consequence. Even in our own times, God help us! how much Christian blood has been shed over the oath and alliance which Pope Julius made between the Emperor Maximilian and King Louis of France, and afterwards broke? How could I tell all the troubles which the popes have stirred up by the devilish presumption with which they annul oaths and vows which have been made between great princes, making a jest of these things, and taking money for it? I have hopes that the judgment day is at the door; nothing can possibly be worse than the Roman See. He suppresses God's commandment, he exalts his own commandment over it; if he is not antichrist, then let someone else tell who he can be! But more of this another time, and better.

24. It is high time that we seriously and honestly consider the case of the Bohemians, and come into union with them so that the terrible slander, hatred and envy on both sides may cease. As befits my folly, I shall be the first to submit an opinion on this subject, with due deference to everyone who may understand the case better than I.

First, we must honestly confess the truth, stop justifying ourselves, and grant the Bohemians that John Hus and Jerome of Prague were burned at Constance in violation of the papal, Christian, imperial safe-conduct and oath; whereby God's commandment was sinned against and the Bohemians were given ample cause for bitterness, and although they ought to have been perfect and to have patiently endured this great injustice and disobedience of God on our part, nevertheless they were not bound to approve of it and to acknowledge that it was well done. Nay, even today they should give up life and limb rather than confess that it is right to violate an imperial, papal, Christian safe-conduct, and faithlessly to act contrary to it. So then, although it is the impatience of the Bohemians which is at fault, yet the pope and his followers are still more to blame for all the trouble, error and loss of souls that have followed upon that council.

I have no desire to pass judgment at this time upon John Hus's articles or to defend his errors, though I have not yet found any errors in his writings, and I am quite prepared to believe that it was neither fair judgment nor honest condemnation which was passed by those who, in their faithless dealing, violated a Christian safe-conduct and a commandment of God. Beyond doubt they were possessed rather by the evil spirit than by the Holy Spirit. No one will doubt that the Holy Spirit does not act contrary to the commandment of God; and no one is so ignorant as not to know that the violation of faith and of a safe-conduct is contrary to the commandment of God, even though they had been promised to the devil himself, still more when the promise was made to a mere heretic. It is also quite evident that such a promise was made to John Hus and the Bohemians and was not kept, but that he was burned in spite of it. I do not wish, however, to make John Hus a saint or a martyr, as do some of the Bohemians, though I confess that injustice was done him, and that his books and doctrines were unjustly condemned; for the judgments of God are secret and terrible, and no one save God alone should undertake to reveal or utter them. All I wish to say is this: though he were never so wicked a heretic, nevertheless he was burned unjustly and against God's commandment, and the Bohemians should not be forced to approve of such conduct, or else we shall never come into unity. Not obstinacy but the open admission of truth must make us one. It is useless to pretend, as was done at that time, that a safe-conduct given to a heretic need not be kept. That is as much as to say

### III. PROPOSALS FOR REFORM

that God's commandments are not to be kept to the end that God's commandments may be kept. The devil made them mad and foolish, so that they did not know what they were saying or doing. God has commanded that a safe-conduct shall be kept. This commandment we should keep though the world fall. How much more, when it is only a question of freeing a heretic! We should vanquish heretics with books, not with burning; for so the ancient fathers did. If it were a science to vanquish the heretics with fire, then the hang-men would be the most learned doctors on earth; we should no longer need to study, but he who overcame another by force might burn him at the stake.

Second, the emperor and the princes should send to the Bohemians some pious and sensible bishops and scholars, but by no means a cardinal or papal legate or inquisitor, for those people are utter ignoramuses as regards things Christian; they seek not the welfare of souls, but, like all the pope's hypocrites, only their own power, profit and glory; indeed, they were the prime movers in this miserable business at Constance. The men thus sent into Bohemia should inform themselves about the faith of the Bohemians, and whether it be possible to unite all their sects. Then the pope should, for their souls' sake, lay aside his supremacy for the time being, and, according to the decree of the most Christian Council of Nicaea, allow the Bohemians to choose one of their number to be Archbishop of Prague, and he should be confirmed by the bishop of Olmütz in Moravia, or the bishop of Gran in Hungary, or the bishop of Gnesen in Poland, or the bishop of Magdeburg in Germany. It will be enough if he is confirmed by one or two of these, as was the custom in the time of St. Cyprian. The pope has no right to oppose such an arrangement, and if he does oppose it, he becomes a wolf and a tyrant; no one should follow him and his ban should be met with a counter-ban.

If, however, it were desired, in honor of the See of St. Peter, to do this with the pope's consent, I should be satisfied, provided it does not cost the Bohemians a heller and the pope does not bind them at all nor make them subject to his tyrannies by oaths and obligations, as he does all other bishops, in despite of God and of justice. If he will not be satisfied with the honor of having his consent asked, then let them not bother anymore about him and his rights, laws, and tyrannies; let the election suffice, and let the blood of all the souls which are endangered cry out against him, for no one should consent to injustice; it is enough to have offered tyranny an honor. If it cannot be otherwise, then an election and approval by the common people can even now be quite as valid as a confirmation by a tyrant, but I hope this will not be necessary. Some of the Romans or the good bishops and scholars will sometime mark and oppose papal tyranny.

I would also advise against compelling them to abolish both kinds in the sacrament, since that is neither unchristian nor heretical, but they should be allowed to retain their own practice, if they wish. Yet the new bishop should be careful that no discord arise because of such a practice, but should kindly instruct them that neither practice is wrong; just as it ought not to cause dissension that the clergy differ from the laity in manner of life and in dress. In like manner if they were unwilling to receive the Roman canon law, they should not be forced to do so, but we should first make sure that they live in accordance with faith and with the Scriptures. For Christian faith and life can well exist without the intolerable laws of the pope, nay, they cannot well exist unless there be fewer of these Roman laws, or none at all. In baptism we have become free and have been made subject to God's Word only; why should any man ensnare us in his words? As St. Paul says, "Ye have become free, be not servants of men," (1 Cor. 7:23; Gal. 5:1) i.e. of those who rule with man-made laws.

If I knew that the Picards held no other error touching the sacrament of the altar except that they believe that the bread and wine are present in their true nature, but that the body and blood of Christ are truly present under them, then I would not condemn them, but would let them enter the obedience of the bishop of Prague. For it is not an article of faith that bread and wine are not essentially and naturally in the sacrament, but this is an opinion of St. Thomas and the pope. On the other hand, it is an article of faith that in the natural bread and wine the true natural body and blood of Christ are present. And so we should tolerate the opinions of both sides until they come to an agreement, because there is no danger in believing that bread is there or is not there. For we have to endure many practices and ordinances so long as they are not harmful to faith. On the other hand, if they had a different faith, I would rather have them outside the Church; yet I would teach them the truth.

Whatever other errors and schisms might be discovered in Bohemia should be tolerated until the archbishop had been restored and had gradually brought all the people together again in one common doctrine. They will assuredly never be united by force, nor by defiance, nor by haste; it will take time and forbearance. Had not even Christ to tarry with His disciples a long while and bear with their unbelief, until they believed His resurrection? If they but had again a regular bishop and church order, without Roman tyranny, I could hope that things would soon be better.

The restoration of the temporal goods which formerly belonged to the Church should not be too strictly demanded, but since we are Christians and each is bound to help the rest, it is in our power, for the sake of unity, to give them these things and let them keep them in the sight of God and men. For Christ says, "Where two are at one with each other on earth, there am I in the midst of them" (Matt. 18:19ff). Would to God that on both sides we were working toward this unity, offering our hands to one another in brotherly humility, and not standing stubbornly on our powers or rights! Love is greater and more necessary than the papacy at Rome, for there can be papacy without love and love without papacy.

With this counsel I shall have done what I could. If the pope or his followers hinder it, they shall render an account for seeking their own things rather than the things of their neighbor, contrary to the love of God (Phil. 2:4). The pope ought to give up his papacy and all his possessions and honors, if he could by that means save one soul; but now he would let the world go to destruction rather than yield a hair's-breadth of his presumptuous authority. And yet he would be the "most holy!" Here my responsibility ends.

25. The universities also need a good, thorough reformation—I must say it no matter whom it vexes—for everything which the papacy has instituted and ordered is directed only towards the increasing of sin and error. What else are the universities, if their present condition remains unchanged, than as the book of Maccabees says, the Gymnasiums of the youths and of Greek glory (2 Macc. 4:9, 12), in which loose living prevails, the Holy Scriptures and the Christian faith are little taught, and the blind, heathen master Aristotle rules alone, even more than Christ. In this regard my advice would be that Aristotle's *Physics*, *Metaphysics*, *On the Soul*, *Ethics*, which have hitherto been thought his best books, should be altogether discarded, together with all the rest of his books which boast of treating the things of nature, although nothing can be learned from them either of the things of nature or the things of the Spirit. Moreover no one has so far understood his meaning, and many souls have been burdened with profitless labor and study, at the cost of much precious time. I venture to say that any potter has more knowledge of nature than is written in these books. It grieves me to the heart that this damned, conceited, rascally heathen has with his false words deluded and made fools of so many of the best Christians. God has sent him as a plague upon us for our sins.

Why, this wretched man, in his best book, *On the Soul*, teaches that the soul dies with the body, although many have tried with vain words to save his reputation. As though we had not the Holy Scriptures,

## III. PROPOSALS FOR REFORM

in which we are abundantly instructed about all things, and of them Aristotle had not the faintest inkling! And yet this dead heathen has conquered and obstructed and almost suppressed the books of the living God, so that when I think of this miserable business I can believe nothing else than that the evil spirit has introduced the study of Aristotle. Again, his book on *Ethics* is the worst of all books. It flatly opposes divine grace and all Christian virtues, and yet it is considered one of his best works. Away with such books! Keep them away from all Christians! Let no one accuse me of exaggeration, or of condemning what I do not understand! My dear friend, I know well whereof I speak. I know my Aristotle as well as you or the likes of you. I have lectured on him and heard lectures on him, and I understand him better than do St. Thomas or Scotus. This I can say without pride, and if necessary I can prove it. I care not that so many great minds have wearied themselves over him for so many hundred years. Such objections do not disturb me as once they did; for it is plain as day that other errors have remained for even more centuries in the world and in the universities.

I should be glad to see Aristotle's books on *Logic*, *Rhetoric*, and *Poetics* retained or used in an abridged form, as textbooks for the profitable training of young people in speaking and preaching. But the commentaries and notes should be abolished, and as Cicero's *Rhetoric* is read without commentaries and notes, so Aristotle's *Logic* should be read as it is, without such a Mass of comments. But now neither speaking nor preaching is learned from it, and it has become nothing but a disputing and a weariness to the flesh. Besides this there are the languages—Latin, Greek, and Hebrew—the mathematical disciplines and history. But all this I give over to the specialists, and, indeed, the reform would come of itself, if we were only seriously bent upon it. In truth, much depends upon it; for it is here that the Christian youth and the best of our people, with whom the future of Christendom lies, are to be educated and trained. Therefore I consider that there is no work more worthy of pope or emperor than a thorough reformation of the universities, and there is nothing worse or more worthy of the devil than unreformed universities.

The medical men I leave to reform their own faculties; the jurists and theologians I take as my share, and I say, in the first place, that it were well if the canon law, from the first letter to the last, and especially the decretals, were utterly blotted out. The Bible contains more than enough directions for all our living, and so the study of the canon law only stands in the way of the study of the Holy Scriptures; moreover, it smacks for the most part of mere avarice and pride. Even though there were much in it that is good, it might as well be destroyed, for the pope has taken the whole canon law captive and imprisoned it in the "chamber of his heart,"[39] so that the study of it is henceforth a waste of time and a farce. At present the canon law is not what is in the books, but what is in the sweet will of the pope and his flatterers. Your cause may be thoroughly established in the canon law; still the pope has his chamber of his heart, and all law and the whole world must be guided by that. Now it is ofttimes a knave, and even the devil himself, who rules this chamber, and they boast that it is ruled by the Holy Spirit! Thus they deal with Christ's unfortunate people. They give them many laws and themselves keep none of them, but others they compel either to keep them or else to buy release.

Since then the pope and his followers have suspended the whole canon law, and since they pay no heed to it, but regard their own wanton will as a law exalting them above all the world, we should follow their example and for our part also reject these books. Why should we waste our time studying them? We could never discover the whole arbitrary will of the pope, which has now become the canon law. The

---

39. Boniface VIII (1294-1303) had decreed that the Roman pontiff has all laws in the chamber of his heart.

canon law has arisen in the devil's name, let it fall in the name of God, and let there be no more doctors of decrees in the world, but only doctor's of the papal chamber, that is, "hypocrites of the pope"! It is said that there is no better temporal rule anywhere than among the Turks, who have neither spiritual nor temporal law, but only their Koran, and we must confess that there is no more shameful rule than among us, with our spiritual and temporal law, so that there is no estate which lives according to the light of nature, still less according to Holy Scripture.

The temporal law—God help us! what a wilderness it has become! Though it is much better, wiser and more rational than the "spiritual law" which has nothing good about it except the name, still there is far too much of it. Surely the Holy Scriptures and good rulers would be law enough; as St. Paul says in 1 Corinthians 6, "Is there no one among you can judge his neighbor's cause, that ye must go to law before heathen courts?" (v. 1). It seems just to me that territorial laws and territorial customs should take precedence of the general imperial laws, and the imperial laws be used only in case of necessity. Would to God that as every land has its own peculiar character, so it were ruled by its own brief laws, as the lands were ruled before these imperial laws were invented, and many lands are still ruled without them! These diffuse and far-etched laws are only a burden to the people, and hinder causes more than they help them. I hope, however, that others have given this matter more thought and attention than I am able to do.

My friends the theologians have spared themselves pains and labor; they leave the Bible in peace and read the Sentences. I should think that the Sentences ought to be the first study of young students in theology and the Bible ought to be the study for the doctors. But now it is turned around; the Bible comes first, and is put aside when the bachelor's degree is reached, and the Sentences come last. They are attached forever to the doctorate, and that with such a solemn obligation that a man who is not a priest may indeed read the Bible, but the Sentences a priest must read. A married man, I observe, could be a doctor of the Bible, but under no circumstances a doctor of the Sentences. What good fortune can we expect if we act so perversely and in this way put the Bible, the holy Word of God, so far to the rear? Moreover the pope commands, with many severe words, that his laws are to be read and used in the schools and the courts, but little is said of the Gospel. Thus it is the custom that in the schools and the courts the Gospel lies idle in the dust under the bench, to the end that the pope's harmful laws may rule alone.

If we are called by the title of teachers of Holy Scripture, then we ought to be compelled, in accordance with our name, to teach the Holy Scriptures and nothing else, although even this title is too proud and boastful and no one ought to be proclaimed and crowned teacher of Holy Scripture. Yet it might be suffered, if the work justified the name; but now, under the despotism of the Sentences, we find among the theologians more of heathen and human opinion than of the holy and certain doctrine of Scripture. What, then, are we to do? I know of no other way than humbly to pray God to give us doctors of Theology; pope, emperor and universities may make doctors of arts, of medicine, of laws, of the Sentences, but be assured that no one will make a doctor of Holy Scripture, save only the Holy Ghost from Heaven, as Christ says in John 6, "They must all be taught of God Himself" (v. 45). Now the Holy Ghost does not concern Himself about red or brown birettas[40] or other decorations, nor does He ask whether one is old or young, layman or priest, monk or secular, virgin or married; nay He spake of old by an ass, against the prophet who rode upon it (Num. 22:28). Would God that we were worthy to have such doctors given us, whether they were layman or priests, married or virgin. True, they now try to force

---

40. The head-dress of the doctors.

the Holy Ghost into pope, bishops, and doctors, although there is no sign or indication whatever that He is in them.

The number of theological books must also be lessened, and a selection made of the best of them. For it is not many books or much reading that makes men learned, but it is good things, however little of them, often read, that make men learned in the Scriptures, and make them godly, too. Indeed the writings of all the holy fathers should be read only for a time, in order that through them we may be led to the Holy Scriptures. As it is, however, we read them only to be absorbed in them and never come to the Scriptures. We are like men who study the sign-posts and never travel the road. The dear fathers wished, by their writings, to lead us to the Scriptures, but we so use them as to be led away from the Scriptures, though the Scriptures alone are our vineyard in which we ought all to work and toil.

Above all, the foremost and most general subject of study, both in the higher and the lower schools, should be the Holy Scriptures, and for the young boys the Gospel. And would to God that every town had a girls' school also, in which the girls were taught the Gospel for an hour each day either in German or Latin. Indeed the schools, monasteries and nunneries began long ago with that end in view, and it was a praiseworthy and Christian purpose, as we learn from the story of St. Agnes and other of the saints. That was the time of holy virgins and martyrs, and then it was well with Christendom, but now they have come to nothing but praying and singing. Ought not every Christian at his ninth or tenth year to know the entire holy Gospel from which he derives his name and his life? A spinner or a seamstress teaches her daughter the trade in her early years; but now even the great, learned prelates and bishops themselves do not know the Gospel.

O how unjustly we deal with these poor young people who are committed to us for direction and instruction! We must give a terrible accounting for our neglect to set the Word of God before them.

They are as Jeremiah says in Lamentations 2: "Mine eyes are grown weary with weeping, my bowels are terrified, my liver is poured out upon the ground, because of the destruction of the daughter of my people, for the youth and the children perish in all the streets of the whole city; they said to their mothers, 'Where is bread and wine?' and they swooned as the wounded in the streets of the city and gave up the ghost in their mothers' bosom" (vv. 11-12). This pitiful evil we do not see—how even now the young folk in the midst of Christendom languish and perish miserably for want of the Gospel, in which we ought to be giving them constant instruction and training.

Moreover, if the universities were diligent in the study of Holy Scripture, we should not send everybody there, as we do when all we ask is numbers, and everyone wishes to have a doctor's degree, but we should send only the best qualified students, who have previously been well trained in the lower schools. A prince or city council ought to see to this, and permit only the well qualified to be sent. But where the Holy Scriptures do not rule, there I advise no one to send his son. Everyone not unceasingly busy with the Word of God must become corrupt; that is why the people who are in the universities and who are trained there are the kind of people they are. For this no one is to blame but the pope, the bishops, and the prelates, who are charged with the training of the youth. For the universities ought to turn out only men who are experts in the Holy Scriptures, who can become bishops and priests, leaders in the fight against heretics, the devil, and all the world. But where do you find this true? I greatly fear that the universities are wide gates of Hell, if they do not diligently teach the Holy Scriptures and impress them on the youth.

26. I know full well that the Roman crowd will make pretensions and great boasts about how the pope took the Holy Roman Empire from the Greek Emperor and bestowed it on the Germans, for which honor and benevolence he is said to have justly deserved and obtained from the Germans submission and thanks and all good things. For

this reason they will, perhaps, undertake to throw to the winds all attempts to reform them, and will not allow us to think about anything but the bestowal of the Roman Empire. For this cause they have heretofore persecuted and oppressed many a worthy emperor so arbitrarily and arrogantly that it is a pity to tell of it, and with the same adroitness they have made themselves overlords of all the temporal powers and authorities, contrary to the Holy Gospel. Of this too I must therefore speak.

There is no doubt that the true Roman Empire, which the writings of the prophets foretold in Numbers 24:24 and in Daniel 2:39ff has long since been overthrown and brought to an end, as Balaam clearly prophesied in Numbers 24, when he said: "The Romans shall come and overthrow the Jews; and afterwards they also shall be destroyed." That was brought to pass by the Goths, but especially when the Turkish Empire arose almost a thousand years ago; then in time Asia and Africa fell away, and finally Venice arose, and there remained to Rome nothing of its former power.

Now when the pope could not subdue to his arrogant will the Greeks and the emperor at Constantinople, who was hereditary Roman Emperor, he bethought himself of this device, namely, to rob him of his empire and his title and turn it over to the Germans, who were at that time warlike and of good repute, so as to bring the power of the Roman Empire under his control and give it away as a fief. So too it turned out. It was taken away from the emperor at Constantinople and its name and title were given to us Germans. Thereby we became the servants of the pope, and there is now a second Roman Empire, which the pope has built upon the Germans; for the other, which was first, has long since fallen, as I have said.

So then the Roman See has its will. It has taken possession of Rome, driven out the German Emperor and bound him with oaths not to dwell at Rome. He is to be Roman Emperor, and yet he is not to have possession of Rome, and besides he is at all times to be dependent upon the caprice of the pope and his followers, so that we have the name and they have the land and cities. They have always abused our simplicity to serve their own arrogance and tyranny, and they call us mad Germans, who let ourselves be made apes and fools at their bidding.

Ah well! For God the Lord it is a small thing to toss empires and principalities to and fro! He is so generous with them that once in a while He gives a kingdom to a knave and takes it from a good man, sometimes by the treachery of wicked, faithless men and sometimes by heredity, as we read of the Kingdoms of Persia and Greece, and of almost all kingdoms; and Daniel 2 and 4 says: "He Who ruleth over all things dwelleth in Heaven, and it is He alone Who changeth kingdoms, tosseth them to and fro, and maketh them" (2:21; 4:14). Since, therefore, no one can think it a great thing to have a kingdom given him, especially if he is a Christian, we Germans too cannot be puffed up because a new Roman Empire is bestowed on us; for in His eyes it is a trifling gift, which He often gives to the most unworthy, as Daniel 4 says: "All who dwell upon the earth are in His eyes as nothing, and He has power in all the kingdoms of men, to give them to whomsoever He will" (v. 35).

But although the pope unjustly and by violence robbed the true emperor of his Roman Empire, or of its name, and gave it to us Germans, it is certain, nevertheless, that in this matter God has used the pope's wickedness to give such an empire to the German nation, and after the all of the first Roman Empire, to set up another, which still exists. And although we gave no occasion to this wickedness of the popes, and did not understand their false aims and purposes, nevertheless, through this papal trickery and roguery, we have already paid too dearly for our empire, with incalculable bloodshed, with the suppression of our liberty, with the risk and robbery of all our goods, especially the goods of the churches and canonries, and with the suffering of unspeakable deception and insult. We have the name of the empire, but the pope has our wealth, honor, body, life, soul, and all that is ours. So we Germans are to be cheated in the trade. What the popes sought was to be emperors, and since they could not manage that, they at least succeeded in setting themselves over the emperors.

Because then, the empire has been given us without our fault, by the providence of God and the plotting of evil men, I would not advise that we give it up, but rather that we rule it wisely and in the fear of God, so long as it shall please Him. For, as has been said, it matters not to Him where an empire comes from; it is His will that it shall be ruled. Though the popes took it dishonestly from others, nevertheless we did not get it dishonestly. It is given us by the will of God through evil-minded men, and we have more regard for God's will than for the treacherous purpose of the popes, who, in bestowing it, wished to be emperors themselves, and more than emperors, and only to fool and mock us with the name. The King of Babylon also seized his empire by robbery and force; yet it was God's will that it should be ruled by the holy princes, Daniel, Hananiah, Azariah, and Mishael (Dan 3:30; 5:29); much more then is it His will that this empire be ruled by the Christian princes of Germany, regardless of whether the pope stole it, or got it by robbery, or made it anew. It is all God's ordering, which came to pass before we knew of it.

Therefore the pope and his followers may not boast that they have done a great favor to the German nation by the bestowal of this Roman Empire. First, because they did not mean it for our good, but were rather taking advantage of our simplicity in order to strengthen themselves in their proud designs against the Roman Emperor at Constantinople, from whom the pope godlessly and lawlessly took this empire, a thing which he had no right to do. Second, because the pope's intention was not to give us the empire, but to get it for himself, that he might bring all our power, our freedom, wealth, body, and soul into subjection to himself and use us (if

God had not prevented) to subdue all the world. He clearly says so himself in his decretals, and he has attempted it, by many evil wiles, with a number of the German emperors. How beautifully we Germans have been taught our German! When we thought to be lords, we became slaves of the most deceitful tyrants; we have the name, title, and insignia of the empire, but the pope has its treasures, its authority, its law, and its liberty. So the pope gobbles the kernel, and we play with the empty hulls.

Now may God, who by the wiles of tyrants has tossed this empire into our lap, and charged us with the ruling of it, help us to live up to the name, title, and insignia, to rescue our liberty, and to show the Romans, for once, what it is that we, through them, have received from God! They boast that they have bestowed on us an empire. So be it, then! If it is true, then let the pope give us Rome and everything else which he has got from the empire; let him free our land from his intolerable taxing and robbing, and give us back our liberty, authority, wealth, honor, body, and soul; let the empire be what an empire should be, and let his words and pretensions be fulfilled!

If he will not do that, then why all this shamming, these false and lying words and juggler's tricks? Is he not satisfied with having so rudely led this noble nation by the nose these many hundred years without ceasing? It does not follow that the pope must be above an emperor because he makes or crowns him. The prophet Samuel at God's command anointed and crowned Kings Saul and David, and yet he was their subject; and the prophet Nathan anointed King Solomon, but was not set over him on that account (1 Sam. 16:1; 16:13); Elisha too had one of his servants anoint Jehu King of Israel (1 Kings 1:38ff), and yet they remained obedient and subject to him (2 Kings 9:1ff). Except in the case of the pope, it has never happened in all the world's history that he who consecrated or crowned the king was over the king. He lets himself be crowned pope by three cardinals, who are under him, and he is nevertheless their superior. Why then should he, contrary to the example which he himself sets and contrary to the custom and teaching of all the world and of the Scriptures, exalt himself above temporal authorities, or the empire, simply because he crowns or consecrates the emperor? It is enough that he should be the emperor's superior in divine things, to wit, in preaching, teaching, and administering the sacraments, in which things, indeed, any bishop or priest is over every other man, as St. Ambrose in his See was over the emperor Theodosius, and the prophet Nathan over David, and Samuel over Saul? Therefore, let the German emperor be really and truly emperor, and let not his authority or his sword be put down by this blind pretension of papal hypocrites, as though they were to be excepted from his dominion and themselves direct the temporal sword in all things.

27. Enough has now been said about the failings of the clergy, though more of them can and will be found if these are properly considered. We would say something too about the failings of the temporal estate.

1. There is great need of a general law and decree of the German nation against the extravagance and excess in dress, by which so many nobles and rich men are impoverished. God has given to us, as to other lands, enough wool, hair, flax and everything else which properly serves for the seemly and honorable dress of every rank, so that we do not need to spend and waste such enormous sums for silk and velvet and golden ornaments and other foreign wares. I believe that even if the pope had not robbed us Germans with his intolerable exactions, we should still have our hands more than full with these domestic robbers, the silk and velvet merchants. In the matter of clothes, as we see, everybody wants to be equal to everybody else, and pride and envy are aroused and increased among us, as we deserve. All this and much more misery would be avoided if our curiosity would only let us be thankful, and be satisfied with the goods which God has given us.

2. In like manner it is also necessary to restrict the spice-traffic, which is another of the great ships in which money is carried out of German lands. There grows among us, by God's grace, more to eat and drink than in any other land, and just as choice and good. Perhaps the proposals that I make may seem foolish and impossible and give the impression that I want to suppress the greatest of all trades, that of commerce, but I am doing what I can. If reforms are not generally introduced, then let everyone who is willing reform himself. I do not see that many good customs have ever come to a land through commerce, and in ancient times God made His people of Israel dwell away from the sea on this account, and did not let them engage much in commerce.

3. But the greatest misfortune of the German nation is certainly the traffic in annuities. If that did not exist many a man would have to leave unbought his silks, velvets, golden ties, spices, and ornaments of every sort. It has not existed much over a hundred years, and has already brought almost all princes, cities, endowed institutions, nobles, and their heirs to poverty, misery, and ruin; if it shall continue for another hundred years Germany cannot possibly have a pfennig left and we shall certainly have to devour one another. The devil invented the practice, and the pope, by confirming it, has injured the whole world. Therefore I ask and pray that everyone open his eyes to see the ruin of himself, his children, and his heirs, which not only stands before the door, but already haunts the house, and that emperor, princes, lords, and cities do their part that this trade be condemned as speedily as possible, and henceforth prevented, regardless whether or not the pope, with all his law and unlaw, is opposed to it, and whether or not benefices or church foundations are based upon it. It is better that there should be in a city one living based on an honest freehold or revenue, than a hundred based on an annuity; indeed a living based on an annuity is worse and more grievous than twenty based on freeholds. In truth this traffic in rents must be a sign and symbol that the

world, for its grievous sins, has been sold to the devil, so that both temporal and spiritual possessions must fail us, and yet we do not notice it at all.

Here, too, we must put a bit in the mouth of the Fuggers and similar corporations. How is it possible that in the lifetime of a single man such great possessions, worthy of a king, can be piled up, and yet everything be done legally and according to God's will?[41] I am not a mathematician, but I do not understand how a man with a hundred gulden can make a profit of twenty gulden in one year, nay, how with one gulden he can make another; and that, too, by another way than agriculture or cattle-raising, in which increase of wealth depends not on human wits, but on God's blessing. I commend this to the men of affairs. I am a theologian, and find nothing to blame in it except its evil and offending appearance, of which St. Paul says, "Avoid every appearance or show of evil" (1 Thes. 5:22). This I know well, that it would be much more pleasing to God if we increased agriculture and diminished commerce, and that they do much better who, according to the Scriptures, till the soil and seek their living from it, as was said to us and to all men in Adam, "Accursed be the earth when thou laborest therein, it shall bear thee thistles and thorns, and in the sweat of thy face shalt thou eat thy bread" (Gen. 3:17ff). There is still much land lying untilled.

4. Next comes the abuse of eating and drinking, which gives us Germans a bad reputation in foreign lands, as though it were our special vice. Preaching cannot stop it; it has become too common, and has got too firmly the upper hand. The waste of money which it causes would be a small thing, were it not followed by other sins—murder, adultery, stealing, irreverence, and all the vices. The temporal sword can do something to prevent it; or else it will be as Christ says: "The last day shall come like a secret snare, when they shall be eating

---

41. Luther is talking about usury.

and drinking, marrying and wooing, building and planting, buying and selling" (Luke 21:34ff). It is so much like that now that I verily believe the judgment day is at the door, though men are thinking least of all about it.

5. Finally, is it not a pitiful thing that we Christians should maintain among us open and common houses of prostitution, though all of us are baptized unto chastity? I know very well what some say to this, to wit, that it is not the custom of any one people, that it is hard to break up, that it is better that there should be such houses than that married women, or maidens, or those of more honorable estate should be outraged. But should not the temporal, Christian government consider that in this heathen way the evil is not to be controlled? If the people of Israel could exist without such an abomination, why could not Christian people do as much? Nay, how do many cities, towns and villages exist without such houses? Why should not great cities also exist without them?

In this, and in the other matters above mentioned, I have tried to point out how many good works the temporal government could do, and what should be the duty of every government, to the end that every one may learn what an awful responsibility it is to rule, and to have high station. What good would it do that an overlord were in his own life as holy as St. Peter, if he have not the purpose diligently to help his subjects in these matters? His very authority will condemn him! For it is the duty of the authorities to seek the highest good of their subjects. But if the authorities were to consider how the young people might be brought together in marriage, the hope of entering the married state would greatly help every one to endure and to resist temptation.

But now every man is drawn to the priesthood or the monastic life, and among them, I fear, there is not one in a hundred who has any other reason than that he seeks a living, and doubts that he will ever be able to support himself in the estate of matrimony. Therefore they live wildly enough beforehand, and wish, as they say, to "wear out their lust," but rather wear it in, as experience shows. I find the proverb true, "Despair makes most of the monks and priests"; and so things are as we see them.

My faithful counsel is that, in order to avoid many sins which have become very common, neither boy nor maid should take the vow of chastity, or of the "spiritual life," before the age of thirty years. It is, as St. Paul says, a peculiar gift (1 Cor. 7). Therefore let him whom God does not constrain, put off becoming a cleric and taking the vows. Nay, I will go farther and say that if you trust God so little that you are not willing to support yourself as a married man, and wish to become a cleric only because of this distrust, then for the sake of your own soul, I beg of you not to become a cleric, but rather a farmer, or whatever else you please. For if to obtain your temporal support you must have one measure of trust in God, you must have ten measures of trust to continue in the life of a cleric. If you do not trust God to support you in the world, how will you trust him to support you in the Church? Alas, unbelief and distrust spoil everything and lead us into all misery, as we see in every estate of life!

Much could be said of this miserable condition. The young people have no one to care for them. They all do as they please, and the government is of as much use to them as if it did not exist; and yet this should be the chief concern of pope, bishops, lords, and councils. They wish to rule far and wide, and yet to help no one. O, what a rare bird will a lord and ruler be in Heaven just on this account, even though he build a hundred churches for God and raise up all the dead!

(Let this suffice for this time! Of what the temporal powers and the nobility ought to do, I think I have said enough in the little book *On Good Works*. There is room for improvement in their lives and in their rule, and yet the abuses of the temporal power are not to be compared with those of the spiritual power, as I have there shown.)

I think too that I have pitched my song in a high key, have made many propositions which will be thought impossible and have attacked many things too sharply. But what am I to do? I am in duty bound to speak. If I were able, these are the things I should wish to do. I prefer the wrath of the world to the wrath of God; they can do no more than take my life. Many times heretofore I have made overtures of peace to my opponents, but as I now see, God has through them compelled me to open my mouth wider and wider and give them enough to say, bark, shout, and write, since they have nothing else to do. Ah well, I know another little song about Rome and if I their ears itch for it I will sing them that song too, and pitch the notes to the top of the scale. Understandest thou, dear Rome, what I mean?

I have many times offered my writings for investigation and judgment, but it has been of no use. To be sure, I know that if my cause is just, it must be condemned on earth, and approved only by Christ in Heaven; or all the Scriptures show that the cause of Christians and of Christendom must be judged by God alone. Such a cause has never yet been approved by men on earth, but the opposition has always been too great and strong. It is my greatest care and fear that my cause may remain uncondemned, by which I should know for certain that it was not yet pleasing to God.

Therefore let them boldly go to work—pope, bishop, priest, monk, and scholar! They are the right people to persecute the truth, as they have ever done.

God give us all a Christian mind, and especially to the Christian nobility of the German nation a right spiritual courage to do the best that can be done for the poor Church. Amen.

Wittenberg, 1520

# THE BABYLONIAN CAPTIVITY OF THE CHURCH

*Translated by A.T.W. Steinhaeuser*

# LUTHER'S INTRODUCTION

Martin Luther, Augustinian, to his friend, Herman Tulich, Greeting

Willy nilly, I am compelled to become every day more learned, with so many and such able masters vying with one another to improve my mind. Some two years ago I wrote a little book on indulgences, which I now deeply regret having published; for at the time I was still sunk in a mighty superstitious veneration for the Roman tyranny and held that indulgences should not be altogether rejected, seeing they were approved by the common consent of men. Nor was this to be wondered at, for I was then engaged single-handed in my Sisyphean[42] task. Since then, however, through the kindness of Sylvester and the friars, who so strenuously defended indulgences, I have come to see that they are nothing but an imposture of the Roman sycophants by which they play havoc with men's faith and fortunes. Would to God I might prevail upon the booksellers and upon all my readers to burn up the whole of my writings on indulgences and to substitute for them this proposition: Indulges are a knavish trick of the Roman sycophants.

---

42. Sisyphus was a character in pagan mythology condemned in Hades to perpetually roll a rock up, only for it to fall back once it reached the place he was taking it.

Next, Eck and Emser, with their fellows, undertook to instruct me concerning the primacy of the pope. Here too, not to prove ungrateful to such learned folk, I acknowledge how greatly I have profited by their labors. For, while denying the divine authority of the papacy, I had yet admitted its human authority. But after hearing and reading the subtle subtleties of these coxcombs with which they adroitly prop their idol—for in these matters my mind is not altogether unteachable—I now know of a certainty that the papacy is the kingdom of Babylon and the power of Nimrod the mighty hunter.[43] Once more, therefore, that all may all out to my friends' advantage, I beg both booksellers and readers to burn what I have published on that subject and to hold to this proposition: The Papacy is the mighty hunting of the Roman bishop. This follows from the arguments of Eck, Emser, and the Leipzig lecturer on the Holy Scriptures.

Now they are putting me to school again and teaching me about communion in both kinds and other weighty subjects. And I must all to with might and main, so as not to hear these my pedagogues without profit. A certain Italian friar of Cremona[44] has written a "Revocation of Martin Luther to the Holy See"—that is, a revocation in which not I revoke anything (as the words declare) but he revokes me. That is the kind of Latin the Italians are now beginning to write. Another friar, a German of Leipzig, that same lecturer, you know, on the whole canon of the Scriptures, has written a book against me concerning the sacrament in both kinds, and is planning, I understand, still greater and more marvelous things. The Italian was canny enough not to set down his name, fearing perhaps the fate of Cajetan and Sylvester. But the Leipzig man, as becomes a fierce and valiant German, boasts on his ample title-page of his name, his career, his

---

43. Babylon is associated with the antichrist in the book of Revelation (chapters 17 and 18). Nimrod was said to be the builder of the tower of Babel (Babylon).
44. Isidore Isolani.

saintliness, his scholarship, his office, glory, honor, aye, almost of his very clogs. Here I shall doubtless gain no little information, since indeed his dedicatory epistle is addressed to the Son of God Himself. On so familiar a footing are these saints with Christ who reigns in Heaven! Moreover, methinks I hear three magpies chattering in this book; the first in good Latin, the second in better Greek, the third in purest Hebrew.[45] What think you, my Herman, is there for me to do but to prick up my ears? The thing emanates from Leipzig, from the Observance of the Holy Cross.

Fool that I was, I had hitherto thought it would be well if a general council decided that the sacrament be administered to the laity in both kinds. The more than learned friar would set me right, and declares that neither Christ nor the apostles commanded or commended the administration of both kinds to the laity; it was, therefore, left to the judgment of the Church what to do or not to do in this matter, and the Church must be obeyed. These are his words.

You will perhaps ask what madness has entered into the man, or against whom he is writing, since I have not condemned the use of one kind, but have left the decision about the use of both kinds to the judgment of the Church—the very thing he attempts to assert and which he turns against me. My answer is that this sort of argument is common to all those who write against Luther; they assert the very things they assail, for they set up a man of straw whom they may attack. Thus Sylvester and Eck and Emser, thus the theologians of Cologne and Louvain; and if this friar had not been of the same kidney he would never have written against Luther.

Yet in one respect this man has been happier than his fellows. For in undertaking to prove that the use of both kinds is neither commanded nor commended, but left to the will of the Church, he brings

---

45. A satiric reference to a section in Alveld's treatise, on the name of Jesus, which he spells IHSVH and brings proofs for this form from the three languages.

forward passages of Scripture to prove that by the command of Christ one kind only was appointed for the laity. So that it is true, according to this new interpreter of the Scriptures, that one kind was not commanded, and at the same time was commanded, by Christ! This novel sort of argument is, as you know, the particular forte of the Leipzig dialecticians. Did not Emser in his earlier book profess to write of me in a friendly spirit, and then, after I had convicted him of filthy envy and foul lying, did he not openly acknowledge in his later book, written to refute my arguments, that he had written in both a friendly and an unfriendly spirit? A sweet fellow, forsooth, as you know.

But hearken to our distinguished distinguisher of "kinds," for whom the will of the Church and a command of Christ, and a command of Christ and no command of Christ, are all one and the same! How ingeniously he proves that only one kind is to be given to the laity, by the command of Christ, that is, by the will of the Church. He puts it in capital letters, thus: THE INFALLIBLE FOUNDATION. Thereupon he treats John 6 with incredible wisdom, in which passage Christ speaks of the bread from Heaven and the bread of life, which is He Himself. The learned fellow not only refers these words to the sacrament of the altar, but because Christ says, "I am the living bread," (John 6:35, 41, 51). and not, "I am the living cup," he actually concludes that we have in this passage the institution of the sacrament in only one kind for the laity. But there follow the words, "My flesh is meat indeed, and my blood is drink indeed," (John 6:55). and, "Except ye eat the flesh of the Son of man, and drink his blood" (John 6:53); and when it dawned upon the good friar that these words speak undeniably for both kinds and against one kind—presto! how happily and learnedly he slips out of the quandary by asserting that in these words Christ means to say only that whoever receives the one kind receives under it both flesh and blood. This he puts for the "infallible foundation" of a structure well worthy of the holy and Heavenly observance.

Now prithee, herefrom learn with me that Christ, in John 6, enjoins the sacrament in one kind, yet in such wise that His commanding it means leaving it to the will of the Church, and further, that Christ is speaking in this chapter only of the laity and not of the priests. For to the latter the living bread from Heaven does not pertain, but presumably the deadly bread from Hell! And how is it with the deacons and subdeacons, who are neither laymen nor priests? According to this brilliant writer, they ought to use neither the one kind nor both kinds! You see, dear Tulich, this novel and observant method of treating Scripture.

But learn this, too: that Christ is speaking in John 6 of the sacrament of the altar, although He Himself teaches that His words refer to faith in the Word made flesh, for He says, "This is the work of God, that ye believe on him whom he hath sent" (v. 29). But our Leipzig professor of the Scriptures must be permitted to prove anything he pleases from any Scripture passage whatsoever. For he is an Anaxagorian, or rather an Aristotelian theologian, for whom nouns and verbs, interchanged, mean the same thing and anything. So aptly does he cite Scripture prooftexts throughout the whole of his book, that if he set out to prove the presence of Christ in the sacrament, he would not hesitate to commence thus: "Here beginneth the book of the Revelation of St. John the Divine." All his quotations are as apt as this one would be, and the wiseacre imagines he is adorning his drivel with the multitude of his quotations. The rest I pass over, lest you should smother in the filth of this vile cloaca.

In conclusion, he brings forward 1 Corinthians 11, where Paul says he received from the Lord, and delivered to the Corinthians, the use of both the bread and the cup (v. 23). Here again our distinguisher of kinds, treating the Scriptures with his usual brilliance, teaches that Paul did not deliver, but permitted both kinds. Do you ask where he gets his proof? Out of his own head, as he did in the case of John 6. For it does not behoove this lecturer to give a reason for his assertions;

he belongs to the order of those who teach and prove all things by their visions. Accordingly we are here taught that the apostle, in this passage, addressed not the whole Corinthian congregation, but the laity alone—but then he "permitted" nothing at all to the clergy, and they are deprived of the sacrament altogether!—and further, that, according to a new kind of grammar, "I have received from the Lord" means "It is permitted by the Lord," and "I have delivered it to you" means "I have permitted it to you." I pray you, mark this well. For by this method, not only the Church, but every passing knave will be at liberty, according to this magister, to turn all the commands, institutions, and ordinances of Christ and the apostles into a mere "permission."

I perceive, therefore, that this man is driven by an angel of Satan, and that he and his partners seek but to make a name for themselves through me, as men who were worthy to cross swords with Luther. But their hopes shall be dashed: I shall ignore them and not mention their names from henceforth even forever. This one reply shall suffice me for all their books. If they be worthy of it, I pray Christ in His mercy to bring them to a sound mind; if not, I pray that they may never leave off writing such books, and that the enemies of the truth may never deserve to read any other. It is a popular and true saying,

> This I know of a truth—whenever with filth I contended,
> Victor or vanquished, alike, came I defiled from the fray.

And, since I perceive that they have an abundance of leisure and of writing-paper, I shall see to it that they may have ample opportunity for writing. I shall run on before, and while they are celebrating a glorious victory over one of my so-called heresies, I shall be meanwhile devising a new one. For I too am desirous that these gallant leaders in battle should win to themselves many titles and decorations. Therefore, while they complain that I laud communion in both kinds, and are happily engrossed in this most important and worthy matter, I will go yet one step farther and undertake to show that all those who deny communion in both kinds to the laity are wicked men. And the more conveniently to do this, I will compose a prelude on the captivity of the Roman Church. In due time I shall have a great deal more to say, when the learned papists have disposed of this book.

I take this course, lest any pious reader who may chance upon this book should be offended at my dealing with such filthy matters, and should justly complain of finding in it nothing to cultivate and instruct his mind or even to furnish good or learned thought. For you know how impatient my friends are because I waste my time on the sordid fictions of these men, which, they say, are amply refuted in the reading; they look for greater things from me, which Satan seeks in this way to hinder. I have at length resolved to follow their counsel and to leave to those hornets the pleasant business of wrangling and hurling invectives.

Of that friar of Cremona I will say nothing. He is an unlearned man and a simpleton, who attempts with a few rhetorical passages to recall me to the Holy See, from which I am not as yet aware of having departed, nor has any one proved it to me. He is chiefly concerned in those silly passages with showing that I ought to be moved by the vow of my order and by the act that the empire has been transferred to us Germans. He seems thus to have set out to write, not my "revocation," but rather the praises of the French people and the Roman pontiff. Let him attest his loyalty in his little book; it is the best he could do. He does not deserve to be harshly treated, for methinks he was not prompted by malice; nor yet to be learnedly refuted, for all his chatter is sheer ignorance and simplicity.

At the outset I must deny that there are seven sacraments, and hold for the present to but three—baptism, penance and the bread. These three have been subjected to a miserable captivity by the Roman curia, and the Church has been deprived of all her liberty. To be sure, if

I desired to use the term in its scriptural sense, I should allow but a single sacrament, with three sacramental signs; but of this I shall treat more fully at the proper time.

# THE SACRAMENT OF THE BREAD

Let me tell you what progress I have made in my studies on the administration of this sacrament. For when I published my treatise on the Eucharist, I clung to the common usage, being in no wise concerned with the question of the right or wrong of the papacy. But now, challenged and attacked, nay, forcibly thrust into the arena, I shall freely speak my mind, let all the papists laugh or weep together.

## FIRST CAPTIVITY: WITHHOLDING OF THE CUP FROM THE LAITY

In the first place, John 6 is to be entirely excluded from this discussion, since it does not refer in a single syllable to the sacrament. For not only was the sacrament not yet instituted, but the whole context plainly shows that Christ is speaking of faith in the Word made flesh, as I have said above. For He says, "My words are spirit, and they are life," (v. 63). which shows that He is speaking of a spiritual eating, whereby whoever eats has life, whereas the Jews understood Him to be speaking of bodily eating and therefore disputed with Him. But no eating can give life save the eating which is by faith, for that is the truly spiritual and living eating. As Augustine also says: "Why make ready teeth and stomach? Believe, and thou hast eaten." For the sacramental eating does not give life, since many eat unworthily. Therefore, He cannot be understood as speaking of the sacrament in this passage.

These words have indeed been wrongly applied to the sacrament, as in the decretal *Dudum* and often elsewhere. But it is one thing to misapply the Scriptures, it is quite another to understand them in their proper meaning. But if Christ in this passage enjoined the sacramental eating, then by saying, "Except ye eat my flesh and drink my blood, ye have no life in you" (John 6:53), He would condemn all infants, invalids, and those absent or in any wise hindered from the sacramental eating, however strong their faith might be. Thus Augustine, in the second book of his *Contra Julianum*, proves from Innocent that even infants eat the flesh and drink the blood of Christ, without the sacrament; that is, they partake of them through the faith of the Church. Let this then be accepted as proved: John 6 does not belong here. For this reason I have elsewhere written that the Bohemians have no right to rely on this passage in support of their use of the sacrament in both kinds.

Now there are two passages that do clearly bear upon this matter: the Gospel narratives of the institution of the Lord's Supper, and Paul in 1 Corinthians 11. These let us examine.

Matthew, Mark, and Luke agree that Christ gave the whole sacrament to all the disciples (Matt. 26; Mark 14; Luke 22), and it is certain that Paul delivered both kinds (1 Cor. 11). No one has ever had the temerity to assert the contrary. Further, Matthew reports that Christ said not of the bread, "Eat ye all of it," (Matt. 26:27). but of the cup, "Drink ye all of it"; and Mark likewise says not, "They all ate of it," but, "They all drank of it" (Mark 14:23). Both Matthew and Mark attach the note of universality to the cup, not to the bread; as though the Spirit saw this schism coming, by which some would be forbidden to partake of the cup, which Christ desired should be common to all. How furiously, think you, would they rave against us, if they had found the word "all" attached to the bread instead of the cup! They would not leave us a loophole to escape, they would cry out upon us and set us down as heretics, they would damn us for schismatics. But now, since it stands on our side and against them, they will not be bound by any force of logic—these men of the most free will, who change and change again even the things that be God's, and throw everything into confusion.

But imagine me standing over against them and interrogating my lords the papists. In the Lord's Supper, I say, the whole sacrament, or communion in both kinds, is given only to the priests or else it is given also to the laity. If it is given only to the priests, as they would have it, then it is not right to give it to the laity in either kind, for it must not be rashly given to any to whom Christ did not give it when He instituted it. For if we permit one institution of Christ to be changed, we make all of His laws invalid, and everyone will boldly claim that he is not bound by any law or institution of His. For a single exception, especially in the Scriptures, invalidates the whole. But if it is given also to the laity, then it inevitably follows that it ought not to be withheld from them in either form. And if any do withhold it from them when they desire it, they act impiously and contrary to the work, example, and institution of Christ.

I confess that I am conquered by this to me unanswerable argument, and that I have neither read, nor heard, nor found anything to advance against it. For here the word and example of Christ stand firm, when He says, not by way of permission but of command, "Drink ye all of it" (Matt. 26:27). For if all are to drink, and the words cannot be understood as addressed to the priests alone, then it is certainly an impious act to withhold the cup from laymen who desire it, even though an angel from Heaven were to do it. For when they say that the distribution of both kinds was left to the judgment of the Church, they make this assertion without giving any reason or it and put it forth without any authority; it is ignored just as readily as it is proved, and does not hold against an opponent who confronts us with the word and work of Christ. Such an one must be refuted with a word of Christ, but this we do not possess.

But if one kind may be withheld from the laity, then with equal right and reason a portion of baptism and penance might also be taken from them by this same authority of the Church. Therefore, just as baptism and absolution must be administered in their entirety, so the sacrament of the bread must be given in its entirety to all laymen, if they desire it. I am amazed to find them asserting that the priests may never receive only the one kind, in the Mass, on pain of committing a mortal sin, and that for no other reason, as they unanimously say, than that both kinds constitute the one complete sacrament, which may not be divided. I pray them to tell me why it may be divided in the case of the laity, and why to them alone the whole sacrament may not be given. Do they not acknowledge by their own testimony either that both kinds are to be given to the laity, or that it is not a valid sacrament when only one kind is given to them? How can the one kind be a complete sacrament or the laity and not a complete sacrament for the priests? Why do they flaunt the authority of the Church and the power of the pope in my face? These do not make void the Word of God and the testimony of the truth.

But further, if the Church can withhold the wine from the laity, it can also withhold the bread from them; it could, therefore, withhold the entire sacrament of the altar from the laity and completely annul Christ's institution so far as they are concerned. I ask, by what authority? But if the Church cannot withhold the bread, or both kinds, neither can it withhold the wine. This cannot possibly be gainsaid, for the Church's power must be the same over either kind as over both kinds, and if she has no power over both kinds, she has none over either kind. I am curious to hear what the Roman sycophants will have to say to this.

What carries most weight with me, however, and quite decides me is this: Christ says: "This is my blood, which is shed for you and for many for the remission of sins" (Matt. 26:28). Here we see very plainly that the blood is given to all those for whose sins it was shed. But who will dare to say it was not shed for the laity? Do you not see whom He addresses when He gives the cup? Does He not give it to all? Does He not say that it is shed for all? "For you," He says—well, we will let these be the priests—"and for many"—these cannot be priests, and yet He says, "Drink ye all of it" (Matt. 26:27). I too could easily trifle here and with my words make a mockery of Christ's words, as my dear trifler does, but they who rely on the Scriptures in opposing us must be refuted by the Scriptures. This is what has prevented me from condemning the Bohemians, who, be they wicked men or good, certainly have the word and act of Christ on their side, while we have neither, but only that hollow device of men—"the Church has appointed it." It was not the Church that appointed these things, but the tyrants of the churches, without the consent of the Church, which is the people of God.

But where in all the world is the necessity, where the religious duty, where the practical use of denying both kinds, i.e., the visible sign, to the laity, when everyone concedes to them the grace of the sacrament without the sign? If they concede the grace, which is the greater, why not the sign, which is the lesser? For in every sacrament the sign as such is of far less importance than the thing signified. What then is to prevent them from conceding the lesser, when they concede the greater? I can see but one reason: it has come about by the permission of an angry God in order to give occasion for a schism in the Church, to bring home to us how, having long ago lost the grace of the sacrament, we contend for the sign, which is the lesser, against that which is the most important and the chief thing, just as some men for the sake of ceremonies contend against love. Nay, this monstrous perversion seems to date from the time when we began for the sake of the riches of this world to rage against Christian love. Thus God would show us by this terrible sign how we esteem signs more than the things they signify. How preposterous would it be to admit that the faith of baptism is granted the candidate for baptism, and yet to deny him the sign of this faith, namely, the water!

Finally, Paul stands invincible and stops every mouth when he says in 1 Corinthians 11, "I have received from the Lord what I also delivered unto you" (v. 23). He does not say, "I permitted unto you," as that friar lyingly asserts. Nor is it true that Paul delivered both kinds on account of the contention in the Corinthian congregation. For, first, the text shows that their contention was not about both kinds, but about the contempt and envy among rich and poor, as it is clearly stated: "One is hungry, and another is drunken, and ye put to shame them that have not" (1 Cor. 11:21). Again, Paul is not speaking of the time when he first delivered the sacrament to them, for he says not, "I *receive* of the Lord and *give* unto you," but, "I received and delivered"—namely, when he first began to preach among them, a long while before this contention. This shows that he delivered both kinds to them; and "delivered" means the same as "commanded," for elsewhere he uses the word in this sense. Consequently there is nothing in the friar's fuming about permission; it is a hotchpotch without Scripture, reason or sense. His opponents do not ask what he has dreamed, but what the Scriptures decree in this matter, and out of the Scriptures he cannot adduce one jot or tittle in support of his dreams, while they can bring forward mighty thunderbolts in support of their faith.

Come hither then, ye popish flatterers, one and all! Fall to and defend yourselves against the charge of godlessness, tyranny, lese-majesty against the Gospel, and the crime of slandering your brethren—ye that decry as heretics those who will not be wise after the vaporings of your own brains in the face of such patent and potent words of Scripture. If any are to be called heretics and schismatics, it is not the Bohemians nor the Greeks, for they take their stand upon the Gospel, but you Romans are the heretics and godless schismatics, for you presume upon your own fictions and fly in the face of the clear Scriptures of God. Parry that stroke, if you can!

But what could be more ridiculous and more worthy of this friar's brain than his saying that the apostle wrote these words and gave this permission, not to the Church universal, but to a particular church, that is, the Corinthian? Where does he get his proof? Out of his one storehouse, his own impious head. If the Church universal receives, reads, and follows this epistle in all points as written for itself, why should it not do the same with this portion of it? If we admit that any epistle, or any part of any epistle, of Paul does not apply to the Church universal, then the whole authority of Paul falls to the ground. Then the Corinthians will say that what he teaches about faith in the epistle to the Romans does not apply to them. What greater blasphemy and madness can be imagined than this! God forbid that there should be one jot or tittle in all of Paul which the whole Church universal is not bound to follow and keep! Not so did the Fathers hold, down to these perilous times, in which Paul foretold there should be blasphemers and blind and insensate men (2 Tim. 3:2), of whom this friar is one, nay the chief.

However, suppose we grant the truth of this intolerable madness. If Paul gave his permission to a particular church, then, even from your own point of view, the Greeks and Bohemians are in the right, for they are particular churches; hence it is sufficient that they do not act contrary to Paul, who at least gave permission. Moreover, Paul could not permit anything contrary to Christ's institution. Therefore I cast in thy teeth, O Rome, and in the teeth of all thy sycophants, these sayings of Christ and Paul, on behalf of the Greeks and the Bohemians. Nor canst thou prove that thou hast received any authority to change them, much less to accuse others of heresy or disregarding thy arrogance; rather dost thou deserve to be charged with the crime of godlessness and despotism.

Furthermore, Cyprian, who alone is strong enough to hold all the Romanists at bay, bears witness, in the fifth book of his treatise *Of the Fallen*, that it was a widespread custom in his church to administer both kinds to the laity, and even to children, yea to give the body of the Lord into their hands, of which he cites many instances. He inveighs, for example, against certain members of the congregation as follows: "The sacrilegious man is angered at the priests because he does not forthwith receive the body of the Lord with unclean hands, or drink the blood of the Lord with defiled lips." He is speaking, as you see, of laymen, and irreverent laymen who desired to receive the body and the blood from the priests. Dost thou find anything to snarl at here, thou wretched flatterer? Say that even this holy martyr, a Church Father preeminent for his apostolic spirit, was a heretic and used that permission in a particular church.

In the same place, Cyprian narrates an incident that came under his own observation. He describes at length how a deacon was administering the cup to a little girl, who drew away from him, whereupon he poured the blood of the Lord into her mouth. We read the same of St. Donatus, whose broken chalice this wretched flatterer so lightly disposes of. "I read of a broken chalice," he says, "but I do not read that the blood was given." It is no wonder! He that finds what he pleases in the Scriptures will also read what he pleases in the histories. But will the authority of the Church be established, or will heretics be refuted in this way? Enough of this! I did not undertake this work to reply to him who is not worth replying to, but to bring the truth of the matter to light.

I conclude, then, that it is wicked and despotic to deny both kinds to the laity, and that this is not in the power of any angel, much less of any pope or council. Nor does the Council of Constance give me pause, for if its authority carries weight, why does not that of the Council of Basel also carry weight? For the latter council decided, on the contrary, after much disputing, that the Bohemians might use both kinds, as the extant records and documents of the council prove. And to that council this ignorant flatterer refers in support of his dream; in such wisdom does his whole treatise abound.

The first captivity of this sacrament, therefore, concerns its substance or completeness, of which we have been deprived by the despotism of Rome. Not that they sin against Christ, who use the one kind, for Christ did not command the use of either kind, but left it to every one's free will, when He said: "As oft as ye do this, do it in remembrance of me" (1 Cor. 11:25). But they sin who forbid the giving of both kinds to such as desire to exercise this free will. The fault lies not with the laity, but with the priests. The sacrament does not belong to the priests, but to all, and the priests are not lords but ministers, in duty bound to administer both kinds to those who desire them, and as oft as they desire them. If they wrest this right from the laity and forcibly withhold it, they are tyrants, but the laity are without fault, whether they lack one kind or both kinds; they must meanwhile be sustained by their faith and by their desire for the complete sacrament. Just as the priests, being ministers, are bound to administer baptism and absolution to whoever seeks them, because he has a right to them, but if they do not administer them, he that seeks them has at least the full merit of his faith, while they will be accused before Christ as wicked servants. In like manner the holy Fathers of old who dwelt in the desert did not receive the sacrament in any form for many years together.

Therefore I do not urge that both kinds be seized by force, as though we were bound to this form by a rigorous command; but I instruct men's consciences that they may endure the Roman tyranny, well knowing they have been deprived of their rightful share in the sacrament because of their own sin. This only do I desire:

that no one justify the tyranny of Rome, as though it did well to forbid one of the two kinds to the laity; we ought rather to abhor it, withhold our consent, and endure it just as we should do if we were held captive by the Turk and not permitted to use either kind. That is what I meant by saying it seemed well to me that this captivity should be ended by the decree of a general council, our Christian liberty restored to us out of the hands of the Roman tyrant, and everyone left free to seek and receive this sacrament, just as he is free to receive baptism and penance. But now they compel us by the same tyranny to receive the one kind year after year, so utterly lost is the liberty which Christ has given us. This is but the due reward of our godless ingratitude.

## SECOND CAPTIVITY: TRANSUBSTANTIATION

The second captivity of this sacrament is less grievous so far as the conscience is concerned, yet the very gravest danger threatens the man who would attack it, to say nothing of condemning it. Here I shall be called a Wyclifite, and a heretic a thousand times over. But what of that? Since the Roman bishop has ceased to be a bishop and become a tyrant, I fear none of his decrees, for I know that it is not in his power, nor even in that of a general council, to make new articles of faith.

Years ago, when I was delving into scholastic theology, the Cardinal of Cambray gave me food for thought, in his comments on the fourth book of the Sentences, where he argues with great acumen that to hold that real bread and real wine, and not their accidents only, are present on the altar, is much more probable and requires fewer unnecessary miracles—if only the Church had not decreed otherwise. When I learned later what church it was that had decreed this— namely, the Church of Thomas, i.e., of Aristotle—I waxed bolder, and after floating in a sea of doubt, at last found rest for my conscience in the above view, namely, that it is real bread and real wine in which Christ's real flesh and blood are present, not otherwise and not less really than they assume to be the case under their accidents. I reached this conclusion because I saw that the opinions of the Thomists, though approved by pope and council, remain but opinions and do not become articles of faith, even though an angel from Heaven were to decree otherwise (Gal. 1:8). For what is asserted without Scripture for an approved revelation may be held as an opinion, but need not be believed. But this opinion of Thomas hangs so completely in the air, devoid of Scripture and reason, that he seems here to have forgotten both his philosophy and his logic. For Aristotle treats so very differently from St. Thomas of subject and accidents that methinks this great man is to be pitied, not only for drawing his opinions in matters of faith from Aristotle, but for attempting to base them on him without understanding his meaning—an unfortunate superstructure upon an unfortunate foundation.

I therefore permit every man to hold either of these views, as he chooses. My one concern at present is to remove all scruples of conscience, so that no one may fear to become guilty of heresy if he should believe in the presence of real bread and real wine on the altar, and that everyone may feel at liberty to ponder, hold, and believe either one view or the other, without endangering his salvation. However, I shall now more fully set forth my own view.

In the first place, I do not intend to listen or attach the least importance to those who will cry out that this teaching of mine is Wyclifite, Hussite, heretical, and contrary to the decision of the Church, for they are the very persons whom I have convicted of manifold heresies in the matter of indulgences, the freedom of the will and the grace of God, good works and sin, etc. If Wyclif was once a heretic, they are heretics ten times over, and it is a pleasure to be suspected and accused by such heretics and perverse sophists, whom to please were the height of godlessness. Besides, the only way in which they can prove their opinions and disprove those of others is by saying, "That is Wyclifite, Hussite, heretical!" They have this feeble retort always on their tongue, and they have nothing else. If you demand a Scripture passage, they say, "This is our opinion, and the decision of the Church—that is, of ourselves!" Thus these men, "reprobate concerning the faith" (2 Tim. 3:8) and untrustworthy have the effrontery to set their own fancies before us in the name of the Church as articles of faith.

But there are good grounds for my view, and this above all: no violence is to be done to the words of God, whether by man or angel, but they are to be retained in their simplest meaning wherever possible, and to be understood in by their grammatical and literal sense unless the context plainly forbids, lest we give our adversaries occasion to make a mockery of all the Scriptures. Thus Origen was repudiated, in olden times, because he despised the grammatical sense and turned the trees, and all things else written concerning Paradise, into allegories, for it might therefrom be concluded that God did not create trees. Even so here, when the Evangelists plainly write that Christ took bread and brake it (Matt. 26:26; Mark 14:22; Luke 22:19; Acts 2:46; 1 Cor. 11:23), and the book of Acts and Paul, in their turn, call it bread, we have to think of real bread, and real wine, just as we do of a real cup, or even they do not maintain that the cup is transubstantiated. But since it is not necessary to assume a transubstantiation wrought by Divine power, it is to be regarded as a figment of the human mind, or it rests neither on Scripture nor on reason, as we shall see.

Therefore it is an absurd and unheard-of juggling with words to understand "bread" to mean "the form, or accidents of bread," and "wine" to mean "the form, or accidents of wine." Why do they not also understand all other things to mean their forms, or accidents? And even if this might be done with all other things, it would yet not be right thus to emasculate the words of God and arbitrarily to empty them of their meaning.

Moreover, the Church had the true faith for more than twelve hundred years, during which time the holy Fathers never once mentioned this transubstantiation—forsooth, a monstrous word for a monstrous idea!—until the pseudophilosophy of Aristotle became rampant in the Church, these last three hundred years, during which many other things have been wrongly defined, as for example, that the Divine essence neither is begotten nor begets; that the soul is the substantial form of the human body, and the like assertions, which are made without reason or sense, as the Cardinal of Cambray himself admits.

Perhaps they will say that the danger of idolatry demands that bread and wine be not really present. How ridiculous! The laymen have never become familiar with their fine-spun philosophy of substance and accidents, and could not grasp it if it were taught them. Besides, there is the same danger in the case of the accidents which remain and which they see, as in the case of the substance which they do not see. For if they do not adore the accidents, but Christ hidden under them, why should they adore the bread, which they do not see?

But why could not Christ include His body in the substance of the bread just as well as in the accidents? The two substances of fire and iron are so mingled in the heated iron that every part is both iron and fire. Why could not much rather Christ's body be thus contained in every part of the substance of the bread?

What will they say? We believe that in His birth Christ came forth out of the unopened womb of His mother. Let them say here too that the flesh of the Virgin was meanwhile annihilated, or as they would more aptly say, transubstantiated, so that Christ, after being enfolded in its accidents, finally came forth through the accidents! The same thing will have to be said of the shut door and of the closed mouth of the sepulcher, through which He went in and out without disturbing them. Hence has risen that hotchpotch of a philosophy of constant quantity distinct from the substance, until it has come to such a pass that they themselves no longer know what are accidents and what is substance. For who has ever proved beyond the shadow of a doubt that heat, color, cold, light, weight or shape are mere accidents? Finally, they have been driven to the fancy that a new substance is created by God for their accidents on the altar—all on account of Aristotle, who says, "It is the essence of an accident to be in something," and endless other monstrosities, of all which they would be rid if they simply permitted real bread to be present. And I rejoice greatly that the simple faith of this sacrament is still to be found at least among the common people, for as they do not understand, neither do they dispute, whether accidents are present or substance, but believe with a simple faith that Christ's body and blood are truly contained in whatever is there, and leave to those who have nothing else to do the business of disputing about that which contains them.

But perhaps they will say that from Aristotle we learn that in an affirmative proposition subject and predicate must be identical, or, to set down the beast's own words, in the sixth book of his *Metaphysics*: "An affirmative proposition demands the agreement of subject and predicate," which they interpret as above. Hence when it is said, "This is my body," the subject cannot be identical with the bread, but must be identical with the body of Christ. What shall we say when Aristotle and the doctrines of men are made to be the arbiters of these lofty and divine matters? Why do we not put by such curiosity, and cling simply to the word of Christ, willing to remain in ignorance of what here takes place, and content with this, that the real body of Christ is present by virtue of the words? Or is it necessary to comprehend the manner of the divine working in every detail?

But what do they say to Aristotle's assigning a subject to whatever is predicated of the attributes, although he holds that the substance is the chief subject? Hence for him, "this white," "this large," etc., are subjects of which something is predicated. If that is correct, I ask: if a transubstantiation must be assumed in order that Christ's body be not predicated of the bread, why not also a transaccidentation in order that it be not predicated of the accidents? For the same danger remains if one understands the subject to be "this white" or "this round" is my body, and for the same reason that a transubstantiation is assumed, a transaccidentation must also be assumed, because of this identity of subject and predicate.

Let us not, however, dabble too much in philosophy. Does not Christ appear to have admirably anticipated such curiosity by saying of the wine, not, "That is my blood," but "This is my blood" (Matt. 26:28)? And yet more clearly, by bringing in the word "cup," when He said, "This cup is the new testament in my blood" (1 Cor. 11:25). Does it not seem as though He desired to keep us in a simple faith, so that we might but believe His blood to be in the cup? For my part, if I cannot fathom how the bread is the body of Christ, I will take my reason captive to the obedience of Christ (2 Cor. 10:5), and clinging simply to His word, firmly believe not only that the body of Christ is in the bread, but that the bread is the body of Christ. For in this I am borne out by the words, "He took bread, and giving thanks, He brake it and said, Take, eat; this (i.e., this bread which He took and brake) is my body" (1 Cor. 11:23). And Paul says: "The bread which we break, is it not the communion of the body of Christ?" (1 Cor. 10:16). He says not, "in the bread," but the bread itself is the communion of the body of Christ. What matters it if philosophy cannot fathom this? The Holy Spirit is greater than Aristotle. Does philosophy fathom that transubstantiation of theirs, of which they themselves admit that here all philosophy breaks down? But the agreement of the pronoun "this" with "body," in Greek and Latin, is owing to the fact that in these languages the two words are of the same gender. But in the Hebrew language, which has no neuter gender, "this" agrees with "bread," so that it would be proper to say, "This is my body." This is proved also by the use of language and by common sense; the subject, forsooth, points to the bread, not to the body, when He says, "*Hoc est corpus meum,*" "*Das ist mein Leib,*" i.e., "This bread is my body."

Therefore it is with the sacrament even as it is with Christ. In order that the Godhead may dwell in Him, it is not necessary that the human nature be transubstantiated and the Godhead be contained under its accidents, but both natures are there in their entirety, and it is truly said, "This man is God," and "This God is man." Even though philosophy cannot grasp this, faith grasps it, and the authority of God's Word is greater than the grasp of our intellect. Even so, in order that the real body and the real blood of Christ may be present in the sacrament, it is not necessary that the bread and wine be transubstantiated and Christ be contained under their accidents, but both remain there together, and it is truly said, "This bread is my body, this wine is my blood," (Matt. 26:26) and *vice versa*. Thus I will for the nonce understand it, or the honor of the holy words of God, which I will not suffer any petty human arguments to override or wrest to meanings foreign to them. At the same time, I permit other men to follow the other opinion, which is laid down in the decree *Firmiter* (*Decretal. Greg.* I.1.1 §3); only let them not press us to accept their opinions as articles of faith, as I said above.

## THIRD CAPTIVITY: THE MASS A GOOD WORK AND A SACRIFICE

The third captivity of this sacrament is that most wicked abuse of all, in consequence of which there is today no more generally accepted and firmly believed opinion in the Church than this: that the Mass is a good work and a sacrifice. And this abuse has brought an endless host of others in its train, so that the faith of this sacrament has sacrifice become utterly extinct and the holy sacrament has been turned into a veritable air, tavern, and place of merchandise. Hence participations, brotherhoods, intercessions, merits, anniversaries, memorial days, and the like wares are bought and sold, traded and bartered in the Church, and from this priests and monks derive their whole living.

I am attacking a difficult matter, and one perhaps impossible to abate, since it has become so firmly entrenched through century-long custom and the common consent of men that it would be necessary to abolish most of the books now in vogue, to alter well-nigh the whole external form of the churches, and to introduce, or rather re-introduce, a totally different kind of ceremonies. But my Christ lives, and we must be careful to give more heed to the Word of God than to all the thoughts of men and of angels. I will perform the duties of my office, and uncover the facts in the case; I will give the truth as I have received it, freely and without malice (Matt. 10:8). For the rest let every man look to his own salvation; I will faithfully do my part that none may cast on me the blame for his lack of faith and knowledge of the truth, when we appear before the judgment-seat of Christ.

In the first place, in order to attain safely and fortunately to a true and unbiased knowledge of this sacrament, we must above all else be careful to put aside whatever has been added by the zeal and devotion of men to the original, simple institution of this sacrament—such things as vestments, ornaments, chants, prayers, organs, candles, and the whole pageantry of outward things; we must turn our eyes and hearts simply to the institution of Christ and to this alone, and set naught before us but the very word of Christ by which He instituted this sacrament, made it perfect, and committed it to us. For in that word, and in that word alone, reside the power, the nature, and the whole substance of the Mass. All else is the work of man, added to the word of Christ, and the Mass can be held and remain a Mass just as well without it. Now the words of Christ, in which He instituted this sacrament, are these:

"And whilst they were at supper, Jesus took bread, and blessed, and brake, and gave to His disciples, and said: 'Take ye and eat. This is my body, which shall be given for you.' And taking the chalice, He gave thanks, and gave to them, saying: 'Drink ye all of this. This is the chalice, the new testament in my blood, which shall be shed for you and for many unto remission of sins. This do for the commemoration of me'" (Matt. 26:26; 1 Cor. 11:24ff; Luke 22:20).

These words the apostle also delivers and more fully expounds in 1 Cor. 11:23ff. On them we must lean and build as on a firm foundation, if we would not be carried about with every wind of doctrine, even as we have hitherto been carried about by the wicked doctrines of men, who turn aside the truth (Titus 1:14). For in these words nothing is omitted that pertains to the completeness, the use and the blessing of this sacrament, and nothing is included that is superfluous and not necessary for us to know. Whoever sets them aside and meditates or teaches concerning the Mass will teach monstrous and wicked doctrines, as they have done who made of the sacrament an *opus operatum*[46] and a sacrifice.

Therefore let this stand at the outset as our infallibly certain proposition: the Mass, or sacrament of the altar, is Christ's testament which He left behind Him at His death, to be distributed among His believers. For that is the meaning of His word—"This is the chalice, the new testament in my blood" (Luke 22:20). Let this truth stand, I say, as the immovable foundation on which we shall base all that we have to say, or we are going to overthrow, as you will see, all the godless opinions of men imported into this most precious sacrament. Christ, who is the Truth, saith truly that this is the new testament in His

---

46. The phrase is Latin for "the work worked" and refers to the Roman idea that the sacrament gives Christ regardless of the faith of the recipient.

blood, which is shed for us. Not without reason do I dwell on this sentence; the matter is of no small moment, and must be most deeply impressed upon us.

Let us inquire, therefore, what a testament is, and we shall learn at the same time what the Mass is, what its use and blessing, and what its abuse. A testament, as every one knows, is a promise made by one about to die, in which he designates his bequest and appoints his heirs. Therefore a testament involves, first, the death of the testator, and secondly, the promise of the bequest and the naming of the heir. Thus St. Paul discusses at length the nature of a testament in Romans 4, Galatians 3 and 4, and Hebrews 9. The same thing is also clearly seen in these words of Christ. Christ testifies concerning His death when He says: "This is my body, which shall be given; this is my blood, which shall be shed" (Luke 22:19ff). He designates the bequest when He says: "Unto remission of sins." And He appoints the heirs when He says: "For you, and for many," i.e., for such as accept and believe the promise of the testator, or here it is faith that makes men heirs, as we shall see.

You see, therefore, that what we call the Mass is the promise of remission of sins made to us by God, and such a promise as has been confirmed by the death of the Son of God. For the one difference between a promise and a testament is that a testament is a promise which implies the death of him who makes it. A testator is a man making a promise who is about to die, whilst he that makes a promise is, if I may so put it, a testator who is not about to die. This testament of Christ was foreshadowed in all the promises of God from the beginning of the world; nay, whatever value those olden promises possessed was altogether derived from this new promise that was to come in Christ. Hence the words "covenant" and "testament of the Lord" occur so frequently in the Scriptures, which words signified that God would one day die. For where there is a testament, the death of the testator must needs follow (Heb. 9). Now God made a testament: therefore it was necessary that He should die (Heb. 9:16). But God could not die unless He became man. Thus both the incarnation and the death of Christ are briefly comprehended in this one word "testament."

From the above it will at once be seen what is the right and what the wrong use of the Mass, what is the worthy and what the unworthy preparation for it. If the Mass is a promise, as has been said, it is to be approached, not with any work or strength or merit, but with faith alone. For where there is the Word of God who makes the promise, there must be the faith of man who takes it. It is plain, therefore, that the first step in our salvation is faith, which clings to the word of the promise made by God, who without any effort on our part, in free and unmerited mercy makes a beginning and offers us the word of His promise. For He sent His Word, and by it healed them (Ps. 107:20). He did not accept our work and thus heal us. God's Word is the beginning of all; on it follows faith, and on faith charity, then charity works every good work, for it worketh no ill, nay, it is the fulfilling of the law (Rom. 13:10). In no other way can man come to God and deal with Him than through faith; that is, not man, by any work of his, but God, by His promise, is the author of salvation, so that all things depend on the word of His power, and are upheld and preserved by it (Heb. 1:3), with which word He begat us, that we should be a kind of firstfruits of His creatures (Jas. 1:18).

Thus, in order to raise up Adam after the Fall, God gave him this promise, addressing the serpent: "I will put enmities between thee and the woman, and thy seed and her seed: she shall crush thy head, and thou shalt lie in wait for her heel" (Gen. 3:15). In this word of promise Adam, with them that were his, was carried as it were in God's bosom, and by faith in it he was preserved, patiently waiting for the woman who should crush the serpent's head, as God had promised. And in that faith and expectation he died, not knowing when or in what guise she would come, yet never doubting that she would come. For such a promise, being the truth of God, preserves, even in Hell, those who believe it and wait for it. After this came another promise, made to Noah—to last until the time of Abraham—when a bow was set as a sign in the clouds (Gen. 9:12), by faith in which Noah and his descendants found a gracious God. After that He promised Abraham that all nations should be blessed in his seed (Gen. 12:3), and this is Abraham's bosom, into which his posterity was carried (Luke 16:22). Then to Moses and the children of Israel, and especially to David, He gave the plain promise of Christ (Deut. 18:18), thereby at last making clear what was meant by the promise to them of old time (2 Sam. 7:6). And so it came finally to the most complete promise of the new testament, in which with plain words life and salvation are freely promised, and granted to such as believe the promise. And He distinguished this testament by a particular mark from the old, calling it the "new testament" (Luke 22:20). For the old testament, which He gave by Moses, was a promise not of remission of sins or of eternal things, but of temporal—namely, the land of Canaan—by which no man was renewed in his spirit, to lay hold on the Heavenly inheritance. Therefore it was also necessary that dumb beasts should be slain, as types of Christ, that by their blood the testament might be confirmed, so that the testament was even as the blood, and the promise even as the sacrifice. But here He says, "The new testament in my blood" (Luke 22:20)—not in another's, but in His own, and by this blood grace is promised through the Spirit unto the remission of sins, that we may obtain the inheritance.

The Mass, according to its substance, is, therefore, nothing else than the aforesaid words of Christ—"Take and eat" (1 Cor. 11:24), as if He said: "Behold, O sinful man and condemned, out of pure and unmerited love wherewith I love thee, and by the will of the Father of all mercies, I promise thee in these words, or ever thou canst desire or deserve them, the forgiveness of all thy sins and life everlasting.

And, that thou mayest be most certainly assured of this my irrevocable promise, I give my body and shed my blood, thus by my very death confirming this promise, and leaving thee my body and blood as a sign and memorial of this same promise. As oft, therefore, as thou partakest of them, remember me, and praise, magnify, and give thanks for my love and largess toward thee."

Herefrom you will see that nothing else is needed for a worthy holding of Mass than a faith that confidently relies on this promise, believes Christ to be true in these words of His, and doubts not that these infinite blessings have been bestowed upon it. Hard on this faith there follows, of itself, a most sweet stirring of the heart, whereby the spirit of man is enlarged and waxes at—that is love, given by the Holy Spirit through faith in Christ—so that he is drawn unto Christ, that gracious and good testator, and made quite another and a new man. Who would not shed tears of gladness, nay well-nigh faint for the joy he hath toward Christ, if he believed with unshaken faith that this inestimable promise of Christ belonged to him! How could one help loving so great a Benefactor, who offers, promises and grants, all unbidden, such great riches, and this eternal inheritance, to one unworthy and deserving of somewhat far different?

Therefore, it is our one misfortune that we have many Masses in the world, and yet none or but the fewest of us recognize, consider, and receive these promises and riches that are offered, although verily we should do nothing else in the Mass with greater zeal (yea, it demands all our zeal) than set before our eyes, meditate, and ponder these words, these promises of Christ, which truly are the Mass itself, in order to exercise, nourish, increase, and strengthen our faith by such daily remembrance. For this is what He commands, saying, "This do in remembrance of me" (1 Cor. 11:24).

This should be done by the preachers of the Gospel, in order that this promise might be faithfully impressed upon the people and commended to them, to the awakening of faith in the same. But how many are there now who know that the Mass is the promise of Christ? I will say nothing of those godless preachers of fables who teach human traditions instead of this promise. And even if they teach these words of Christ, they do not teach them as a promise or testament, and, therefore, not to the awakening of faith.

O the pity of it! Under this captivity, they take every precaution that no layman should hear these words of Christ, as if they were too sacred to be delivered to the common people. So mad are we priests that we arrogantly claim that the so-called words of consecration may be said by ourselves alone, as secret words, yet so that they do not profit even us, or we too fail to regard them as promises or as a testament, for the strengthening of faith. Instead of believing them, we reverence them with I know not what superstitious and godless fancies. This misery of ours, what is it but a device of Satan to remove every trace of the Mass out of the Church? Although he is meanwhile at work filing every nook and corner on earth with Masses, that is, abuses and mockeries of God's testament, and burdening the world more and more heavily with grievous sins of idolatry, to its deeper condemnation. For what worse idolatry can there be than to abuse God's promises with perverse opinions and to neglect or extinguish faith in them?

For God does not deal, nor has He ever dealt, with man otherwise than through a word of promise, as I have said; again, we cannot deal with God otherwise than through faith in the word of His promise. He does not desire works, nor has He need of them; we deal with men and with ourselves on the basis of works. But He has need of this—that we deem Him true to His promises, wait patiently for Him, and thus worship Him with faith, hope, and love. Thus He obtains His glory among us, since it is not of ourselves who run, but of Him who showeth mercy (Ps. 115:1), promiseth and giveth, that we have and hold every blessing (Rom. 9:16). That is the true worship and service of God which we must perform in the Mass. But if the words of promise are not proclaimed, what exercise of faith can there be? And without faith, who can have hope or love? Without faith, hope, and love, what service can there be? There is no doubt, therefore, that in our day all priests and monks, together with all their bishops and superiors, are idolaters and in a most perilous state, by reason of this ignorance, abuse, and mockery of the Mass, or sacrament, or testament of God.

For any one can easily see that these two—the promise and faith—must go together. For without the promise there is nothing to believe, while without faith the promise, remains without effect; for it is established and fulfilled through faith. From this everyone will readily gather that the Mass, which is nothing else than the promise, is approached and observed only in this faith, without which whatever prayers, preparations, works, signs of the cross, or genuflections are brought to it, are incitements to impiety rather than exercises of piety, for they who come thus prepared are wont to imagine themselves on that account justly entitled to approach the altar, when in reality they are less prepared than at any other time and in any other work, by reason of the unbelief which they bring with them. How many priests will you find every day offering the sacrifice of the Mass, who accuse themselves of a horrible crime if they—wretched men!—commit a trifling blunder, such as putting on the wrong robe or forgetting to wash their hands or stumbling over their prayers, but that they neither regard nor believe the Mass itself, namely, the divine promise—this causes them not the slightest qualms of conscience. O worthless religion of this our age, the most godless and thankless of all ages!

Hence the only worthy preparation and proper use of the Mass is faith in the Mass, that is to say, in the divine promise. Whoever, therefore, is minded to approach the altar and to receive the sacrament, let him beware of appearing empty before the Lord God (Exod. 23:15; 34:20). But he will appear empty unless he has faith in the Mass, or this new testament. What godless work that he could commit would be a more grievous crime against the truth of God, than this unbelief of his, by which, as much as in him lies, he convicts God of being a liar and a maker of empty promises? The safest course, therefore, will be to go to Mass in the same spirit in which you would go to hear any other promise of God, that is, not to be ready to perform and bring many works, but to believe and receive all that is there promised, or proclaimed by the priest as having been promised to you. If you do not go in this spirit, beware of going at all; you will surely go to your condemnation.

I was right then in saying that the whole power of the Mass consists in the words of Christ, in which He testifies that the remission of sins is bestowed on all those who believe that His body is given and His blood shed for them. For this reason nothing is more important for those who go to hear Mass than diligently and in full faith to ponder these words. Unless they do this, all else that they do is in vain.

But while the Mass is the word of Christ, it is also true that God is wont to add to well-nigh every promise of His a certain sign as a mark or memorial of His promise, so that we may thereby the more faithfully hold to His promise and be the more forcibly admonished by it. Thus, to his promise to Noah that He would not again destroy the world by a flood, He added His bow in the clouds, to show that He would be mindful of His covenant (Gen. 9:13). And after promising Abraham the inheritance in his seed, He gave him the sign of circumcision as the seal of his righteousness by faith. Thus, to Gideon He granted the sign of the dry and the wet fleece, to confirm His promise of victory over the Midianites (Judges 6:36ff). And to Ahaz He offered a sign through Isaiah concerning his victory over the kings of Syria and Samaria, to strengthen his faith in the promise (Is. 7:10ff). And many such signs of the promises of God do we find in the Scriptures.

Thus also to the Mass, that crown of all His promises. He adds His body and blood in the bread and wine as a memorial sign of this great promise, as He says, "This do in remembrance of me" (1 Cor. 11:24). Even so in baptism He adds to the words of the promise, the sign of immersion in water. We learn from this that in every promise of God two things are presented to us—the word and the sign—so that we are to understand the word to be the testament, but the sign to be the sacrament. Thus in the Mass, the word of Christ is the testament, and the bread and wine are the sacrament. And as there is greater power in the word than in the sign, so there is greater power in the testament than in the sacrament, for a man can have and use the word, or testament, apart from the sign, or sacrament. "Believe," says Augustine, "and thou hast eaten." But what does one believe save the word of promise? Therefore I can hold Mass every day, yea, every hour, for I can set the words of Christ before me, and with them refresh and strengthen my faith, as often as I choose. That is a truly spiritual eating and drinking.

Here you may see what great things our theologians of the Sentences have produced. That which is the principal and chief thing, namely, the testament and word of promise, is not treated by one of them; thus they have obliterated faith and the whole power of the Mass. But the second part of the Mass—the sign, or sacrament—this alone do they discuss, yet in such a manner that here too they teach not faith but their preparations and *opera operata*, participations and fruits, as though these were the Mass, until they have fallen to babbling of transubstantiation and endless other metaphysical quibbles, and have destroyed the proper understanding and use of both sacrament and testament, altogether abolished faith, and caused Christ's people to forget their God, as the prophet says, days without number (Jer. 2:32). But do you let the others tell over the manifold fruits of hearing Mass, and turn hither your mind, and say and believe with the prophet that God here prepares a table before you against all those that afflict you, at which your soul may eat and grow fat (Ps. 23:5). But your faith is fed only with the word of divine promise, for "not in bread alone doth man live, but in every word that proceedeth from the mouth of God" (Deut. 8:3; Matt. 4:4). Hence in the Mass you must above all things pay closest heed to the word of promise, as to your rich banquet, green pasture, and sacred refreshment; you must esteem this word higher than all else, trust in it above all things, and cling firmly to it even through the midst of death and all sins. By thus doing you will attain not merely to those tiny drops and crumbs of "fruits of the Mass," which some have superstitiously imagined, but to the very fountainhead of life, which is faith in the word, from which every blessing flows, as it is said in John, "He that believeth in me, out of his belly shall flow rivers of living water" (John 7:38), and again, "He that shall drink of the water that I will give him, it shall become in him a fountain of living water, springing up into life everlasting" (John 4:14).

Now there are two things that commonly tempt us to lose the fruits of the Mass: first, the fact that we are sinners and unworthy of such great things because of our exceeding vileness, and, secondly, the act that, even if we were worthy, these things are so high that our faint-hearted nature dare not aspire to them or ever hope to attain to them. For to have God for our Father, to be His sons and heirs of all His goods—these are the great blessings that come to us through the forgiveness of sins and life everlasting. And who that regarded them aright must not rather stand aghast before them than desire to possess them? Against this twofold faintness of ours we must lay hold on the word of Christ and fix our gaze on it much more firmly than on those thoughts of our weakness. For "great are the works of the Lord" (Ps. 111:2), wrought out according to all His wills, "who is able to do exceeding abundantly above all that we ask or think" (Eph. 3:20). If they did not surpass our worthiness, our grasp and all our thoughts, they would not be divine. Thus Christ also encourages us when He says: "Fear not, little flock, for it hath pleased your Father to give you a kingdom" (Luke 17:32). For it is just this overflowing goodness of the incomprehensible God, lavished upon us through Christ, that moves us to love Him again with our whole heart above all things, to be drawn to Him with all confidence, to despise all things else, and be ready to suffer all things for Him; wherefore this sacrament is well styled "a fount of love."

Let us take an illustration of this from everyday life. If a thousand gulden were bequeathed by a rich lord to a beggar or an unworthy and wicked servant, it is certain that he would boldly claim and take them regardless of his unworthiness and the greatness of the bequest. And if anyone should seek to oppose him by casting in his teeth his unworthiness and the large amount of the legacy, what do you suppose he would say? He would say, forsooth, "What is that to you? What I accept, I accept not on my merits or by any right that I may personally have to it; I know that I am unworthy and receive more than I have deserved, nay, I have deserved the very opposite. But I claim it because it is so written in the will, and on the score of another's goodness. If it was not an unworthy thing for him to bequeath so great a sum to an unworthy person, why should I refuse to accept it because of my unworthiness? Nay, the more unworthy I am, the more reason have I to accept this other man's gracious gift." With such thoughts we need to fortify the consciences of men against all qualms and scruples that they may lay hold on the promise of Christ with unwavering faith, and take the greatest care to approach the sacrament, not trusting in their confession, prayer, and preparation, but rather despairing of these and with a proud confidence in Christ who gives the promise. For, as we have said again and again, the word of promise must here reign supreme in a pure and unalloyed faith, and such faith is the one and all-sufficient preparation.

Hence we see how angry God is with us in that He has permitted godless teachers to conceal the words of this testament from us, and thereby, as much as in them lay, to extinguish faith. And the inevitable result of this extinguishing of faith is even now plainly to be seen—namely, the most godless superstition of works. For when faith dies and the word of faith is silent, works, and the traditions of works immediately crowd into their place. By them we have been carried away out of our own land, as in a Babylonian captivity, and despoiled of all our precious possessions. This has been the fate of the Mass; it has been converted by the teaching of godless men into a good work, which they themselves call an *opus operatum*, and by which they presumptuously imagine themselves all-powerful with God. Thereupon they proceeded to the very height of madness, and having invented the lie that the Mass works *ex opere operate*, they asserted further that it is none the less profitable to others, even if it be harmful to the wicked priest celebrating it. On such a foundation of sand they base their applications, participations, sodalities, anniversaries, and numberless other money-making schemes.

These lures are so powerful, widespread, and firmly entrenched that you will scarcely be able to prevail against them unless you keep before you with unremitting care the real meaning of the Mass, and bear well in mind what has been said above. We have seen that the Mass is nothing else than the divine promise or testament of Christ, sealed with the sacrament of His body and blood. If that is true, you will understand that it cannot possibly be a work, and that there is nothing to do in it, nor can it be dealt with in any other way than by faith alone. And faith is not a work, but the mistress and the life of all works. Where in all the world is there a man so foolish as to regard a promise made to him, or a testament given to him, as a good work which by his acceptance of it he renders to the testator? What heir will imagine he is doing his departed father a kindness by accepting the terms of the will and the inheritance bequeathed to him? What godless audacity is it, therefore, when we who are to receive the testament of God come as those who would perform a good work for Him! This ignorance of the testament, this captivity of the sacrament—are they not too sad for tears? When we ought to be grateful for benefits received, we come in our pride to give that which we ought to take, mocking with unheard-of perversity the mercy of the giver by giving as a work the thing we receive as a gift, so that the testator, instead of being the dispenser of His own goods, becomes the recipient of ours. Out upon such godless doings!

Who has ever been so mad as to regard baptism as a good work, or to believe that by being baptized he was performing a work which he might offer to God or himself and communicate to others? If, therefore, there is no good work that can be communicated to others in this one sacrament or testament, neither will there be any in the Mass, since it too is nothing else than a testament and sacrament. Hence it is a manifest and wicked error to offer or apply Masses for sins or satisfactions for the dead, or for any necessity whatsoever of one's own or of others. You will readily see the obvious truth of this if you but hold firmly that the Mass is a divine promise, which can profit no one, be applied to no one, intercede for no one, and be communicated to no one, save him alone who believes with a faith of his own. Who can receive or apply in behalf of another the promise of God, which demands the personal faith of every individual? Can I give to another what God has promised, even if he does not believe? Can I believe for another, or cause another to believe? But this is what I must do if I am able to apply and communicate the Mass to others, for there are but two things in the Mass—the promise of God, and the faith of man which takes that which the promise offers. But if it is true that I can do this, then I can also hear and believe the Gospel for others, I can be baptized for another, I can be absolved from sins for another, I can also partake of the sacrament of the altar for another, and—to run the gamut of their sacraments also—I can marry a wife for another, be ordained for another, receive confirmation and extreme unction for another! In fine, why did not Abraham believe for all the Jews? Why was faith in the promise made to Abraham demanded of every individual Jew?

Therefore, let this irrefutable truth stand fast. Where there is a divine promise everyone must stand upon his own feet, everyone's personal faith is demanded, everyone will give an account for himself and will bear his own burden (Gal. 6:5), as it is said in the last chapter of Mark: "He that believeth and is baptized shall be saved, but he that believeth not shall be damned" (Mark 16:16). Even so every one may derive a blessing from the Mass for himself alone and only by his own faith, and no one can commune for any other, just as the priest cannot administer the sacrament to any one in another's stead, but administers the same sacrament to each individual by himself. For in consecrating and administering, the priests are our ministers, through whom we do not offer a good work or commune (in the active), but receive the promises and the sign and are communed (in the passive). That has remained to this day the custom among the laity, for they are not said to do good, but to receive it. But the priests have departed into godless ways; out of the sacrament and testament of God, the source of blessings to be received, they have made a good work which they may communicate and offer to others.

But you will say: how is this? Will you not overturn the practice and teaching of all the churches and monasteries by virtue of which they have flourished these many centuries? For the Mass is the foundation of their anniversaries, intercessions, applications, communications, etc., that is to say, of their income. I answer this is the very thing that has constrained me to write of the captivity of the Church, for in this manner the adorable testament of God has been subjected to the bondage of a godless traffic, through the opinions and traditions of wicked men, who, passing over the Word of God, have put forth the thoughts of their own hearts and misled the whole world. What do I care for the number and influence of those who are in this error? The truth is mightier than they all. If you are able to gainsay Christ, according to whom the Mass is a testament and sacrament, then I will admit that they are in the right. Or if you can bring yourself to say that that man is doing a good work who receives the benefit of the testament or who uses this sacrament of promise in order to receive it, then I will gladly condemn my teachings. But since you can do neither, why do you hesitate to turn your back on the multitude who go after evil, and to give God the glory and confess His truth? Which is, indeed, that all priests today are perversely mistaken, who regard the Mass as a work whereby they may relieve their own necessities and those of others, dead or alive. I am uttering unheard-of and startling things, but if you will consider the meaning of the Mass, you will realize that I have spoken the truth. The fault lies with our utter supineness, in which we have become blind to the wrath of God that is raging against us.

I am ready, however, to admit that the prayers which we pour out before God when we are gathered together to partake of the Mass are good works or benefits, which we impart, apply, and communicate to one another, and which we offer for one another, as James teaches us to pray for one another that we may be saved (Jas. 5:16), and as Paul in 1 Timothy 2 commands that supplications, prayers, and intercessions be made for all men, for kings, and for all that are in high station (1 Tim. 2:1ff). These are not the Mass, but works of the Mass—if the prayers of heart and lips may be called works—for they flow from the faith that is kindled or increased in the sacrament. For the Mass, being the promise of God, is not fulfilled by praying, but only by believing; but when we believe, we shall also pray and perform every good work. But what priest of them all offers the sacrifice of the Mass in this sense and believes that he is offering up naught but the prayers? They all imagine themselves to be offering up Christ Himself, as all-sufficient sacrifice, to God the Father, and to be performing a good work for all whom they have the intention to benefit. For they put their trust in the work which the Mass accomplishes, and they do not ascribe this work to prayer. Thus gradually the error has grown, until they have come to ascribe to the sacrament what belongs to the prayers, and to offer to God what should be received as a benefit.

It is necessary, therefore, to make a sharp distinction between the testament or sacrament itself and the prayers which are there offered, and no less necessary to bear in mind that the prayers avail nothing, either for him who offers them or for those for whom they are offered, unless the sacrament be first received in faith, so that it is faith that offers the prayers, for it alone is heard, as James teaches in his first chapter (Jas. 1:6ff). So great is the difference between prayer and the Mass. The prayer may be extended to as many persons as one desires, but the Mass is received by none but the person who believes for himself, and only in proportion to his faith. It cannot be given either to God or to men, but God alone gives it by the ministration of the priest to such men as receive it by faith alone, without any works or merits. For no one would dare to make the mad assertion that a ragged beggar does a good work when he comes to receive a gift from a rich man. But the Mass is, as has been said, the gift and promise of God, offered to all men by the hand of the priest. It is certain, therefore, that the Mass is not a work which may be communicated to others, but it is the object, as it is called, of faith, for the strengthening and nourishing of the personal faith of each individual.

But there is yet another stumbling-block that must be removed, and this is much greater and the most dangerous of all. It is the common belief that the Mass is a sacrifice which is offered to God. Even the words of the canon tend in this direction, when they speak of "these gifts," "these offerings," "this holy sacrifice," and farther on, of "this oblation." Prayer also is made, in so many words, "that the sacrifice may be accepted even as the sacrifice of Abel," etc., and hence Christ is termed the "sacrifice of the altar." In addition to this there are the sayings of the holy Fathers, the great number of examples, and the constant usage and custom of all the world.

To all of this, firmly entrenched as it is, we must resolutely oppose the words and example of Christ. For unless we hold fast to the truth, that the Mass is the promise or testament of Christ, as the words clearly say, we shall lose the whole Gospel and all our comfort. Let us permit nothing to prevail against these words, even though an angel from Heaven should teach otherwise (Gal. 1:8). For there is nothing said in them of a work or a sacrifice. Moreover, we have also the example of Christ on our side. For at the Last Supper, when He instituted this sacrament and established this testament, Christ did not offer Himself to God the Father, nor did He perform a good work on behalf of others, but He set this testament before each of them that sat at table with Him and offered him the sign. Now, the more closely our Mass resembles that first Mass of all, which Christ performed at the Last Supper, the more Christian will it be. But Christ's Mass was most simple, without the pageantry of vestments, genuflections, chants, and other ceremonies. Indeed, if it were necessary to offer the Mass as a sacrifice, then Christ's institution of it was not complete.

Not that anyone should revile the Church universal for embellishing and amplifying the Mass with many additional rites and ceremonies. But this is what we contend for; no one should be deceived by the glamour of the ceremonies and entangled in the multitude of pompous forms, and thus lose the simplicity of the Mass itself, and indeed practice a sort of transubstantiation—losing sight of the simple substance of the Mass and clinging to the manifold accidents of outward pomp. For whatever has been added to the word and example of Christ is an accident of the Mass, and ought to be regarded just as we regard the so-called monstrances and corporal cloths in which the host itself is contained. Therefore, as distributing a testament or accepting a promise differs diametrically from offering a sacrifice, so it is a contradiction in terms to call the Mass a sacrifice, for the former is something that we receive, while the latter is something that we offer. The same thing cannot be received and offered at the same time, nor can it be both given and taken by the same person, just as little as our prayer can be the same as that which our prayer obtains, or the act of praying the same as the act of receiving the answer to our prayer.

What shall we say, then, of the canon of the Mass and the sayings of the Fathers? First of all, if there were nothing at all to be said against them, it would yet be the safer course to reject them all rather than admit that the Mass is a work or a sacrifice, lest we deny the word of Christ and overthrow faith together with the Mass. Nevertheless, not to reject altogether the canons and the Fathers, we shall say the following: the apostle instructs us in 1 Corinthians 11 that it was customary for Christ's believers, when they came together to Mass, to bring with them meat and drink, which they called "collections" and distributed among all who were in want (1 Cor. 11:20ff), after the example of the apostles in Acts 4:34ff. From this store was taken the portion of bread and wine that was consecrated for use in the sacrament. And since all this store of meat and drink was sanctified by the word and by prayer (1 Tim. 4:5), being "lifted up" according to the Hebrew rite of which we read in Moses (Lev. 8:27), the words and the rite of this lifting up, or for offering, have come down to us, although the custom of collecting that which was offered, or lifted up, has fallen long since into disuse. Thus, in Isaiah 37, Hezekiah commanded Isaiah to lift up his prayer in the sight of God for the remnant (v. 4). The Psalmist sings: "Lift up your hands to the holy places" (Ps. 134:2); and: "To Thee will I lift up my hands" (Ps. 63:4). And in 1 Timothy 2 we read: "Lifting up pure hands in every place" (v. 8). For this reason the words "sacrifice" and "oblation" must be taken to refer, not to the sacrament and testament, but to these collections, whence also the word "collect" has come down to us, as meaning the prayers said in the Mass.

The same thing is indicated when the priest elevates the bread and the chalice immediately after the consecration, whereby he shows that he is not offering anything to God, for he does not say a single word here about a victim or an oblation. But this elevation is either a survival of that Hebrew rite of lifting up what was received with thanksgiving and returned to God, or else it is an admonition to us, to provoke us to faith in this testament which the priest has set forth and exhibited in the words of Christ, so that now he shows us also the sign of the testament. Thus the oblation of the bread properly accompanies the demonstrative this in the words, "This is my body," by which sign the priest addresses us gathered about him, and in like manner the oblation of the chalice accompanies the demonstrative this in the words, "This chalice is the new testament, etc." For it is faith that the priest ought to awaken in us by this act of elevation. And would to God that, as he elevates the sign, or sacrament, openly before our eyes, he might also sound in our ears the words of the testament with a loud, clear voice, and in the language of the people, whatever it may be, in order that faith may be the more effectively awakened. For why may Mass be said in Greek and Latin and Hebrew, and not also in German or in any other language?

Let the priests, therefore, who in these corrupt and perilous times offer the sacrifice of the Mass, take heed, first, that the words of the greater and the lesser canon together with the collects, which smack too strongly of sacrifice, be not referred by them to the sacrament, but to the bread and wine which they consecrate, or to the prayers which they say. For the bread and wine are offered at the first, in order that they may be blessed and thus sanctified by the Word and by prayer, but after they have been blessed and consecrated, they are no longer offered, but received as a gift from God. And let the priest bear in mind that the Gospel is to be set above all canons and collects devised by men, and the Gospel does not sanction the calling of the Mass a sacrifice, as has been shown.

Further, when a priest celebrates a public Mass, he should determine to do naught else through the Mass than to commune himself and others, yet he may at the same time offer prayers for himself and for others, but he must beware lest he presume to offer the Mass. But let him that holds a private Mass determine to commune himself. The private Mass does not differ in the least from the ordinary communion which any layman receives at the hand of the priest, and has no greater effect, apart from the special prayers and the act that the priest consecrates the elements for himself and administers them to himself. So far as the blessing of the Mass and sacrament is concerned, we are all of us on an equal footing, whether we be priests or laymen.

If a priest be requested by others to celebrate so-called votive Masses,[47] let him beware of accepting a reward for the Mass, or of presuming to offer a votive sacrifice; he should be at pains to refer all to the prayers which he offers for the dead or the living, saying within himself, "I will go and partake of the sacrament for myself alone, and while partaking I will say a prayer for this one and that." Thus he will take his reward—to buy him food and clothing—not for the Mass, but for the prayers. And let him not be disturbed because all the world holds and practices the contrary. You have the most sure Gospel, and relying on this you may well despise the opinions of men. But if you despise me and insist upon offering the Mass and not the prayers alone, know that I have faithfully warned you and will be without blame on the day of judgment; you will have to bear your sin alone. I have said what I was bound to say as brother to brother for his soul's salvation; yours will be the gain if you observe it, yours the loss if you neglect it. And if some should even condemn what I have said, I reply in the words of Paul: "But evil men and seducers shall grow worse and worse: erring and driving into error" (2 Tim. 3:13).

---

47. Masses celebrated by special request or in honor of certain mysteries (e. g., of the Holy Trinity, of the Holy Spirit, or of angels).

From the above every one will readily understand what there is in that oft quoted saying of Gregory's: "A Mass celebrated by a wicked priest is not to be considered of less effect than one celebrated by any godly priest, and St. Peter's Mass would not have been better than Judas the traitor's, if they had offered the sacrifice of the Mass," which saying has served many as a cloak to cover their godless doings, and because of it they have invented the distinction between *opus operati* and *opus operantis*,[48] so as to be free to lead wicked lives themselves and yet to benefit other men. But Gregory speaks truth, only they misunderstand and pervert his words. For it is true beyond a question that the testament or sacrament is given and received through the ministration of wicked priests no less completely than through the ministration of the most saintly. For who has any doubt that the Gospel is preached by the ungodly? Now the Mass is part of the Gospel, nay, its sum and substance, for what is the whole Gospel but the good tidings of the forgiveness of sins? But whatever can be said of the forgiveness of sins and the mercy of God is all briefly comprehended in the word of this testament. Wherefore the popular sermons ought to be naught else than expositions of the Mass, that is, a setting forth of the divine promise of this testament; that would be to teach faith and truly to edify the Church. But in our day the expounders of the Mass play with the allegories of human rites and play the fool with the people.

Therefore, just as a wicked priest may baptize, that is, apply the word of promise and the sign of the water to a candidate for baptism, so he may also set forth the promise of this sacrament and administer it to those who partake, and even himself partake, like Judas the traitor, at the Lord's Supper. It still remains always the same sacrament and testament, which works in the believer its own work, in the unbeliever a "strange work" (Is. 28:21). But when it comes to offering a

---

48. The work worked is worked by the words of consecration and not because of the holiness of the one offering the work.

sacrifice the case is quite different. For not the Mass but the prayers are offered to God, and therefore it is as plain as day that the offerings of a wicked priest avail nothing, but, as Gregory says again, when an unworthy intercessor is chosen, the heart of the judge is moved to greater displeasure. We must, therefore, not confound these two—the Mass and the prayers, the sacrament and the work, the testament and the sacrifice, for the one comes from God to us, through the ministration of the priest, and demands our faith, the other proceeds from our faith to God, through the priest, and demands His answer. The former descends, the latter ascends. Therefore the former does not necessarily require a worthy and godly minister, but the latter does indeed require such a one, because God heareth not sinners (John 9:31). He knows how to send down blessings through evildoers, but He does not accept the work of any evildoer, as He showed in the case of Cain (Gen. 4:5), and as it is said in Proverbs 15, "The victims of the wicked are abominable to the Lord" (v. 8); and in Romans 14, "All that is not of faith is sin" (v. 23).

But in order to make an end of this first part, we must take up one remaining point against which an opponent might arise. From all that has been said we conclude that the Mass was provided only for such as have a sad, afflicted, disturbed, perplexed, and erring conscience, and that they alone commune worthily. For, since the word of divine promise in this sacrament sets forth the remission of sins, that man may fearlessly draw near, whoever he be whose sins distress him, either with remorse for past or with temptation to future wrongdoing. For this testament of Christ is the one remedy against sins, past, present, and future, if you but cling to it with unwavering faith and believe that what the words of the testament declare is freely granted to you. But if you do not believe this, you will never, nowhere, and by no works or efforts of your own find peace of conscience. For faith alone sets the conscience at peace, and unbelief alone keeps the conscience troubled.

# THE SACRAMENT OF BAPTISM

Blessed be God and the Father of our Lord Jesus Christ, who according to the riches of His mercy hath preserved in His Church this sacrament at least, untouched and untainted by the ordinances of men, and hath made it free unto all nations and every estate of mankind, nor suffered it to be oppressed by the filthy and godless monsters of greed and superstition. For He desired that by it little children, incapable of greed and superstition, might be initiated and sanctified in the simple faith of His Word, for whom even today baptism hath its chief blessing. But if this sacrament were to be given to such as had arrived at man's estate, methinks it could not possibly have retained its power and its glory against the tyranny of greed and superstition which has everywhere laid waste things divine. Doubtless the wisdom of the flesh would here too have devised its preparations and worthinesses, its reservations, restrictions, and I know not what other snares for taking money, until water fetched as high a price as parchment does now.

But Satan, though he could not quench the power of baptism in little children, nevertheless succeeded in quenching it in all adults, so that there are scarce any who call to mind their baptism and still fewer who glory in it, so many other ways have they discovered of ridding themselves of their sins and of reaching Heaven. The source of these false opinions is that dangerous saying of St. Jerome's—either unhappily phrased or wrongly interpreted—in which he terms penance "the second plank" after the shipwreck, as if baptism were not penance. Accordingly, when men fall into sin, they despair of "the first plank," which is the ship, as though it had gone under, and fasten all their faith on the second plank, that is, penance. This has produced those endless burdens of vows, religious works, satisfactions, pilgrimages, indulgences, and sects, whence has arisen that flood of books, questions, opinions and human traditions which the world cannot contain, so that this tyranny plays worse havoc with the Church of God than any tyrant ever did with the Jewish people or with any other nation under Heaven.

It was the duty of the pontiffs to abate this evil, and with all diligence to lead Christians to the true understanding of baptism, so that they might know what manner of men they are and how it becomes Christians to live. But instead of this, their work is now to lead the people as far astray as possible from their baptism, to immerse all men in the flood of their oppression, and to cause the people of Christ, as the prophet says, to forget Him days without number (Jer. 2:32). O unhappy, all who bear the name of priest today! They not only do not know nor do what becometh priests, but they are ignorant of what they ought to know and do. They fulfill the saying in Isaiah 56: "His watchmen are all blind, they are all ignorant: the shepherds themselves knew no understanding; all have declined into their own way, every one after his own gain" (Is. 56:10).

## THE FIRST PART OF BAPTISM: THE DIVINE PROMISE

Now, the first thing in baptism to be considered is the divine promise, which says: "He that believeth and is baptized shall be saved." This promise must be set far above all the glitter of works, vows, religious orders, and whatever man has added thereto, for on it all our salvation depends (Mark 16:16). But we must so consider it as to exercise our faith therein and in nowise doubt that we are saved when we are baptized. For unless this faith be present or be conferred in baptism, baptism will profit us nothing, nay, it becomes a hindrance to us, not only in the moment of its reception, but all the days of our life, for such unbelief accuses God's promise of being a lie, and this is the blackest of all sins. If we set ourselves to this exercise of faith, we shall at once perceive how difficult it is to believe this promise of God. For our human weakness, conscious of its sins, finds nothing more difficult to believe than that it is saved or will be saved, and yet unless it does believe this, it cannot be saved, because it does not believe the truth of God that promiseth salvation.

This message should have been untiringly impressed upon the people and this promise dinned without ceasing in their ears; their baptism should have been called again and again to their mind, and faith constantly awakened and nourished. For, just as the truth of this divine promise, once pronounced over us, continues unto death, so our faith in the same ought never to cease, but to be nourished and strengthened until death by the continual remembrance of this promise made to us in baptism. Therefore, when we rise from sins or repent, we do but return to the power and the faith of baptism from whence we fell, and find our way back to the promise then made to us, from which we departed when we sinned. For the truth of the promise once made remains steadfast, ever ready to receive us back with open arms when we return. This, if I mistake not, is the real meaning of the obscure saying that baptism is the beginning and foundation of all the sacraments, without which none of the others may be received.

It will, therefore, be no small gain for a penitent to lay hold before all else on the memory of his baptism, confidently to call to mind the promise of God, which he has forsaken, and to plead it with His Lord, rejoicing that he is baptized and therefore is yet within the fortress of salvation, and abhorring his wicked ingratitude in falling away from its faith and truth. His soul will find wondrous comfort, and will be encouraged to hope or mercy when he considers that the divine promise which God made to him and which cannot possibly lie, still stands unbroken and unchanged, yea, unchangeable by any sins; as Paul says in 2 Timothy 2, "If we believe not, He continueth faithful, He cannot deny Himself" (2 Tim. 2:13). Aye, this truth of God will sustain him, so that if all else should sink in ruins, this truth, if he believe it, will not ail him. For in it he has a shield against all assaults of the enemy, an answer to the sins that disturb his conscience, an antidote for the dread of death and judgment, and a comfort in every temptation—namely, this one truth—and he can say, "God is faithful that promised" (Heb. 10:23), whose sign I have received in my baptism. "If God be for me, who is against me?" (Rom. 8:31).

The children of Israel, whenever they repented of their sins, turned their thoughts first of all to the exodus from Egypt, and remembering this, returned to God who had brought them out. This memory and this refuge were many times impressed upon them by Moses, and afterward repeated by David. How much rather ought we to call to mind our exodus from Egypt, and, remembering, turn back again to Him who led us forth through the washing of regeneration (Titus 3:5), which we are bidden remember for this very purpose. And this we can do most fittingly in the sacrament of bread and wine. Indeed, in olden times these three sacraments—penance, baptism, and the bread—were all celebrated at the same service, and one supplemented and assisted the other. We read also of a certain holy virgin who in every time of temptation made baptism her sole defense, saying simply, "I am a Christian," and straightway the adversary led from her, or he knew the power of her baptism and of her faith which clung to the truth of God's promise.

Lo, how rich therefore is a Christian, or one who is baptized! Even if he would, he cannot lose his salvation, however much he sin, unless he will not believe. For no sin can condemn him save unbelief alone. All other sins—if faith in God's promise made in baptism return or remain—all other sins, I say, are immediately blotted out through that same faith, or rather through the truth of God, because He cannot deny Himself if you but confess Him and cling believing to Him that promises. But as for contrition, confession of sins, and satisfaction—with all those carefully thought-out exercises of men—if you turn your attention to them and neglect this truth of God, they will suddenly fail you and leave you more wretched than before. For whatever is done without faith in the truth of God is vanity of vanities and vexation of spirit (Eccl. 1:2, 14).

Again, how perilous, nay, how false it is to suppose that penance is the second plank after the shipwreck! How harmful an error it is to believe that the power of baptism is broken, and the ship has foundered, because we have sinned! Nay, that one solid and unsinkable ship remains, and is never broken up into floating timbers; it carries all those who are brought to the harbor of salvation; it is the truth of God giving us its promise in the sacraments. Many, indeed, rashly leap overboard and perish in the waves; these are they who depart from faith in the promise and plunge into sin. But the ship herself remains intact and holds her steady course, and if one be able somehow to return to the ship, it is not on any plank but in the good ship herself that he is borne to life. Such an one is he who through faith returns to the sure promise of God that abideth forever. Therefore Peter, in his second epistle, rebukes them that sin, because they have forgotten that they were purged from their old sins (2 Peter 1:9), in which words he doubtless chides their ingratitude for the baptism they had received and their wicked unbelief.

What is the good, then, of making many books on baptism and yet not teaching this faith in the promise? All the sacraments were instituted for the purpose of nourishing faith, but these godless men so completely pass over this faith that they even assert a man dare not be certain of the forgiveness of sins, that is, of the grace of the sacraments. With such wicked teachings they delude the world, and not only take captive but altogether destroy the sacrament of baptism, in which the chief glory of our conscience consists. Meanwhile they madly rage against the miserable souls of men with their contritions, anxious confessions, circumstances, satisfactions, works, and endless other absurdities. Read, therefore, with great caution the Master of the Sentences in his fourth book, or, better yet, despise him together with all his commentators, who at their best write only of the material and form of the sacraments, that is, they treat of the dead and death-dealing letter of the sacraments, but pass over in utter silence the spirit, life, and use, that is, the truth of the divine promise and our faith.

Beware, therefore, lest the external pomp of works and the deceits of human traditions mislead you, so that you may not wrong the divine truth and your faith. If you would be saved, you must begin with the faith of the sacraments, without any works whatever, but on faith the works will follow, only do not think lightly of faith, which is a work, and of all works the most excellent and the most difficult to do. Through it alone you will be saved, even if you should be compelled to do without any other works. For it is a work of God, not of man, as Paul teaches (Eph. 2:8). The other works He works through us and with our help, but this one He works in us and without our help.

From this we can clearly see the difference, in baptism, between man the minister and God the Doer. For man baptizes and does not baptize: he baptizes, for he performs the work, immersing the person to be baptized; he does not baptize, for in that act he officiates not by his own authority, but in the stead of God. Hence, we ought to receive baptism at the hands of a man just as if Christ Himself, nay, God Himself, were baptizing us with His own hands. For it is not man's baptism, but Christ's and God's baptism which we receive by the hand of a man, just as every other created thing that we make use of by the hand of another is God's alone. Therefore beware of dividing baptism in such a way as to ascribe the outward part to man and the inward part to God. Ascribe both to God alone, and look upon the person administering it as the instrument in God's hands, by which the Lord sitting in Heaven thrusts you under the water with His own hands, and speaking by the mouth of His minister promises you, on earth with a human voice, the forgiveness of your sins.

This the words themselves indicate, when the priest says: "I baptize thee in the name of the Father, and of the Son, and of the Holy Ghost. Amen"—and not: "I baptize thee in my own name." It is as though he said: "What I do, I do not by my own authority, but in the name and stead of God, so that you should regard it just as if our Lord Himself had done it in a visible manner. The Doer and the minister are different persons, but the work of both is the same work, or, rather, it is the work of the Doer alone, through my ministry." For I hold that "in the name of" refers to the person of the Doer, so that the name of the Lord is not only to be uttered and invoked while the work is being done, but the work itself is to be done not as one's own work, but in the name and stead of another. In this sense Christ says, "Many shall come in my name," (Matt. 24:5), and in Romans 1 it is said, "By whom we have received grace and apostleship for obedience to the faith, in all nations, for His name" (Rom. 1:5).

This view I heartily endorse, for there is much of comfort and a mighty aid to faith in the knowledge that one has been baptized not by man, but by the Triune God Himself through a man acting among us in His name. This will dispose of that fruitless quarrel about the "form" of baptism, as these words are called. The Greeks say, "May the servant of Christ be baptized," while the Latins say, "I baptize." Others again, pedantic triflers, condemn the use of the words, "I baptize thee in the name of Jesus Christ"—although it is certain that the apostles used this formula in baptizing, as we read in the Acts of the apostles (2:38; 8:12, 16; 10:48; 19:5)—and would allow no other form to be valid than this: "I baptize thee in the name of the Father, and of the Son, and of the Holy Ghost." But their contention is in vain, for they bring no proof, but merely assert their own dreams. Baptism truly saves in whatever way it is administered, if only it be not administered in the name of man but of God. Nay, I have no doubt that if one received baptism in the name of the Lord, even though the wicked minister should not give it in the name of the Lord, he would yet be truly baptized in the name of the Lord. For the effect of baptism depends not so much on the faith or use of him that confers it as on the faith or use of him that receives it, of which we have an illustration in the case of the play-actor who was baptized in jest. Such anxious disputings and questionings are aroused in us by those who ascribe nothing to faith and everything to works and forms, whereas we owe everything to faith alone and nothing to forms, and faith makes us free in spirit from all those scruples and fancies.

## THE SECOND PART OF BAPTISM: THE SIGN, OR SACRAMENT

The second part of baptism is the sign, or sacrament, which is that immersion into water whence also it derives its name, for the Greek *baptizo* means I immerse, and *baptisma* means immersion. For, as has been said, signs are added to the divine promises to represent that which the words signify, for, as they now say, that which the sacrament "effectively signifies." We shall see how much of truth there is in this. The great majority have supposed that there is some hidden spiritual power in the word or in the water, which works the grace of God in the soul of the recipient. Others deny this and hold that there is no power in the sacraments, but that grace is given by God alone, who according to His covenant aids the sacraments He has instituted. Yet all are agreed that the sacraments are effective signs of grace, and they reach this conclusion by this one argument: if the sacraments of the New Law merely "signified," it would not be apparent in what respect they surpassed the sacraments of the Old Law. Hence they have been driven to attribute such great power to the sacraments of the New Law that in their opinion they benefit even such men as are in mortal sins, and that they do not require faith or grace; it is sufficient not to oppose a "bar," that is, an actual intention to sin again.

But these views must be carefully avoided and shunned, because they are godless and infidel, being contrary to faith and to the nature of the sacraments. For it is an error to hold that the sacraments of the New Law differ from those of the Old Law in the efficacy of their "signifying." The "signifying" of both is equally efficacious. The same God who now saves me by baptism saved Abel by his sacrifice, Noah by the bow, Abraham by circumcision, and all the others by their respective signs. So far as the "signifying" is concerned, there is no difference between a sacrament of the Old Law and one of the New, provided that by the Old Law you mean that which God wrought among the patriarchs and other fathers in the days of the law. But those signs which were given to the patriarchs and fathers must be sharply distinguished from the legal types which Moses instituted in his law, such as the priestly rites concerning robes, vessels, meats, dwellings, and the like. Between these and the sacraments of the New Law there is a vast difference, but no less between them and those signs that God from time to time gave to the fathers living as judges under the law, such as the sign of Gideon's fleece (Judg. 6:36), Manoah's sacrifice (Judg. 13:19), or the sign which Isaiah offered to Ahaz, in Isaiah 7:10, for to these signs God attached a certain promise which required faith in Him.

This, then, is the difference between the legal types and the new and old signs—the former have not attached to them any word of promise requiring faith. Hence they are not signs of justification, for they are not sacraments of the faith that alone justifies, but only sacraments of works; their whole power and nature consisted in works, not in faith, and he that observed them fulfilled them, even if he did it without faith. But our signs, or sacraments, as well as those of the fathers, have attached to them a word of promise, which requires faith, and they cannot be fulfilled by any other work. Hence they are signs or sacraments of justification, for they are the sacraments of justifying faith and not of works. Their whole efficacy, therefore, consists in faith itself, not in the doing of a work, for whoever believes them fulfills them, even if he should not do a single work. Whence has arisen the saying, "Not the sacrament but the faith of the sacrament justifies." Thus circumcision did not justify Abraham and his seed, and yet the apostle calls it the seal of the righteousness of faith (Rom. 4:11), because faith in the promise, to which circumcision was added, justified him and fulfilled that which circumcision signified. For faith was the spiritual circumcision of the foreskin of the heart (Deut. 10:16; Jer. 4:4), which was symbolized by the literal circumcision of the flesh. And in the same manner it was obviously not Abel's sacrifice that justified him, but it was his faith, by which he offered himself wholly to God and which was symbolized by the outward sacrifice.

Even so it is not baptism that justifies or benefits anyone, but it is faith in the word of promise, to which baptism is added. This faith justifies, and fulfills that which baptism signifies. For faith is the submersion of the old man and the emerging of the new. Therefore it cannot be that the new sacraments differ from the old, for both have the divine promise and the same spirit of faith, although they do differ vastly from the olden types on account of the word of promise, which is the one decisive point of difference. Even so, today, the outward show of vestments, holy places, meats and of all the endless ceremonies has doubtless a fine symbolical meaning, which is to be spiritually fulfilled, and yet because there is no word of divine promise attached to these things, they can in nowise be compared with the signs of baptism and of the bread, nor do they in any way justify or benefit one, since they are fulfilled in the very observance, apart from faith. For while they are taking place or are being performed, they are being fulfilled, as the apostle says of them, in Colossians 2, "Which are all to perish with the using, after the commandments and doctrines of men" (v. 22). The sacraments, on the contrary, are not fulfilled when they are observed, but when they are believed.

It cannot be true, therefore, that there is in the sacraments a power efficacious for justification, or that they are effective signs of grace. All such assertions tend to destroy faith, and arise from ignorance of the divine promise. Unless you should call them effective in the sense that they certainly and efficaciously impart grace, where faith is unmistakably present. But it is not in this sense that efficacy is now ascribed to them, as witness the act that they are said to benefit all men, even the godless and unbelieving, provided they do not oppose a "bar"—as if such unbelief were not in itself the most obstinate and hostile of all bars to grace. So firmly bent are they on turning the sacrament into a command, and faith into a work. For if the sacrament confers grace on me because I receive it, then indeed I obtain grace by virtue of my work and not of faith; I lay hold not on the promise in the sacrament, but on the sign instituted and commanded by God. Do you not see, then, how completely the sacraments have been misunderstood by our sententious theologians? They have taken no account, in their discussions on the sacraments, of either faith or the promise, but cling only to the sign and the use of the sign, and draw us away from faith to the work, from the word to the sign. Thus they have not only carried the sacraments captive (as I have said), but have completely destroyed them, as far as they were able.

Therefore, let us open our eyes and learn to give more heed to the word than to the sign, and to faith than to the work, for the use of the sign, remembering that wherever there is a divine promise there faith is required, and that these two are so necessary to each other that neither can be efficacious apart from the other. For it is not possible to believe unless there be a promise, and the promise is not established unless it be believed. But where these two meet, they give a real and most certain efficacy to the sacraments. Hence, to seek the efficacy of the sacrament apart from the promise and apart from faith is to labor in vain and to find damnation. Thus Christ says: "He that believeth and is baptized shall be saved; he that believe not shall be damned" (Mark 16:16). He shows us in this word that faith is so necessary a part of the sacrament that it can save even without the sacrament; for which reason He did not see it to say: "He that believeth not, *and is not baptized....*"

Baptism, then, signifies two things—death and resurrection; that is, full and complete justification. The minister's immersing the child in the water signifies death; his drawing it forth again signifies life. Thus Paul expounds it in Romans 6, "We are buried together with Christ by baptism into death; that as Christ is risen from the dead by the glory of the Father, so we also may walk in newness of life" (v. 4). This death and resurrection we call the new creation, regeneration, and the spiritual birth. And this must not be understood only in a figurative sense, of the death of sin and the life of grace, as many understand it, but of actual death and resurrection. The significance of baptism is not an imaginary significance, and sin does not completely die, nor does grace completely rise, until the body of sin that we carry about in this life is destroyed, as the apostle teaches in the same chapter (Rom. 6:6). For as long as we are in the flesh, the desires of the flesh stir and are stirred. Wherefore, as soon as ever we begin to believe, we also begin to die to this world and to live unto God in the life to come, so that faith is truly a death and a resurrection, that is, it is that spiritual baptism in which we go under and come forth.

Hence it is indeed correct to say that baptism is a washing from sins, but that expression is too weak and mild to bring out the full significance of baptism, which is rather a symbol of death and resurrection. For this reason I would have the candidates for baptism completely immersed in the water, as the word says and as the sacrament signifies. Not that I deem this necessary, but it were well to give to so perfect and complete a things a perfect and complete sign; thus it was also doubtless instituted by Christ. The sinner does not so much need to be washed as he needs to die, in order to be wholly renewed and made another creature, and to be conformed to the death and resurrection of Christ, with whom, through baptism, he dies and rises again. Although you may properly say that Christ was washed clean of mortality when He died and rose again, yet that is a weaker way of putting it than if you said He was completely changed and renewed. In the same way it is far more forceful to say that baptism signifies our utter dying and rising to eternal life, than to say that it signifies merely our being washed clean from sins.

Here, again, you see that the sacrament of baptism, even in respect to its sign, is not the matter of a moment, but continues for all time. Although its administration is soon over, yet the thing it signifies continues until we die, nay, until we rise at the last day. For as long as we live we are continually doing that which our baptism signifies—we die and rise again. We die, that is, not only spiritually and in our affections, by renouncing the sins and vanities of this world, but we die in very truth, we begin to leave this bodily life and to lay hold on the life to come, so that there is, as they say, a real and even a bodily going out of this world to the Father.

We must, therefore, beware of those who have reduced the power of baptism to such a vanishing point as to say that the grace of God is indeed inpoured in baptism, but afterwards poured out again through sin, and that thereupon one must reach Heaven by another way, as if baptism had then become entirely useless. Do not you hold to such a view, but know that baptism signifies your dying and living again, and therefore, whether it be by penance or by any other way, you can but return to the power of your baptism, and do afresh that which you were baptized to do and which your baptism signified. Never does baptism lose its power, unless you despair and refuse to return to its salvation. You may, indeed, for a season wander away from the sign, but that does not make the sign of none effect. You have, thus, been baptized once in the sacrament, but you must be constantly baptized again through faith, you must constantly die, you must constantly live again. Baptism swallowed up your whole body, and gave it forth again; even so that which baptism signifies should swallow up your whole life in body and soul, and give it forth again at the last day, clad in robes of glory and immortality. We are, therefore, never without the sign of baptism nor yet without the thing it signifies; nay, we must be baptized ever more and more completely, until we perfectly fulfill the sign at the last day.

Therefore, whatever we do in this life that avails for the mortifying of the flesh and the giving life to the spirit, belongs to baptism; and the sooner we depart this life the sooner do we fulfill our baptism, and the greater our sufferings the more closely do we conform to our baptism. Hence those were the Church's halcyon days, when the martyrs were being killed every day and accounted as sheep for the slaughter (Ps. 44:22; Rom. 8:36); for then the power of baptism reigned supreme in the Church, which power we have today lost sight of amid the multitude of works and doctrines of men. For all our life should be baptism, and the fulfilling of the sign, or sacrament, of baptism; we have been set free from all else and wholly given over to baptism alone, that is, to death and resurrection.

This glorious liberty of ours, and this understanding of baptism have been carried captive in our day, and whom have we to thank for this but the Roman pontiff with his despotism? More than all others, it was his first duty, as chief shepherd, to preach and defend this liberty and this knowledge, as Paul says in 1 Corinthians: "Let a man so account of us as of the ministers of Christ, and the dispensers of the mysteries, or sacraments, of God" (1 Cor. 4:1). Instead of this, he seeks only to oppress us with his decrees and his laws, and to enslave and ensnare us in the tyranny of his power. By what right, in God's name, does the pope impose his laws upon us? To say nothing of his wicked and damnable neglect to teach these mysteries. Who gave him power to despoil us of this liberty, granted us in baptism? One thing only (as I have said) has been enjoined upon us all the days of our life—to be baptized, that is, to be put to death and to live again, through faith in Christ, and this faith alone should have been taught, especially by the chief shepherd. But now there is not a word said about faith, and the Church is laid waste with endless laws concerning works and ceremonies, the power and right understanding of baptism are put by, and faith in Christ is prevented.

Therefore I say that neither pope nor bishop nor any other man has the right to impose a single syllable of law upon a Christian man without his consent, and if he does, it is done in the spirit of tyranny. Therefore the prayers, fasts, donations, and whatever else the pope decrees and demands in all of his decretals, as numerous as they are iniquitous, he demands and decrees without any right whatever, and he sins against the liberty of the Church whenever he attempts any such thing. Hence it has come to pass that the churchmen of our day are indeed such vigorous defenders of the liberty of the Church, that is, of wood and stone, of land and rents—for "churchly" is nowadays the same as "spiritual"—yet with such fictions they not only take captive but utterly destroy the true liberty of the Church, and deal with us far worse than the Turk, in opposition to the word of the apostle, "Be not made the bondslaves of men" (1 Cor. 7:23). For, verily, to be subjected to their statutes and tyrannical laws is to be made the bondslaves of men.

This impious and desperate tyranny is fostered by the pope's disciples, who here drag in and pervert that saying of Christ, "He that heareth you heareth me" (Luke 10:16). With puffed cheeks they blow up this saying to a great size in support of their traditions. Though Christ spake it to the apostles when they went forth to preach the

Gospel, and though it applies solely to the Gospel, they pass over the Gospel and apply it only to their fables. He says in John 10: "My sheep hear my voice, but the voice of a stranger they hear not" (v. 27); and to this end He left us the Gospel, that His voice might be uttered by the pontiffs. But they utter their own voice, and themselves desire to be heard. Moreover, the apostle says that he was not sent to baptize but to preach the Gospel (1 Cor. 1:17). Therefore, no one is bound to the traditions of the pope, nor does he need to give ear to him unless he teaches the Gospel and Christ, and the pope should teach nothing but faith without any restrictions. But since Christ says, "He that heareth you heareth me," (Luke 10:16), and does not say to Peter only, "He that heareth thee," why does not the pope also hear others? In fine, where there is true faith there must also be the word of faith. Why then does not an unbelieving pope now and then hear a believing servant of his, who has the word of faith? It is blindness, sheer blindness, that holds the popes in its power.

But others, more shameless still, arrogantly ascribe to the pope the power to make laws, on the basis of Matthew 16, "Whatsoever thou shalt bind," etc. (v. 19), though Christ treats in this passage of binding and loosing sins, not of taking the whole Church captive and oppressing it with laws. So this tyranny treats everything with its own lying words and violently wrests and perverts the words of God. I admit indeed that Christians ought to bear this accursed tyranny just as they would bear any other violence of this world, according to Christ's word: "If one strike thee on thy right cheek, turn to him also the other" (Matt. 5:39). But this is my complaint: that the godless pontiffs boastfully claim the right to do this, that they pretend to be seeking the Church's welfare with this Babylon of theirs, and that they foist this fiction upon all mankind. For if they did these things, and we suffered their violence, well knowing, both of us, that it was godlessness and tyranny, then we might number it among the things that tend to the mortifying of this life and the fulfilling of our baptism, and might with a good conscience glory in the inflicted injury. But now they seek to deprive us of this consciousness of our liberty, and would have us believe that what they do is well done, and must not be censured or complained of as wrongdoing. Being wolves, they masquerade as shepherds; being antichrists, they would be honored as Christ.

Solely in behalf of this freedom of conscience, I lift my voice and confidently cry: no laws may by any right be laid upon Christians, whether by men or angels, without their consent; for we are free from all things. And if any laws are laid upon us, we must bear them in such a way as to preserve the consciousness of our liberty, and know and certainly affirm that the making of such laws is an injustice, which we will bear and glory in, giving heed not to justify the tyrant nor yet to rebel against his tyranny. "For who is he," says Peter, "that will harm you, if ye be followers of that which is good?" (1 Pet. 3:13). "All things work together or good to the elect" (Rom. 8:28).

Nevertheless, since but few know this glory of baptism and the blessedness of Christian liberty, and cannot know them because of the tyranny of the pope, I for one will clear my skirts and salve my conscience by bringing this charge against the pope and all his papists: Unless they will abolish their laws and traditions, and restore to Christ's churches their liberty and have it taught among them, they are guilty of all the souls that perish under this miserable captivity, and the papacy is of a truth the kingdom of Babylon, yea, of very antichrist! For who is "the man of sin" and "the son of perdition" (2 Thes. 2:3ff) but he that with his doctrines and his laws increases sins and the perdition of souls in the Church, while he sitteth in the Church as if he were God? All this the papal tyranny has fulfilled, and more than fulfilled, these many centuries; it has extinguished faith, obscured the sacraments, and oppressed the Gospel, but its own laws, which are not only impious and sacrilegious, but even barbarous and foolish, it has enjoined and multiplied world without end.

Behold, then, our miserable captivity; how the city doth sit solitary that was full of people! How the mistress of the Gentiles is become as a widow: the princess of provinces made tributary! There is none to comfort her, all her friends have despised her (Lam. 1:1ff). So many orders, so many rites, so many sects, so many professions, exertions, and works in which Christians are engaged, until they lose sight of their baptism, and for this swarm of locusts, cankerworms, and caterpillars (Joel 1:4) not one of them is able to remember that he is baptized or what blessings his baptism brought him. We should be even as little children, newly baptized, who are engaged in no efforts and no works, but are free in every way, secure, and saved solely through the glory of their baptism. For we are indeed little children, continually baptized anew in Christ.

In contradiction of what has been said, some will perhaps point to the baptism of infants, who do not grasp the promise of God and cannot have the faith of baptism, so that either faith is not necessary or else infant baptism is without effect. Here I say what all say: infants are aided by the faith of others, namely, those who bring them to baptism. For the Word of God is powerful, when it is uttered, to change even a godless heart, which is no less deaf and helpless than any infant. Even so the infant is changed, cleansed, and renewed by inpoured faith, through the prayer of the Church that presents it for baptism and believes, to which prayer all things are possible (Mark 9:23). Nor should I doubt that even a godless adult might be changed, in any of the sacraments, if the same Church prayed and presented him, as we read in the Gospel of the man sick of the palsy, who was healed through the faith of others (Matt. 9:1ff). I should be ready to admit that in this sense the sacraments of the New Law are efficacious to confer grace, not only to those who do not, but even to those who do most obstinately, oppose, and bar. What obstacle will not the faith of the Church and the prayer of faith remove? Do we not believe that Stephen by this powerful means converted Paul the apostle? But then the sacraments accomplish what they do not by their own power, but by the power of faith, without which they accomplish nothing at all, as has been said.

There remains the question, whether it is right to baptize an infant not yet born, with only a hand or a foot presenting. Here I will decide nothing hastily, and confess my ignorance. I am not sure whether the reason given by some is sufficient—that the soul resides in its entirety in every part of the body, or it is not the soul but the body that is externally baptized with water. Nor do I share the view of others that he who is not yet born cannot be born again, even though it has considerable force. I leave these matters to the teaching of the Spirit, and meanwhile permit everyone to abound in his own sense (Rom. 14:15).

## VOWS AND OTHER WORKS

One thing I will add—and would to God I might persuade all to do it!—to wit, completely to abolish or avoid all vows, be they vows to enter religious orders, to make pilgrimages, or to do any works whatsoever, that we may remain in the liberty of our baptism, which is the most religious and rich in works. It is impossible to say how greatly that widespread delusion of vows lowers baptism and obscures the knowledge of Christian liberty, to say nothing now of the unspeakable and infinite peril of souls which that mania for making vows and that ill-advised rashness daily increase. O most godless pontiffs and unhappy pastors, who slumber on unheeding and indulge your evil lusts, without pity or this "affliction of Joseph" (Amos 6:4-6) so dreadful and fraught with peril!

Vows should either be abolished by a general edict, particularly such as are taken for life, and all men diligently recalled to the vows of baptism, or else everyone should be warned not to take a vow rashly, and no one encouraged to do so, nay, permission be given only with difficulty and reluctance. For we have vowed enough in baptism, nay, more than we can ever fulfill; if we give ourselves to the keeping of this one vow, we shall have all we can do. But now we compass earth and sea to make many proselytes (Matt. 23:15); we fill the world with priests, monks, and nuns, and imprison them all in life-long vows. You will find those who argue and decide that a work done in fulfillment of a vow ranks higher than one done without a vow, and is to be rewarded with I know not what great rewards in Heaven. Blind and godless Pharisees, who measure righteousness and holiness by the greatness, number, or other quality of the works! But God measures them by faith alone, and with Him there is no difference between works except that which is wrought by faith.

With such bombast these wicked men advertise their inventions and puff up human works, to lure on the unthinking populace, who are almost always led by the glitter of works to make shipwreck of their faith, to forget their baptism and do despite to their Christian liberty. For a vow is a kind of law or requirement; therefore when vows are multiplied, laws and works are necessarily multiplied, and when this is done, faith is extinguished and the liberty of baptism taken captive. Others, not content with these wicked allurements, add yet this and say that entrance into a religious order is a new baptism, as it were, which may afterward be repeated as often as the purpose to live the religious life is renewed. Thus these "votaries" have appropriated to themselves all righteousness, salvation, and glory, and let to those who are merely baptized nothing to compare with them. Nay, the Roman pontiff, that fountain and source of all superstitions, confirms, approves, and adorns this mode of life with high-sounding bulls and dispensations, while no one deems baptism worthy of even a thought. And with such glittering pomp (as we have said) they drive the easily led people of Christ into certain disaster, so that in their ingratitude toward baptism they presume to achieve greater things by their works than others achieve by their faith.

Therefore, God again shows Himself froward to the froward (Ps. 18:26), and to repay the makers of vows for their ingratitude and pride, causes them to break their vows or to keep them only with prodigious labor; to remain sunk in them, never coming to the knowledge of the grace of faith and baptism; to continue in their hypocrisy unto the end, since their spirit is not approved of God; and at last to become a laughing-stock to the whole world, ever ensuing righteousness and never attaining unto righteousness, so that they fulfill the word of Isaiah: "The land is full of idols" (Is. 2:8)

I am indeed far from forbidding or discouraging anyone who may desire to take a vow privately and of his own free choice, for I would not altogether despise and condemn vows. But I would most strongly advise against setting up and sanctioning the making of vows as a public mode of life. It is enough that everyone should have the private right to take a vow at his peril, but to commend the vowing of vows as a public mode of life—this I hold to be most harmful to the Church and to simple souls. And I hold this, first, because it runs directly counter to the Christian life, for a vow is a certain ceremonial law and a human tradition or presumption, and from these the Christian has been set free through baptism. For a Christian is subject to no laws but the law of God. Again, there is no instance in Scripture of such a vow, especially of life-long chastity, obedience, and poverty. But whatever is without warrant of Scripture is hazardous and should by no means be commended to anyone, much less established as a common and public mode of life, although whoever will must be permitted to make the venture at his own peril. For certain works are wrought by the Spirit in a few men, but they must not be made an example or a mode of life for all.

Moreover, I greatly fear that these modes of life of the religious orders belong to those things which the apostle foretold: "They shall teach a life in hypocrisy, forbidding to marry, to abstain from meats, which God hath created to be received with thanksgiving" (1 Tim.

4:2ff). Let no one retort by pointing to saints Bernard, Francis, Dominic and others, who founded or fostered monastic orders. Terrible and marvelous is God in His counsels toward the sons of men. He could keep Daniel, Hananiah, Azariah, and Mishael holy at the court of the king of Babylon (Dan 1:6ff), that is, in the midst of godlessness; why could He not sanctify those men also in their perilous mode of living or guide them by the special operation of His Spirit, yet without desiring it to be an example to others? Besides, it is certain that none of them was saved through his vows and his "religious" life; they were saved through faith alone, by which all men are saved, and with which that splendid slavery of vows is more than anything else in conflict.

But everyone may hold to his own view of this (Rom. 14:5). I will return to my argument. Speaking now in behalf of the Church's liberty and the glory of baptism, I feel myself in duty bound publicly to set forth the counsel I have learned under the Spirit's guidance. I therefore counsel the magnates of the churches, first of all, to abolish all those vows, or at least not to approve and extol them. If they will not do this, then I counsel all men who would be assured of their salvation to abstain from all vows, above all from the great and life-long vows; I give this counsel especially to all growing boys and youths. This I do, first, because this manner of life has no witness or warrant in the Scriptures, as I have said, but is puffed up solely by the bulls (and they truly are "bulls") of human popes. And, secondly, because it greatly tends to hypocrisy, by reason of its outward show and its unusual character, which engender conceit and a contempt of the common Christian life. And if there were no other reason for abolishing these vows, this one were reason enough, namely, that through them, faith and baptism are slighted and works are exalted, which cannot be done without harmful results. For in the religious orders there is scarce one in many thousands, who is not more concerned about works than about faith, and on the basis of this madness they have even made distinctions among themselves, such as "the more strict" and "the more lax," as they call them.

Therefore I advise no one to enter any religious order or the priesthood—nay, I dissuade everyone, unless he be forearmed with this knowledge and understand that the works of monks and priests, be they never so holy and arduous, differ no whit in the sight of God from the works of the rustic toiling in the field or the woman going about her household tasks, but that all works are measured before Him by faith alone; as Jeremiah says: "O Lord, thine eyes are upon faith" (Jer. 5:3); and Ecclesiasticus: "In every work of thine regard thy soul in faith, for this is the keeping of the commandments" (Eccl. 32:27). Nay, he should know that the menial housework of a maidservant or manservant is ofttimes more acceptable to God than all the fastings and other works of a monk or a priest, because the latter lacks faith. Since, therefore, vows seem to tend nowadays only to the glorification of works and to pride, it is to be feared that there is nowhere less of faith and of the Church than among the priests, monks, and bishops, and that these men are in truth heathen or hypocrites, who imagine themselves to be the Church or the heart of the Church, and "spiritual," and the Church's leaders, when they are everything else but that. And it is to be feared that this is indeed "the people of the captivity," (Ps. 64:1) among whom all things freely given us in baptism are held captive, while "the people of the earth" are left behind in poverty and in small numbers, and, as is the lot of married folk, appear vile in their eyes.

From what has been said we learn that the Roman pontiff is guilty of two glaring errors. In the first place, he grants dispensations from vows, and does it as though he alone of all Christians possessed this authority; such is the temerity and audacity of wicked men. If it be possible to grant a dispensation from a vow, then any brother may grant one to his neighbor or even to himself. But if one's neighbor cannot grant a dispensation, neither can the pope by any right. For whence has he his authority? From the power of the keys? But the keys belong to all, and avail only for sins (Matt. 18:15ff). Now they themselves claim that vows are "of divine right." Why then does the pope deceive and destroy the poor souls of men by granting dispensations in matters of divine right, in which no dispensations can be granted? He babbles indeed, in the section "Of vows and their redemption"(*Decretal. Greg.* III.3.3.34.7), of having the power to change vows, just as in the law the firstborn of an ass was changed or a sheep (Exod.13:13)—as if the firstborn of an ass, and the vow he commands to be everywhere and always offered, were one and the same thing, or as if when God decrees in His law that a sheep shall be changed or an ass, the pope, a mere man, may straightway claim the same power, not in his own law but in God's! It was not a pope, but an ass changed for a pope, that made this decretal, so egregiously senseless and godless is it.

The other error is this. The pope decrees, on the other hand, that marriage is dissolved if one party enter a monastery even without the consent of the other, provided the marriage be not yet consummated. Gramercy, what devil puts such monstrous things into the pope's mind! God commands men to keep faith and not break their word to one another, and again, to do good with that which is their own; for He hates "robbery in a sacrifice," (Is. 61:8), as he says by the mouth of Isaiah. But one spouse is bound by the marriage contract to keep faith with the other, and he is not his own. He cannot break his faith by any right, and whatever he does with himself is robbery if it be without the other's consent. Why does not one who is burdened with debts follow this same rule and obtain admission to an order, so as to be released from his debts and be free to break his word? O more than blind! Which is greater: the faith commanded by God or a vow devised and chosen by man? Thou art a shepherd of souls, O pope? And ye that teach such things are doctors of sacred theology? Why then do ye teach them? Because, forsooth, ye have decked out your vow as a better work than marriage, and do not exalt faith, which alone exalts all things, but ye exalt works, which are naught in the sight of God, or which are all alike so far as any merit is concerned.

I have no doubt, therefore, that neither men nor angels can grant a dispensation from vows, if they be proper vows. But I am not fully clear in my own mind whether all the things that men nowadays vow come under the head of vows. For instance, it is simply foolish and stupid for parents to dedicate their children, before birth or in early infancy, to "the religious life," or to perpetual chastity; nay, it is certain that this can by no means be termed a vow. It seems a mockery of God to vow things which it is not at all in one's power to keep. As to the triple vow of the monastic orders, the longer I consider it, the less I comprehend it, and I marvel whence the custom of exacting this vow has arisen. Still less do I understand at what age vows may be taken in order to be legal and valid. I am pleased to find them unanimously agreed that vows taken before the age of puberty are not valid. Nevertheless, they deceive many young children who are ignorant both of their age and of what they are vowing; they do not observe the age of puberty in receiving such children, who after making their profession are held captive and devoured by a troubled conscience, as though they had afterward given their consent. As if a vow which was invalid could afterward become valid with the lapse of time.

It seems absurd to me that the terms of a legal vow should be prescribed to others by those who cannot prescribe them for themselves. Nor do I see why a vow taken at eighteen years of age should be valid, and not one taken at ten or twelve years. It will not do to say that at eighteen a man feels his carnal desires. How is it when he scarcely feels them at twenty or thirty, or when he feels them more keenly at thirty than at twenty? Why do they not also set a certain age-limit for the vows of poverty and obedience? But at what age will you say a man should feel his greed and pride? Even the most spiritual hardly become aware of these emotions. Therefore, no vow will ever become binding and valid until we have become spiritual, and no longer have any need of vows. You see, these are uncertain and perilous matters, and it would therefore be a wholesome counsel to leave such lofty modes of living, unhampered by vows, to the Spirit alone, as they were of old, and by no means to change them into a rule binding for life. But let this suffice for the present concerning baptism and its liberty; in due time I may treat of the vows at greater length. Of a truth they stand sorely in need of it.

# THE SACRAMENT OF PENANCE

We come in the third place to the sacrament of penance. On this subject I have already given no little offence by my published treatises and disputations, in which I have amply set forth my views. These I must now briefly rehearse, in order to unmask the tyranny that is rampant here no less than in the sacrament of the bread. For because these two sacraments furnish opportunity for gain and profit, the greed of the shepherds rages in them with incredible zeal against the flock of Christ, although baptism, too, has sadly declined among adults and become the servant of avarice, as we have just seen in our discussion of vows.

This is the first and chief abuse of this sacrament: they have utterly abolished the sacrament itself, so that there is not a vestige of it left. For they have overthrown both the word of divine promise and our faith, in which this as well as other sacraments consists. They have applied to their tyranny the word of promise which Christ spake in Matthew 16, "Whatsoever thou shalt bind," etc. (v. 19), in Matthew 18, "Whatsoever ye shall bind," etc. (v. 18), and in John, the last chapter, "Whosesoever sins ye remit, they are remitted unto them," (John 20:23) etc. In these words the faith of penitents is aroused to the obtaining of remission of sins. But in all their writing, teaching, and preaching their sole concern has been, not to teach Christians what is promised in these words or what they ought to believe and what great comfort they might find in them, but only to extend their own tyranny far and wide through force and violence, until it has come to such a pass that some of them have begun to command the very angels in Heaven and to boast in incredible mad wickedness of having in these words obtained the right to a Heavenly and an earthly rule, and of possessing the power to bind even in Heaven. Thus they say nothing of the saving faith of the people, but babble only of the despotic power of the pontiffs, whereas Christ speaks not at all of power, but only of faith.

For Christ hath not ordained principalities or powers or lordships, but ministries, in the Church; as we learn from the apostle, who says: "Let a man so account of us as of the ministers of Christ, and the dispensers of the mysteries of God" (1 Cor. 4:1). Now when He said: "He that believeth and is baptized shall be saved" (Mark 16:16). He called forth the faith of those to be baptized, so that by this word of promise a man might be certain of being saved if he believed and was baptized. In that word there is no impartation of any power whatever, but only the institution of the ministry of those who baptize. Similarly, when He says here: "Whatsoever thou shalt bind," etc. (Matt. 16:19), he calls forth the faith of the penitent, so that by this word of promise he may be certain of being truly absolved in Heaven, if he be absolved and believe. Here there is no mention at all of power, but of the ministry of him that absolves. It is a wonder these blind and overbearing men missed the opportunity of arrogating a despotic power to themselves from the promise of baptism. But if they do not do this in the case of baptism, why should they have presumed to do it in the case of the promise of penance? For in both there is a like ministry, a similar promise, and the same kind of sacrament. So that, if baptism does not belong to Peter alone, it is undeniably a wicked usurpation of power to claim the keys for the pope alone. Again, when Christ says: "Take, eat; this is my body, which is given for you. Take, drink;

this is the chalice of my blood," etc. (1 Cor. 11:24ff), He calls forth the faith of those who eat, so that through these words their conscience may be strengthened by faith and they may rest assured of receiving the forgiveness of sins, if they have eaten. Here, too, He says nothing of power, but only of a ministry.

Thus the promise of baptism remains in some sort, at least to infants; the promise of bread and the cup has been destroyed and made subservient to greed, faith becoming a work and the testament a sacrifice, while the promise of penance has fallen prey to the most oppressive despotism of all and serves to establish a more than temporal rule.

Not content with these things, this Babylon of ours has so completely extinguished faith that it insolently denies its necessity in this sacrament; nay, with the wickedness of antichrist it calls it heresy if anyone should assert its necessity. What more could this tyranny do that it has not done (Is. 5:4)? "Verily, by the rivers of Babylon we sit and weep, when we remember thee, O Zion. We hang our harps upon the willows in the midst thereof" (Ps. 137:1-2). The Lord curse the barren willows of those streams! Amen.

Now let us see what they have put in the place of the promise and the faith which they have blotted out and overthrown. Three parts have they made of penance—contrition, confession, and satisfaction, yet so as to destroy whatever of good there might be in any of them and to establish here also their covetousness and tyranny.

## I. CONTRITION

In the first place, they teach that contrition precedes faith in the promise; they hold it much too cheap, making it not a work of faith, but a merit; nay, they do not mention it at all. So deep are they sunk in works and in those instances of Scripture that show how many obtained grace by reason of their contrition and humility of heart, but they take no account of the faith which wrought such contrition and sorrow of heart, as it is written of the men of Nineveh in Jonah 3, "And the men of Nineveh believed in God, and they proclaimed a fast," (v. 5). etc. Others, again, more bold and wicked, have invented a so-called "attrition," which is converted into contrition by virtue of the power of the keys, of which they know nothing. This attrition they grant to the wicked and unbelieving and thus abolish contrition altogether. O the intolerable wrath of God, that such things should be taught in the Church of Christ! Thus, with both faith and its work destroyed, we go on secure in the doctrines and opinions of men— yea, we go on to our destruction. A contrite heart is a precious thing, but it is found only where there is a lively faith in the promises and the threats of God. Such faith, intent on the immutable truth of God, startles and terrifies the conscience and thus renders it contrite, and afterwards, when it is contrite, raises it up, consoles and preserves it, so that the truth of God's threatening is the cause of contrition, and the truth of His promise the cause of consolation, if it be believed. By such faith a man merits the forgiveness of sins. Therefore faith should be taught and aroused before all else, and when faith is obtained, contrition and consolation will follow inevitably and of themselves.

Therefore, although there is something of truth in their teaching that contrition is to be attained by what they call the recollection and contemplation of sins, yet their teaching is perilous and perverse so long as they do not teach first of all the beginning and cause of contrition: the immutable truth of God's threatening and promise, to the awakening of faith, so that men may learn to pay more heed to the truth of God, whereby they are cast down and lifted up, than to the multitude of their sins, which will rather irritate and increase the sinful desires than lead to contrition, if they be regarded apart from the truth of God. I will say nothing now of the intolerable burden they have bound upon us with their demand that we should frame a contrition for every sin. That is impossible; we can know only the smaller part of our sins, and even our good works are found to be sins, according to Psalm 143, "Enter not into judgment with thy servant; for in thy sight shall no man living be justified" (v. 2). It is enough to lament the sins which at the present moment distress our conscience, as well as those which we can readily call to mind. Whoever is in this frame of mind is without doubt ready to grieve and fear for all his sins, and will do so whenever they are brought to his knowledge in the future.

Beware, then, of putting your trust in your own contrition and of ascribing the forgiveness of sins to your own sorrow. God does not have respect to you because of that, but because of the faith by which you have believed His threatenings and promises, and which wrought such sorrow within you. Thus we owe whatever of good there may be in our penance, not to our scrupulous enumeration of sins, but to the truth of God and to our faith. All other things are the works and fruits of this, which follow of their own accord, and do not make a man good, but are done by a man already made good through faith in the truth of God. Even so, "a smoke goeth up in His wrath, because He is angry and troubleth the mountains and kindleth them" (Ps. 18:8). First comes the terror of His threatening, which burns up the wicked, then faith, accepting this, sends up the cloud of contrition, etc.

## II. CONFESSION

Contrition, however, is less exposed to tyranny and gain than wholly given over to wickedness and pestilent teaching. But confession and satisfaction have become the chief workshop of greed and violence. Let us first take up confession. There is no doubt that confession is necessary and commanded of God. Thus we read in Matthew 3: "They were baptized of John in Jordan, confessing their sins" (v. 6). And in 1 John 1: "If we confess our sins, he is faithful and just to forgive us our sins.... If we say that we have not sinned, we make him a liar, and his word is not in us" (v. 9). If the saints may not deny their sin, how much more ought those who are guilty of open and great sins to make confession! But most effectively of all does Matthew 18 prove the institution of confession, in which passage Christ teaches that a sinning brother should be rebuked, haled before the Church, accused and, if he will not hear, excommunicated. But he hears when, heeding the rebuke, he acknowledges and confesses his sin (Matt. 18:15).

Of private confession, which is now observed, I am heartily in favor, even though it cannot be proved from the Scriptures; it is useful and necessary, nor would I have it abolished—nay, I rejoice that it exists in the Church of Christ, for it is a cure without an equal for distressed consciences. For when we have laid bare our conscience to our brother and privately made known to him the evil that lurked within, we receive from our brother's lips the word of comfort spoken by God Himself, and, if we accept it in faith, we find peace in the mercy of God speaking to us through our brother. This alone do I abominate—that this confession has been subjected to the despotism and extortion of the pontiffs. They reserve to themselves even hidden sins, and command that they be made known to confessors named by them, only to trouble the consciences of men. They merely play the pontiff, while they utterly despise the true duties of pontiffs, which are to preach the Gospel and to care for the poor. Yea, the godless despots leave the great sins to the plain priests, and reserve to themselves those sins only which are of less consequence, such as those ridiculous and fictitious things in the bull *Coena Domini*. Nay, to make the wickedness of their error the more apparent, they not only do not reserve, but actually teach and approve the sins against the service of God, against faith and the chief commandments, such as their running on pilgrimages, the perverse worship of the saints, the lying saints' legends, the various forms of trust in works and ceremonies, and the practicing of them, by all of which faith in God is extinguished and idolatry encouraged, as we see in our day. We have the same kind of priests today as Jeroboam ordained of old in Dan and Beersheba (1 Kings 12:26ff)—ministers of the golden calves, men who are ignorant of the law of God, of faith, and of whatever pertains to the feeding of Christ's sheep, and who inculcate in the people nothing but their own inventions with terror and violence.

Although my advice is that we bear this outrage of reserved cases, even as Christ bids us bear all the tyranny of men, and teaches us that we must obey these extortioners, nevertheless I deny that they have the right to make such reservations, nor do I believe they can bring one jot or tittle of proof that they have it. But I am going to prove the contrary. In the first place, Christ, speaking in Matthew 18 of open sins, says that if our brother shall hear us when we rebuke him, we have saved the soul of our brother, and that he is to be brought before the Church only if he refuse to hear us, so that his sin may be corrected among brethren. How much more will it be true of hidden sins that they are forgiven if one brother freely makes confession to another? So that it is not necessary to tell it to the Church, that is, as these babblers interpret it, the prelate or priest. We have another proof of this in Christ's words in the same chapter: "Whatsoever you shall bind on earth shall be bound also in Heaven, and whatsoever you shall loose on earth shall be loosed in Heaven" (Matt. 18:18). For this is said to each and every Christian. Again, He says in the same place: "Again I say to you, that if two of you shall consent upon earth, concerning anything whatsoever that they shall ask, it shall be done to them by my Father who is in Heaven" (Matt 18:19). Now, the brother who lays his hidden sins before his brother and craves pardon, certainly consents with his brother upon earth in the truth, which is Christ. Of which Christ says yet more clearly, confirming His preceding words: "Verily I say unto you, where two or three are gathered together in my name, there am I in the midst of them" (Matt. 18:20).

Hence, I have no doubt but that every one is absolved from his hidden sins when he has made confession, either of his own accord or after being rebuked, has sought pardon and amended his ways, privately before any brother, however much the violence of the pontiffs may rage against it; for Christ has given to every one of His believers the power to absolve even open sins. Add yet this little point: if any reservation of hidden sins were valid, so that one could not be saved unless they were forgiven, then a man's salvation would be prevented most of all by those aforementioned good works and idolatries which are nowadays taught by the popes. But if these most grievous sins do not prevent one's salvation, how foolish it is to reserve those lighter sins! Verily, it is the foolishness and blindness of the pastors that produce these monstrous things in the Church. Therefore I would admonish these princes of Babylon and bishops of Bethaven (Hos. 4:15; 10:5) to refrain from reserving any cases whatsoever. Let them, moreover, permit all brothers and sisters freely to hear the confession of hidden sins, so that the sinner may make his sins known to whomever he will and seek pardon and comfort, that is, the word of Christ, by the mouth of his neighbor. For with these presumptions of theirs they only ensnare the consciences of the weak without necessity, establish their wicked despotism, and fatten their avarice on the sins and ruin of their brethren. Thus they stain their hands with the blood of souls, sons are devoured by their parents, Ephraim devours Judah, and Syria Israel with open mouth, as Isaiah saith (Is. 9:20).

To these evils they have added the "circumstances," and also the mothers, daughters, sisters, brothers-in-law, and sisters-in-law, branches and fruits of sins, since, forsooth, astute and idle men have worked out a kind of family tree of relationships and affinities even among sins, so prolific is wickedness coupled with ignorance. For this conceit, whatever rogue be its author, has like many another become a public law. Thus do the shepherds keep watch over the Church of

Christ; whatever new work or superstition those stupid devotees may have dreamed of, they straightway drag to the light of day, deck out with indulgences, and safeguard with bulls; so far are they from suppressing it and preserving to God's people the true faith and liberty. For what has our liberty to do with the tyranny of Babylon? My advice would be to ignore all circumstances utterly. With Christians there is only one circumstance—that a brother has sinned. For there is no person to be compared with a Christian brother. And the observance of places, times, days, persons, and all other superstitious moonshine, only magnifies the things that are nothing, to the injury of those which are everything, as if aught could be greater or of more importance than the glory of Christian brotherhood! Thus they bind us to places, days, and persons, that the name of brother may be lightly esteemed, and we may serve in bondage instead of being free—we to whom all days, places, persons, and all external things are one and the same.

## III. SATISFACTION

How unworthily they have dealt with satisfaction, I have abundantly shown in the controversies concerning indulgences. They have grossly abused it, to the ruin of Christians in body and soul. To begin with, they taught it in such a manner that the people never learned what satisfaction really is, namely, the renewal of a man's life. Then they so continually harp on it and emphasize its necessity that they leave no room for faith in Christ. With these scruples they torture poor consciences to death, and one runs to Rome, one to this place, another to that, this one to Chartreuse, that one to some other place, one scourges himself with rods, another ruins his body with fasts and vigils, and all cry with the same mad zeal, "Lo here is Christ! Lo there!" (Luke 17:20ff), believing that the kingdom of Heaven, which is within us, will come with observation.

For these monstrous things we are indebted to thee, O Roman See, and thy murderous laws and ceremonies, with which thou hast corrupted all mankind, so that they think by works to make satisfaction for sin to God, Who can be satisfied only by the faith of a contrite heart! This faith thou not only keepest silent with this uproar of thine, but even oppressest, only so thy insatiable horseleech have those to whom it may say, "Bring, bring!" (Prov. 30:15) and may traffic in sins.

Some have gone even farther and have constructed those instruments for driving souls to despair—their decrees that the penitent must rehearse all sins anew for which he neglected to make the imposed satisfaction. Yea, what would not they venture to do, who were born for the sole purpose of carrying all things into a tenfold captivity? Moreover, how many are possessed with the notion that they are in a saved state and are making satisfaction for their sins if they but mumble over, word for word, the prayers the priest has imposed, even though they give never a thought meanwhile to amending their life! They believe that their life is changed in the one moment of contrition and confession, and it remains only to make satisfaction for their past sins. How should they know better, when they are not taught otherwise? No thought is given here to the mortifying of the flesh, no value is attached to the example of Christ, who absolved the woman taken in adultery and said to her, "Go, and sin no more!" (John 8:11), thereby laying upon her the cross—the mortifying of her flesh. This perverse error is greatly encouraged by our absolving sinners before the satisfaction has been completed, so that they are more concerned about completing the satisfaction which lies before them than they are about contrition, which they suppose to be past and over when they have made confession. Absolution ought rather to follow on the completion of satisfaction, as it did in the ancient Church, with the result that, after completing the work, penitents gave themselves with greater diligence to faith and the living of a new life.

But this must suffice in repetition of what I have more fully said on indulgences, and in general this must suffice for the present concerning the three sacraments, which have been treated, and yet not treated, in so many harmful books, theological as well as juristic. It remains to attempt some discussion of the other sacraments also, lest I seem to have rejected them without cause.

# THE SACRAMENT OF CONFIRMATION

I wonder what could have possessed them to make a sacrament of confirmation out of the laying on of hands, which Christ employed when He blessed young children (Mark 10:16), and the apostles when they imparted the Holy Spirit (Acts 8:17; Acts 19:6; Acts 6:6; Mark 16:18), ordained elders and cured the sick, as the apostle writes to Timothy, "Lay hands suddenly on no man" (1 Tim. 5:22). Why have they not also turned the sacrament of the bread into confirmation? For it is written in Acts 9, "And when he had taken meat he was strengthened," and in Psalm 104, "And that bread may cheer man's heart" (v. 15). Confirmation would thus include three sacraments—the bread, ordination, and confirmation itself. But if everything the apostles did is a sacrament, why have they not rather made preaching a sacrament?

I do not say this because I condemn the seven sacraments, but because I deny that they can be proved from the Scriptures. Would to God we had in the Church such a laying on of hands as there was in apostolic times, whether we called it confirmation or healing! But there is nothing left of it now but what we ourselves have invented to adorn the office of the bishops, that they may have at least something to do in the Church. For after they relinquished to their inferiors those arduous sacraments together with the Word, as being too common for themselves—since, forsooth, whatever the divine Majesty has instituted must needs be despised of men!—it was no more than right that we should discover something easy and not too burdensome for such delicate and great heroes to do, and should by no means entrust it to the lower clergy as something common, for whatever human wisdom has decreed must needs be held in honor among men! Therefore, as are the priests, so let their ministry and duty be. For a bishop who does not preach the Gospel or care for souls (1 Cor. 8:4), what is he but an idol in the world, having but the name and appearance of a bishop?

But we seek, instead of this, sacraments that have been divinely instituted, among which we see no reason for numbering confirmation. For, in order that there be a sacrament, there is required above all things a word of divine promise, whereby faith may be trained. But we read nowhere that Christ ever gave a promise concerning confirmation, although He laid hands on many and included the laying on of hands among the signs in Mark 16: "They shall lay their hands on the sick, and they shall recover" (v. 18). Yet no one referred this to a sacrament, nor can this be done. Hence it is sufficient to regard confirmation as a certain churchly rite or sacramental ceremony, similar to other ceremonies, such as the blessing of holy water and the like. For if every other creature is sanctified by the word and by prayer (1 Tim. 4:4ff), why should not much rather man be sanctified by the same means? Still, these things cannot be called sacraments of faith, because there is no divine promise connected with them, neither do they save, but sacraments do save those who believe the divine promise.

# THE SACRAMENT OF MARRIAGE

Not only is marriage regarded as a sacrament without the least warrant of Scripture, but the very traditions which extol it as a sacrament have turned it into a farce. Let me explain.

We said that there is in every sacrament a word of divine promise, to be believed by whoever receives the sign, and that the sign alone cannot be a sacrament. Now we read nowhere that the man who marries a wife receives any grace of God. Nay, there is not even a divinely instituted sign in marriage, for nowhere do we read that marriage was instituted by God to be a sign of anything. To be sure, whatever takes place in a visible manner may be regarded as a type or figure of something invisible, but types and figures are not sacraments in the sense in which we use this term. Furthermore, since marriage existed from the beginning of the world and is still found among unbelievers, it cannot possibly be called a sacrament of the New Law and the exclusive possession of the Church. The marriages of the ancients were no less sacred than are ours, nor are those of unbelievers less true marriages than those of believers, and yet they are not regarded as sacraments. Besides, there are even among believers married folk who are wicked and worse than any heathen. Why should marriage be called a sacrament in their case and not among the heathen? Or are we going to prate so foolishly of baptism and the Church as to hold that marriage is a sacrament only in the Church, just as some make the mad claim that temporal power exists only in the Church? That is childish and foolish talk, by which we expose our ignorance and our arrogance to the ridicule of unbelievers.

But they will say: the apostle writes in Ephesians 5, "They shall be two in one flesh. This is a great sacrament" (Eph. 5:31ff). Surely you are not going to contradict so plain a statement of the apostle! I reply: This argument, like the others, betrays great shallowness and a negligent and thoughtless reading of Scripture. Nowhere in Holy Scripture is this word sacrament employed in the meaning to which we are accustomed; it has an entirely different meaning. For wherever it occurs it signifies not the sign of a sacred thing, but a sacred, secret, hidden thing. Thus Paul writes in 1 Corinthians 4, "Let a man so account of us as the ministers of Christ, and dispensers of the mysteries—i.e., sacraments—of God" (1 Cor. 4:1). Where we have the word *sacrament* the Greek text reads *mystery*, which word our version sometimes translates and sometimes retains in its Greek form. Thus our verse reads in the Greek: "They shall be two in one flesh; this is a great *mystery*" (Eph. 5:31). This explains how they came to find a sacrament of the New Law here—a thing they would never have done if they had read the word *mystery*, as it is in the Greek. Thus Christ Himself is called a sacrament in 1 Timothy 3, "And evidently great is the sacrament—i.e., mystery—of godliness, which was manifested in the flesh, was justified in the spirit, appeared unto angels, hath been preached unto the Gentiles, is believed by the world, is taken up in glory" (1 Tim. 3:16). Why have they not drawn out of this passage an eighth sacrament of the New Law, since they have the clear authority of Paul? But if they restrained themselves here, where they had a most excellent opportunity to unearth a new sacrament, why are they so wanton in the former passage? It was their ignorance, forsooth, of both words and things; they clung to the mere sound of the words, nay, to their own fancies. For, having once arbitrarily taken the word sacrament to mean a sign, they straightway, without thought or scruple, made a sign of it every time they came upon it in the sacred Scriptures. Such new meanings of words and such human customs they have also elsewhere dragged into Holy Writ and conformed it to their dreams, making anything out of any passage whatsoever. Thus they continually chatter nonsense about the terms: good and evil works, sin, grace, righteousness, virtue, and well-nigh every one of the fundamental words and things. For they employ them all after their own arbitrary judgment, learned from the writings of men, to the detriment both of the truth of God and of our salvation.

Therefore, *sacrament* or *mystery* in Paul's writings is that wisdom of the Spirit, hidden in a mystery, as he says in 1 Corinthians 2:7ff, which is Christ, who is for this very reason not known to the princes of this world, wherefore they also crucified Him, and who still is to them foolishness, an offense, a stone of stumbling (1 Cor. 1:23; Rom. 9:33), and a sign which is spoken against (Luke 2:34). The preachers he calls dispensers of these mysteries because they preach Christ, the power and the wisdom of God (1 Cor. 1:23ff; 4:1), yet so that one cannot receive this unless one believe. Therefore, a sacrament is a mystery, or secret thing, which is set forth in words and is received by the faith of the heart. Such a sacrament is spoken of in the verse before us—"They shall be two in one flesh. This is a great sacrament"(Eph 5:31)—which they understand as spoken of marriage, whereas Paul wrote these words of Christ and the Church, and clearly explained his meaning by adding, "But I speak in Christ and in the Church." Aye, how well they agree with Paul! He declares he is setting forth a great sacrament in Christ and the Church, but they set it forth in a man and a woman! If such wantonness be permitted in the sacred Scriptures, it is small wonder if one find there anything one please, even a hundred sacraments.

Christ and the Church are, therefore, a mystery, that is, a great and secret thing, which it was possible and proper to represent by marriage as by a certain outward allegory, but that was no reason for their calling marriage a sacrament. The Heavens are a type of the apostles, as Psalm 19 declares; the sun is a type of Christ; the waters, of the peoples (Ps. 19:1ff), but that does not make those things sacraments, for in every case there are lacking both the divine institution and the divine promise which constitute a sacrament. Hence Paul, in Ephesians 5, following his own mind, applies to Christ these words in Genesis 2 about marriage, or else, following the general view, he teaches that the spiritual marriage of Christ is also contained therein, saying, "As Christ cherisheth the Church: because we are members of his body, of his flesh and of his bones. For this cause shall a man leave his father and mother, and shall cleave to his wife, and they shall be two in one flesh. This is a great sacrament; I speak in Christ and in the Church" (Eph. 5:29ff). You see, he would have the whole passage apply to Christ, and is at pains to admonish the reader to find the sacrament in Christ and the Church, and not in marriage.

Therefore we grant that marriage is a type of Christ and the Church, and a sacrament, yet not divinely instituted, but invented by men in the Church, carried away by their ignorance both of the word and of the thing. Which ignorance, since it does not conflict with the faith, is to be charitably borne with, just as many other practices of human weakness and ignorance are borne with in the Church, so long as they do not conflict with the faith and with the Word of God. But we are now dealing with the certainty and purity of the faith and the Scriptures, so that our faith be not exposed to ridicule, when after affirming that a certain thing is contained in the sacred Scriptures and in the articles of our faith, we are refuted and shown that it is not contained therein, and, being found ignorant of our own affairs, become a stumbling-block to our opponents and to the weak, nay, that we destroy not the authority of the Holy Scriptures. For those things which have been delivered to us by God in the sacred Scriptures must be sharply distinguished from those that have been invented by men in the Church, it matters not how eminent they be for saintliness and scholarship.

So far concerning marriage itself. But what shall we say of the wicked laws of men by which this divinely ordained manner of life is ensnared and tossed to and fro? Good God! It is dreadful to contemplate the audacity of the Roman despots, who wantonly tear marriages asunder and again force them together. Prithee, is mankind given over to the wantonness of these men, for them to mock and in every way abuse and make of them whatever they please for filthy lucre's sake?

There is circulating far and wide and enjoying a great reputation a book whose contents have been poured together out of the cesspool of all human traditions, and whose title is "The Angelic Sum," though it ought rather to be "The More than Devilish Sum." Among endless other monstrosities which are supposed to instruct the confessors, while they most mischievously confuse them, there are enumerated in this book eighteen hindrances to marriage. If you will examine these with the just and unprejudiced eye of faith, you will see that they belong to those things which the apostle foretold: "There shall be those that give heed to spirits of devils, speaking lies in hypocrisy, forbidding to marry" (1 Tim. 4:1ff). What is forbidding to marry if it is not this—to invent all those hindrances and set those snares, in order to prevent men from marrying or, if they be married, to annul their marriage? Who gave this power to men? Granted that they were holy men and impelled by godly zeal, why should another's holiness disturb my liberty? Why should another's zeal take me captive? Let whoever will be a saint and a zealot, and to his heart's content, only let him not bring harm upon another, and let him not rob me of my liberty!

Yet I am glad that those shameful laws have at length attained to their full measure of glory, which is this: the Romanists of our day have through them become merchants. What is it they sell? The shame of men and women—merchandise, forsooth, most worthy of such merchants, grown altogether filthy and obscene through greed and godlessness. For there is nowadays no hindrance that may not be legalized upon the intercession of mammon, so that these laws of men seem to have sprung into existence for the sole purpose of serving those grasping and robbing Nimrods as snares for taking money and as nets for catching souls, and in order that that "abomination" might stand "in the holy place" (Matt. 24:15), the Church of God, and openly sell to men the shame of either sex, or as the Scriptures say, "shame and nakedness" (Lev. 13:6ff), of which they had previously robbed them by means of their laws. O worthy trade for our pontiffs to ply, instead of the ministry of the Gospel, which in their greed and pride they despise, being delivered up to a reprobate sense with utter shame and infamy (Rom. 1:28).

But what shall I say or do? If I enter into details, the treatise will grow to inordinate length, for everything is in such dire confusion one does not know where to begin, whither to go on, or where to leave off. I know that no state is well governed by means of laws. If the magistrate be wise, he will rule more prosperously by natural bent than by laws. If he be not wise, he will but further the evil by means of laws, for he will not know what use to make of the laws nor how to adapt them to the individual case. More stress ought, therefore, to be laid, in civil affairs, on putting good and wise men in office than on making laws, for such men will themselves be the very best laws, and will judge every variety of case with lively justice. And if there be knowledge of the divine law combined with natural wisdom, then written laws will be entirely superfluous and harmful. Above all, love needs no laws whatever.

Nevertheless I will say and do what I can. I admonish and pray all priests and brethren, when they encounter any hindrance from which the pope can grant dispensation and which is not expressly contained in the Scriptures, by all means to confirm any marriage that may have been contracted in any way contrary to the ecclesiastical or pontifical laws. But let them arm themselves with the divine law, which says, "What God hath joined together, let no man put asunder" (Matt. 19:6). For the joining together of a man and a woman is of divine law and is binding, however it may conflict with the laws of men: the laws of men must give way before it without hesitation. For if a man leaves father and mother and cleaves to his wife, how much more will he tread underfoot the silly and wicked laws of men in order to cleave to his wife! And if pope, bishop, or official annul any marriage because it was contracted contrary to the laws of men, he is antichrist, he does violence to nature, and is guilty of lese-majesty toward God, because this word stands: "What God hath joined together, let no man put asunder" (Matt. 19:6).

Besides this, no man had the right to frame such laws, and Christ has granted to Christians a liberty which is above all laws of men, especially where a law of God conflicts with them. Thus it is said in Mark 2, "The Son of man is lord also of the sabbath," (v. 28). and, "The sabbath was made for man, not man for the sabbath" (v. 27). Moreover, such laws were condemned beforehand by Paul, when he foretold that there would be men forbidding to marry (1 Tim. 4:3). Here, therefore, those cruel hindrances arising from affinity, spiritual or legal relationship, and consanguinity must give way, so far as the Scriptures permit, in which the second degree of consanguinity alone is prohibited. Thus it is written in Leviticus 18, in which chapter there are twelve persons a man is prohibited from marrying: namely, his mother, his mother-in-law, his full sister, his half-sister by either parent, his granddaughter, his father's or mother's sister, his daughter-in-law, his brother's wife, his wife's sister, his stepdaughter, and his uncle's wife (Lev. 18:6ff). Here only the first degree of affinity and the second degree of consanguinity are forbidden, yet not without exception, as will appear on closer examination, for the brother's or sister's daughter, or the niece, is not included in the prohibition, although she is in the second degree. Therefore, if a marriage has been contracted outside of these degrees, it should by no means be annulled on account of the laws of men, since it is nowhere written in the Bible that any other degrees were prohibited by God. Marriage itself, as of divine institution, is incomparably superior to any laws, so that marriage should not be annulled for the sake of the laws, rather should the laws be broken for the sake of marriage.

That nonsense about conpaternities, conmaternities, confraternities, consororities, and confilieties must therefore be altogether abolished when a marriage has been contracted. What was it but the superstition of men that invented those spiritual relationships? If one may not marry the person one has baptized or stood sponsor for, what right has any Christian to marry any other Christian? Is the relationship that grows out of the external rite or the sign of the sacrament more intimate than that which grows out of the blessing of the sacrament itself? Is not a Christian man brother to a Christian woman, and is not she his sister? Is not a baptized man the spiritual brother of a baptized woman? How foolish we are! If a man instruct his wife in the Gospel and in faith in Christ and thus become truly her father in Christ, would it not be right for her to remain his wife? Would not Paul have had the right to marry a maiden out of the Corinthian congregation, of whom he boasts that he has begotten them all in Christ (1 Cor. 4:15)? Lo, thus has Christian liberty been suppressed through the blindness of human superstition.

There is even less in the legal relationship, and yet they have set it above the divine right of marriage. Nor would I recognize that hindrance which they term "disparity of religion," and which forbids one to marry any unbaptized person, even on condition that she become converted to the faith. Who made this prohibition? God or man? Who gave to men the power to prohibit such a marriage? The spirits, forsooth, that speak lies in hypocrisy, as Paul says (1 Tim 4:1). Of them it must be said, "The wicked have told me fables, but not as thy law" (Ps. 119:85). The heathen Patricius married the Christian Monica, the mother of St. Augustine. Why should not the same be permitted nowadays?

The same stupid, nay, wicked cruelty is seen in "the hindrance of crime," as when a man has married a woman with whom he had lived in adultery, or when he plotted to bring about the death of a woman's husband in order to be able to wed the widow. I pray you, whence comes this cruelty of man toward man, which even God never demanded? Do they pretend not to know that Bathsheba, the wife of Uriah, was wed by David, a most saintly man, after the double crime of adultery and murder? If the divine law did this, what do these despotic men to their fellow servants?

Another hindrance is that which they call "the hindrance of a tie," as when a man is bound by being betrothed to another woman. Here they decide that, if he has had carnal knowledge of the second, the betrothal with the first becomes null and void. This I do not understand at all. I hold that he who has betrothed himself to one woman belongs no longer to himself, and because of this act, by the prohibition of the divine law, he belongs to the first, though he has not known her, even if he has known the second. For it was not in his power to give the latter what was no longer his own; he deceived her and actually committed adultery. But they regard the matter differently because they pay more heed to the carnal union than to the divine command, according to which the man, having plighted his troth to the first, is bound to keep it forever. For whoever would give anything must give of that which is his own. And God forbids a man to overreach or circumvent his brother in any matter (1 Thes. 4:6). This prohibition must be kept, over and above all the traditions of all men. Therefore, the man in the above case cannot with a good conscience live in marriage with the second woman, and this hindrance should be completely overthrown. For if a monastic vow make a man to be no longer his own, why does not a promise of betrothal given and received do the same?—since this is one of the precepts and fruits of the Spirit (Gal. 5:22ff; Eph. 5:9), while a monastic vow is of human invention. And if a wife may claim her husband despite the act that he has taken a monastic vow, why may not a bride claim her betrothed, even though he has known another? But we said above that he who has plighted his troth to a maiden ought not to take a monastic vow, but is in duty bound to keep faith with her, which faith he cannot break for any tradition of men, because it is commanded by God. Much more should the man here keep faith with his first bride, since he could not plight his troth to a second save with a lying heart, and therefore did not really plight it, but deceived her, his neighbor, against God's command. Therefore, the "hindrance of error" enters in here, by which his marriage to the second woman is rendered null and void.

The "hindrance of ordination" also is a lying invention of men, especially since they prate that even a contracted marriage is annulled by it. Thus they constantly exalt their traditions above the commands of God. I do not indeed sit in judgment on the present state of the priestly order, but I observe that Paul charges a bishop to be the husband of one wife (1 Tim. 3:2); hence no marriage of deacon, priest, bishop, or any other order can be annulled—although it is true that Paul knew nothing of this species of priests, and of the orders that we have today. Perish those cursed human traditions which have crept into the Church only to multiply perils, sins, and evils! There exists, therefore, between a priest and his wife a true and indissoluble marriage, approved by the divine commandment. But what if wicked men in sheer despotism prohibit or annul it? So be it! Let it be wrong among men; it is nevertheless right before God, whose command must needs take precedence if it conflicts with the commands of men.

An equally lying invention is that "hindrance of public decency," by which contracted marriages are annulled. I am incensed at that barefaced wickedness which is so ready to put asunder what God hath joined together that one may well scent antichrist in it, for it opposes all that Christ has done and taught. What earthly reason is there for holding that no relative of a deceased husband, even to the fourth degree, may marry the latter's widow? That is not a judgment of public decency, but ignorance of public decency. Why was not this judgment of public decency found among the people of Israel, who were endowed with the best laws, the laws of God? On the contrary, the next of kin was even compelled by the law of God to marry the widow of his relative (Deut. 25:5). Must the people of Christian liberty be burdened with severer laws than the people of legal bondage? But, to make an end of these figments, rather than hindrances—thus far there seem to me to be no hindrances that may justly annul a contracted marriage save these: impotence of the husband, ignorance of a previously contracted marriage, and a vow of chastity. Still, concerning the last, I am to this day so far from certain that I do not know at what age such a vow is to be regarded as binding, as I also said above in discussing the sacrament of baptism. Thus you may learn, from this one question of marriage, how wretchedly and desperately all the activities of the Church have been confused, hindered, ensnared, and subjected to danger through the pestilent, ignorant, and wicked traditions of men, so that there is no hope of betterment unless we abolish at one stroke all the laws of all men, restore the Gospel of liberty, and by it judge and rule all things. Amen.

We have to speak, then, of sexual impotence, that we may the more readily advise the souls that are in peril. But first I wish to state that what I have said of hindrances is intended to apply after a marriage has been contracted; no marriage should be annulled by any such hindrance. But as to marriages which are to be contracted, I would briefly repeat what I said above. Under the stress of youthful passion or of any other necessity for which the pope grants dispensation, any brother may grant a dispensation to another or even to himself, and following that counsel snatch his wife out of the power of the tyrannical laws as best he can. For with what right am I deprived of my liberty by another's superstition and ignorance? If the pope grants a dispensation for money, why should not I, for my soul's salvation, grant a dispensation to myself or to my brother? Does the pope set up laws? Let him set them up or himself, and keep hands off my liberty, else I will take it by stealth! Now let us discuss the matter of impotence.

Take the following case. A woman, wed to an impotent man, is unable to prove her husband's impotence before court, or perhaps she is unwilling to do so with the Mass of evidence and all the notoriety which the law demands, yet she is desirous of having children or is unable to remain continent. Now suppose I had counseled her to demand a divorce from her husband in order to marry another, satisfied that her own and her husband's conscience and their experience were ample testimony of his impotence, but the husband refused his consent to this. Then suppose I should further counsel her, with the consent of the man (who is not really her husband, but merely a dweller under the same roof with her), to give herself to another, say her husband's brother, but to keep this marriage secret, and to ascribe the children to the so-called putative father. The question is: is such a woman in a saved state? I answer, certainly, because in this case the error and ignorance of the man's impotence are a hindrance to the marriage; the tyranny of the laws permits no divorce; the woman is free through the divine law, and cannot be compelled to remain continent. Therefore the man ought to yield her this right, and let another man have her as wife whom he has only in outward appearance.

Moreover, if the man will not give his consent, or agree to this division—rather than allow the woman to burn or to commit adultery, I should counsel her to contract a marriage with another and flee to distant parts unknown. What other counsel could be given to one constantly in danger from lust? Now I know that some are troubled by the act that then the children of this secret marriage are not the rightful heirs of their putative father. But if it was done with the consent of the husband, then the children will be the rightful heirs.

If, however, it was done without his knowledge or against his will, then let unbiased Christian reason, nay, let Christian charity decide which of the two has done the greater injury to the other. The wife alienates the inheritance, but the husband has deceived his wife and is completely defrauding her of her body and her life. Is not the sin of the man who wastes his wife's body and life a greater sin than that of the woman who merely alienates the temporal goods of her husband? Let him, therefore, agree to a divorce, or else be satisfied with strange heirs, for by his own fault he deceived the innocence of a maiden and defrauded her of the proper use of her body, besides giving her a well-nigh irresistible opportunity to commit adultery. Let both be weighed in the same scales. Certainly, by every right deceit should fall back on the deceiver, and whoever has done an injury must make it good. What is the difference between such a husband and the man who holds another's wife captive together with her husband? Is not such a tyrant compelled to support wife and children and husband, or else to set them free? Why should not the same hold here? Therefore I maintain that the man should be compelled either to submit to a divorce or to support the other man's child as his heir. Doubtless this would be the judgment of charity. In that case, the impotent man, who is not really the husband, should support the heirs of his wife in the same spirit in which he would at great cost wait on his wife if she fell sick or suffered some other ill, for it is by his fault and not by his wife's that she suffers this ill. This have I set forth to the best of my ability, for the strengthening of anxious consciences, being desirous to bring my afflicted brethren in this captivity what little comfort I can.

As to divorce, it is still a moot question whether it be allowable. For my part I so greatly detest divorce that I should prefer bigamy to it,[49]

---

49. Ironically, this is exactly what Luther did do in the case of Philip of Hesse, and it greatly soiled the reputation of the Protestants for a time, because it made them look like libertines.

but whether it be allowable, I do not venture to decide. Christ Himself, the Chief Pastor, says in Matthew 5, "Whosoever shall put away his wife, excepting for the cause of fornication, maketh her commit adultery; and he that shall marry her that is put away, committeth adultery" (v. 32). Christ, then, permits divorce, but for the cause of fornication only. The pope must, therefore, be in error whenever he grants a divorce for any other cause, and no one should feel safe who has obtained a dispensation by this temerity (not authority) of the pope. Yet it is a still greater wonder to me why they compel a man to remain unmarried after being separated from his wife, and why they will not permit him to remarry. For if Christ permits divorce for the cause of fornication and compels no one to remain unmarried, and if Paul would rather have one marry than burn (1 Cor. 7:9), then He certainly seems to permit a man to marry another woman in the stead of the one who has been put away. Would to God this matter were thoroughly threshed out and decided, so that counsel might be given in the infinite perils of those who, without any fault of their own, are nowadays compelled to remain unmarried, that is, of those whose wives or husbands have run away and deserted them, to come back perhaps after ten years, perhaps never. This matter troubles and distresses me; I meet cases of it every day, whether it happen by the special malice of Satan or because of our neglect of the Word of God.

I, indeed, who alone against all can decide nothing in this matter would yet greatly desire at least the passage in 1 Corinthians 7 to be applied here: "But if the unbeliever depart, let him depart. For a brother or sister is not under servitude in such cases" (v. 15). Here the apostle gives permission to put away the unbeliever who departs and to set the believing spouse free to marry again. Why should not the same hold true when a believer—that is, a believer in name, but in truth as much an unbeliever as the one Paul speaks of—deserts his wife, especially if he never intends to return? I certainly can see no difference between the two. But I believe that if in the apostle's day an unbelieving deserter had returned and had become a believer or had promised to live again with his believing wife, he would not have been taken back, but he too would have been given the right to marry again. Nevertheless, in these matters I decide nothing, as I have said, although there is nothing I would rather see decided, since nothing at present more grievously perplexes me and many more with me. I would have nothing decided here on the mere authority of the pope or the bishops, but if two learned and pious men agreed in the name of Christ and published their opinion in the spirit of Christ (Matt. 18:19ff), I should prefer their judgment even to such councils as are nowadays assembled, famous only for numbers and authority, not for scholarship and saintliness. Herewith I hang up my harp (Ps. 137:2), until another and a better man shall take up this matter with me.

# THE SACRAMENT OF ORDINATION

Of this sacrament the Church of Christ knows nothing: it is an invention of the church of the pope. Not only is there nowhere any promise of grace attached to it, but there is not the least mention of it in the whole New Testament. Now it is ridiculous to put forth as a sacrament of God that which cannot be proved to have been instituted by God. I do not hold that this rite, which has been observed for so many centuries, should be condemned, but in sacred things I am opposed to the invention of human fictions, nor is it right to give out as divinely instituted what was not divinely instituted, lest we become a laughing-stock to our opponents. We ought to see to it that every article of faith of which we boast be certain, pure, and based on clear passages of Scripture. But that we are utterly unable to do in the case of the sacrament under consideration.

The Church has no power to make new divine promises, as some prate, who hold that what is decreed by the Church is of no less authority than what is decreed by God, since the Church is under the guidance of the Holy Spirit. But the Church owes its life to the word of promise through faith, and is nourished and preserved by this same word. That is to say, the promises of God make the Church, not the Church the promise of God. For the Word of God is incomparably superior to the Church, and in this Word the Church, being a creature, has nothing to decree, ordain, or make, but only to be decreed, ordained, and made. For who begets his own parent? Who first brings forth his own maker? This one thing indeed the Church can do—it can distinguish the Word of God from the words of men, as Augustine confesses that he believed the Gospel, moved thereto by the authority of the Church, which proclaimed, this is the Gospel. Not that the Church is, therefore, above the Gospel; if that were true, she would also be above God, in whom we believe because she proclaims that He is God. But, as Augustine elsewhere says, the truth itself lays hold on the soul and thus renders it able to judge most certainly of all things, but the truth it cannot judge, but is forced to say with unerring certainty that it is the truth. For example, our reason declares with unerring certainty that three and seven are ten, and yet it cannot give a reason why this is true, although it cannot deny that it is true; it is taken captive by the truth and does not so much judge the truth as it is judged by the truth. Thus it is also with the mind of the Church (1 Cor. 2:16), when under the enlightenment of the Spirit she judges and approves doctrines; she is unable to prove it, and yet is most certain of having it. For as in philosophy no one judges general conceptions, but all are judged by them, so it is in the Church with the mind of the Spirit, that judgeth all things and is judged by none, as the apostle says (1 Cor. 2:15). But of this another time.

Let this then stand fast: the Church can give no promises of grace; that is the work of God alone. Therefore she cannot institute a sacrament. But even if she could, it yet would not follow that ordination is a sacrament. For who knows which is the Church that has the Spirit? Since when such decisions are made there are usually only a few bishops or scholars present; it is possible that these may not be really of the Church, and that all may err, as councils have repeatedly erred, particularly the Council of Constance, which fell into the most wicked error of all. Only that which has the approval of the Church universal, and not of the Roman church alone, rests on a trustworthy foundation. I therefore admit that ordination is a certain churchly rite, on a par with many others introduced by the Church Fathers, such as the blessing of vases, houses, vestments, water, salt, candles, herbs, wine, and the like. No one calls any of these a sacrament, nor is there in them any promise. In the same manner, to anoint a man's hands with oil or to shave his head and the like is not to administer a sacrament, since there is no promise given to those things; he is simply prepared, like a vessel or an instrument, for a certain work.

But you will reply: 'What do you say to Dionysius, who in his *Ecclesiastical Hierarchy* enumerates six sacraments, among which he also includes orders?' I answer that I am well aware that this is the one writer of antiquity who is cited in support of the seven sacraments, although he omits marriage and thus has only six. We read simply nothing about these "sacraments" in the other Fathers, nor do they ever refer to them as sacraments, for the invention of sacraments is of recent date. Indeed, to speak more boldly, the setting so great store by this Dionysius, whoever he may have been, greatly displeases me, for there is scarce a line of sound scholarship in him. Prithee, by what authority and with what reasons does he establish his hotchpotch about the angels in his *Celestial Hierarchy*?—a book over which many curious and superstitious spirits have cudgeled their brains. If one were to read and judge fairly, is not all shaken out of his sleeve and very like a dream? But in his *Mystic Theology*, which certain most ignorant theologians greatly puff, he is downright dangerous, being more of a Platonist than a Christian, so that, if I had my way, no believing mind would give the least attention to these books. So far from learning Christ in them you will lose even what you know of Him. I know whereof I speak. Let us rather hear Paul, that we may learn Jesus Christ and Him crucified (1 Cor. 2:2). He is the way, the life, and the truth; He is the ladder by which we come unto the Father, as He saith: "No man cometh unto the Father but by me" (John 14:6).

And in the *Ecclesiastical Hierarchy*, what does this Dionysius do but describe certain churchly rites and play round them with his allegories without proving them? Just as among us the author of the book entitled *Rationale divinorum*. Such allegorical studies are the work of idle men. Think you I should find it difficult to play with allegories round anything in creation? Did not Bonaventure by allegory draw the liberal arts into theology? And Gerson even converted the smaller Donatus into a mystic theologian. It would not be a difficult task for me to compose a better hierarchy than that of Dionysius, for he knew nothing of pope, cardinals, and archbishops, and put the bishop at the top. Nay, who has so weak a mind as not to be able to launch into allegories? I would not have a theologian give himself to allegorizing until he has perfected himself in the grammatical and literal interpretation of the Scriptures, otherwise his theology will bring him into danger, as Origen discovered.

Therefore a thing does not need to be a sacrament simply because Dionysius describes it. Otherwise, why not also make a sacrament of the processions, which he describes in his book, and which continue to this day? There will then be as many sacraments as there have been rites and ceremonies multiplied in the Church. Standing on so unsteady a foundation, they have nevertheless invented "characters," which they attribute to this sacrament of theirs and which are indelibly impressed on those who are ordained. Whence do such ideas come? By what authority, with what reasons, are they established? We do not object to their being free to invent, say, and give out whatever they please, but we also insist on our liberty and demand that they shall not arrogate to themselves the right to turn their ideas into articles of faith, as they have hitherto presumed to do. It is enough that we accommodate ourselves to their rites and ceremonies for the sake of peace, but we refuse to be bound by such things as though they were necessary to salvation, when they are not. Let them put by their despotic demands, and we shall yield free obedience to their opinions, and thus live at peace with them. It is a shameful and wicked slavery for a Christian man, who is free, to be subject to any but Heavenly and divine traditions.

We come now to their strongest argument. It is this: Christ said at the Last Supper: "Do this in remembrance of me" (1 Cor. 11:24). Here, they say Christ ordained the apostles to the priesthood. From this passage they also concluded, among other things, that both kinds are to be administered to the priests alone. In fine, they have drawn out of this passage whatever they pleased, as men who might arrogate to themselves the free will to prove anything whatever from any words of Christ, no matter where found. But is that interpreting the words of God? Pray, answer me! Christ gives us no promise here, but only commands that this be done in remembrance of Him. Why do they not conclude that He also ordained priests when He laid upon them the office of the Word and of baptism, saying, "Go ye into all the world, and preach the Gospel to every creature, baptizing them in the name" (Mark 16:15; Matt. 28:19) etc.? For it is the proper duty of priests to preach and to baptize. Or, since it is nowadays the chief and, as they say, indispensable duty of priests to read the canonical hours,[50] why have they not discovered the sacrament of ordination in those passages in which Christ, in many places and particularly in the garden, commanded them to pray that they might not enter into temptation (Matt. 26:41)? But perhaps they will evade this argument by saying that it is not commanded to pray; it is enough to read the canonical hours. Then it follows that this priestly work can be proved nowhere in the Scriptures, and thus their praying priesthood is not of God, as indeed it is not.

But which of the ancient Fathers claimed that in this passage priests were ordained? Whence comes this novel interpretation? I will tell you. They have sought by this device to set up a nursery of

---

50. The stated daily prayers, fixed by canon, of the clergy.

implacable discord, whereby clerics and laymen should be separated from each other farther than Heaven from earth, to the incredible injury of the grace of baptism and the confusion of our fellowship in the Gospel. Here, indeed, are the roots of that detestable tyranny of the clergy over the laity; trusting in the external anointing by which their hands are consecrated, in the tonsure and in vestments, they not only exalt themselves above lay Christians, who are only anointed with the Holy Spirit, but regard them almost as dogs and unworthy to be included with them in the Church. Hence they are bold to demand, to exact, to threaten, to urge, to oppress, as much as they please. In short, the sacrament of ordination has been and is a most approved device for the establishing of all the horrible things that have been wrought hitherto and will yet be wrought in the Church. Here Christian brotherhood has perished, here shepherds have been turned into wolves, servants into tyrants, churchmen into worse than worldlings.

If they were forced to grant that as many of us as have been baptized are all priests without distinction, as indeed we are, and that to them was committed the ministry only, yet with our consent, they would presently learn that they have no right to rule over us except in so far as we freely concede it. For thus it is written in 1 Peter 2, "Ye are a chosen generation, a royal priesthood, and a priestly kingdom" (v. 9). Therefore we are all priests, as many of us as are Christians. But the priests, as we call them, are ministers chosen from among us, who do all that they do in our name. And the priesthood is nothing but a ministry, as we learn from 1 Corinthians 4, "Let a man so account of us as of the ministers of Christ, and the dispensers of the mysteries of God" (v. 1).

It follows herefrom that whoever does not preach the Word, called by the Church to this very thing, is no priest at all. And further, that the sacrament of ordination can be nothing else than a certain rite of choosing preachers in the Church. For thus is a priest defined in Malachi 2, "The lips of the priest shall keep knowledge, and they shall seek the law at his mouth, because he is the angel of the Lord of hosts" (v. 7). You may be certain, then, that whoever is not an angel of the Lord of hosts, or whoever is called to anything else than such angelic service—if I may so term it—is never a priest; as Hosea says, "Because thou hast rejected knowledge, I will reject thee, that thou shalt not do the office of priesthood to me" (Hos. 4:6). They are also called pastors because they are to pasture, that is, to teach. Therefore, they who are ordained only to read the canonical hours and to offer Masses are indeed papist, but not Christian priests, because they not only do not preach, but are not called to preach; nay, it comes to this: that such a priesthood is a different estate altogether from the office of preaching. Thus they are hour-priests and Mass-priests, that is, a sort of living idol, having the name of priest, while they are in reality such priests as Jeroboam ordained in Bethaven of the off-scouring of the people, and not of the tribe of Levi (1 Kings 12:31).

Lo, whither hath the glory of the Church departed! The whole earth is filled with priests, bishops, cardinals, and clerics, and yet not one of them preaches by virtue of his office, unless he be called to do so by another and a different call besides his sacramental ordination. Everyone thinks he is doing full justice to his sacrament by mumbling the vain repetitions of his prescribed prayers and by celebrating Masses; moreover, by never really praying those hours, or if he does pray them, by praying them for himself, and by offering his Masses as a sacrifice—which is the height of perversity!—whereas the Mass consists in the use of the sacrament. It is clear, therefore, that the ordination which as a sacrament makes clerics of this sort of men is in truth nothing but a mere fiction, devised by men who understand nothing about the Church, the priesthood, the ministry of the Word, or the sacraments. And as is the sacrament, so are the priests it makes. To such errors and such blindness has come a still worse captivity: in order to separate themselves still farther from other Christians, whom they deem profane, they have unmanned themselves, like the priests of Cybele, and taken upon them the burden of a pretended celibacy.

It was not enough for this hypocrisy and error to forbid bigamy, namely, the having of two wives at the same time, as it was forbidden in the law, and as is the accepted meaning of the term, but they have called it bigamy if a man married two virgins, one after the other, or if he married a widow. Nay, so holy is the holiness of this most holy sacrament that no married man can become a priest as long as his wife lives. And—here we reach the very summit of holiness—even he is prevented from entering the priesthood, who without his knowledge or by an unfortunate chance married a fallen woman. But if one have defiled a thousand harlots or ravished countless matrons and virgins or even kept numerous Ganymedes,[51] that would be no hindrance to his becoming bishop or cardinal or pope. Moreover, the apostle's word, "the husband of one wife" (1 Tim. 3:2) must be interpreted to mean, "the prelate of one church," and this has given rise to the "incompatible benefices." At the same time the pope, that munificent dispenser, may join to one man three, twenty, one hundred wives—I should say churches—if he be bribed with money or power—I should say, moved by godly charity and constrained by the care of the churches!

O pontiffs worthy of this holy sacrament of ordination! O princes, not of the catholic churches, but of the synagogues, nay, the black dens, of Satan (Rev. 2:9)! I would cry out with Isaiah: "Ye scornful men, who rule over my people that is in Jerusalem" (28:14), and with Amos: "Woe to you that are wealthy in Zion, and to you that have confidence in the mountain of Samaria: ye great men, heads of the people, that go in with state into the house of Israel" (6:1). O the reproach that such monstrous priests bring upon the Church of God! Where are there any bishops or priests who know the Gospel, not

---

51. Ganymede was a boy raped by Zeus, and Luther is referring to pederasty here.

to speak of preaching it? Why then do they boast of being priests? Why do they desire to be regarded as holier and better and mightier than other Christians, who are merely laymen? To read the hours, what unlearned men, or, as the apostle says, what men speaking with tongues, cannot do that (1 Cor. 14:23)? But to pray the hours—that belongs to monks, hermits, and men in private life, all of them laymen. The duty of the priest is to preach, and if he does not preach he is as much a priest as a painted man is a man. Does ordaining such babbling priests make one a bishop? Or blessing churches and bells? Or confirming boys? Certainly not. Any deacon or layman could do as much. The ministry of the Word makes the priest and the bishop.

Therefore my advice is: flee, all ye that would live in safety; begone, young men, and do not enter upon this holy estate, unless you are determined to preach the Gospel and are able to believe that you are not made one whit better than the laity through this sacrament of ordination! For to read the hours is nothing, and to offer Mass is to receive the sacrament. What then is there left to you that every layman does not have? Tonsure and vestments? A sorry priest, forsooth, who consists of tonsure and vestment! Or the oil poured on your fingers? But every Christian is anointed and sanctified with the oil of the Holy Spirit, both in body and soul, and in ancient times touched the sacrament with his hands no less than the priests do now. But today our superstition counts it a great crime if the laity touch either the bare chalice or the *corporale*; not even a nun who is a pure virgin would be permitted to wash the palls[52] and sacred linens of the altar. O God! how the sacrosanct sanctity of this sacrament of ordination has grown and grown. I anticipate that ere long the laity will not be permitted to touch the altar except when they offer their money. I can scarce contain myself when I contemplate the wicked tyrannies of these desperate men, who with their farcical

---

52. Covers for the chalice.

and childish fancies mock and overthrow the liberty and the glory of the Christian religion.

Let everyone, therefore, who knows himself to be a Christian be assured of this, and apply it to himself: that we are all priests, and there is no difference between us, that is to say, we have the same power in respect to the Word and all the sacraments. However, no one may make use of this power except by the consent of the community or by the call of a superior. For what is the common property of all, no individual may arrogate to himself, unless he be called. And therefore this sacrament of ordination, if it have any meaning at all, is nothing else than a certain rite whereby one is called to the ministry of the Church. Furthermore, the priesthood is properly nothing but the ministry of the Word, mark you, of the Word—not of the law, but of the Gospel. And the diaconate is not the ministry of reading the gospel or the epistle, as is the present practice, but the ministry of distributing the Church's alms to the poor, so that the priests may be relieved of the burden of temporal matters and may give themselves more freely to prayer and the Word. For this was the purpose of the institution of the diaconate, as we read in Acts 6:4. Whoever, therefore, does not know or preach the Gospel, is not only not a priest or bishop, but he is a plague of the Church, who under the false title of priest or bishop—in sheep's clothing, forsooth—oppresses the Gospel and plays the wolf in the Church. Therefore, unless those priests and bishops with whom the Church is now filled work out their salvation in some other way, that is, realize that they are not priests or bishops and bemoan the fact that they bear the name of an office whose duties they either do not know or cannot fulfill, and thus with prayers and tears lament their wretched hypocritical life—unless they do this, they are truly the people of eternal perdition, and the words of Isaiah are fulfilled in them: "Therefore is my people led away captive, because they had not knowledge, and their nobles have perished with famine, and their multitude were dried up with thirst. Therefore hath

Hell enlarged her soul and opened her mouth without any bounds, and their strong ones, and their people, and their high and generous ones shall go down into it" (Is. 5:13ff). What a dreadful word for our age, in which Christians are sucked down into so deep an abyss!

Since, therefore, what we call the priesthood is a ministry, so far as we can learn from the Scriptures, I cannot understand why one who has been made a priest cannot again become a layman, for the sole difference between him and a layman is his ministry. But to depose a man from the ministry is so far from impossible that it is even now the usual penalty imposed upon guilty priests: they are either suspended for a season or permanently deprived of their office. For that lying "indelible character" has long since become a laughing-stock. I admit that the pope imparts this character, but Christ knows nothing of it, and a priest who is consecrated with it becomes thereby the life-long servant and captive, not of Christ, but of the pope, as it is in our day. Moreover, unless I am greatly mistaken, if this sacrament and this life fall, the papacy itself with its characters will scarcely survive; our joyous liberty will be restored to us; we shall realize that we are all equal by every right, and having cast of the yoke of tyranny shall know that he who is a Christian has Christ, and that he who has Christ has all things that are Christ's and is able to do all things (Phil. 4:13). Of this I will write more, and more tellingly, as soon as I perceive that the above has displeased my friends the papists.

# THE SACRAMENT OF EXTREME UNCTION

To the rite of anointing the sick our theologians have made two additions which are worthy of them; first, they call it a sacrament, and secondly, they make it the last sacrament. So that it is now the sacrament of extreme unction, which may be administered only to such as are at the point of death. Being such subtle dialecticians, perchance they have done this in order to relate it to the first unction of baptism and the two succeeding unctions of confirmation and ordination. But here they are able to cast in my teeth that in the case of this sacrament there are, on the authority of James the Apostle, both promise and sign, which, as I have all along maintained, constitute a sacrament. For does not James say: "Is any man sick among you? Let him bring in the priests of the church, and let them pray over him, anointing him with oil in the name of the Lord. And the prayer of faith shall raise him up, and if he be in sins, they shall be forgiven him" (Jas. 5:14ff). There, say they, you have the promise of the forgiveness of sins, and the sign of the oil.

But I reply: if ever there was a mad conceit, here is one indeed. I will say nothing of the fact that many assert with much probability that this epistle is not by James the apostle, nor worthy of an apostolic spirit, although, whoever be its author, it has come to be esteemed as authoritative. But even if the apostle James did write it, I yet should say, no apostle has the right on his own authority to institute a sacrament, that is, to give a divine promise with a sign attached, for this belongs to Christ alone. Thus Paul says that he received from the Lord the sacrament of the Eucharist, and that he was not sent to baptize but to preach the Gospel (1 Cor. 11:23; 1 Cor. 1:17). And we read nowhere in the Gospel of this sacrament of extreme unction. But let us also waive that point. Let us examine the words of the apostle, or whoever was the author of the epistle, and we shall at once see how little heed these multipliers of sacraments have given to them.

In the first place, then, if they believe the apostle's words to be true and binding, by what right do they change and contradict them? Why do they make an extreme and a particular kind of unction of that which the apostle wished to be general? For he did not desire it to be an extreme unction or administered only to the dying, but he says quite generally: "If any man be sick"—not, "If any man be dying." I care not what learned discussions Dionysius has on this point in his *Ecclesiastical Hierarchy*; the apostle's words are clear enough, on which words he as well as they rely without, however, following them. It is evident, therefore, that they have arbitrarily and without any authority made a sacrament and an extreme unction out of the misunderstood words of the apostle, to the detriment of all other sick persons, whom they have deprived of the benefit of the unction which the apostle enjoined.

But what follows is still better. The apostle's promise expressly declares that the prayer of faith shall save the sick man, and the Lord shall raise him up. The apostle commands us to anoint the sick man and to pray, in order that he may be healed and raised up, that is, that he may not die, and that it may not be an extreme unction. This is proved also by the prayers which are said during the anointing for the recovery of the one who is sick. But they say, on the contrary, that the unction must be administered to none but the dying, that is, that they may not be healed and raised up. If it were not so serious a matter, who could help laughing at this beautiful, apt, and sound exposition of the apostle's words? Is not the folly of the sophists here shown in its true colors? As here, so in many other places, they affirm what the Scriptures deny, and deny what they affirm. Why should we not give thanks to these excellent magisters of ours? I therefore spoke truth when I said they never conceived a crazier notion than this.

Furthermore, if this unction is a sacrament it must necessarily be, as they say, an effective sign of that which it signifies and promises. Now it promises health and recovery to the sick, as the words plainly say: "The prayer of faith shall save the sick man, and the Lord shall raise him up." But who does not see that this promise is seldom if ever fulfilled? Scarce one in a thousand is restored to health, and when one is restored nobody believes that it came about through the sacrament, but through the working of nature or the medicine, or to the sacrament they ascribe the opposite power. What shall we say then? Either the apostle lies in making this promise or else this unction is no sacrament. For the sacramental promise is certain, but this promise deceives in the majority of cases. Indeed—and here again we recognize the shrewdness and foresight of these theologians—for this very reason they would have it to be extreme unction, that the promise should not stand, in other words, that the sacrament should be no sacrament. For if it is extreme unction, it does not heal, but gives way to the disease, but if it heals, it cannot be extreme unction. Thus, by the interpretation of these magisters, James is shown to have contradicted himself, and to have instituted a sacrament in order not to institute one, for they must have an extreme unction just to make untrue what the apostle intends, namely, the healing of the sick. If that is not madness, pray what is?

These people exemplify the word of the apostle in 1 Timothy 1, "Desiring to be teachers of the law, understanding neither the things they say, nor whereof they affirm" (v. 7). Thus they read and follow all things without judgment. With the same thoughtlessness they have also found auricular confession in our apostle's words "Confess your sins one to another" (Jas. 5:16). But they do not observe the command of the apostle, that the priests of the Church be called, and prayer be made for the sick. Scarce a single priestling is sent nowadays, although the apostle would have many present, not because of the unction but of the prayer. Wherefore he says: "The prayer of faith shall save the sick man," etc. I have my doubts, however, whether he would have us understand priests when he says presbyters, that is, elders. For one who is an elder is not therefore a priest or minister, so that the suspicion is justified that the apostle desired the older and graver men in the Church to visit the sick; these should perform a work of mercy and pray in faith and thus heal him. Still it cannot be denied that the ancient churches were ruled by elders, chosen for this purpose, without these ordinations and consecrations, solely on account of their age and their long experience.

Therefore, I take it, this unction is the same as that which the apostles practiced in Mark 6, "They anointed with oil many that were sick, and healed them" (v. 13). It was a ceremony of the early Church, by which they wrought miracles on the sick, and which has long since ceased, even as Christ, in the last chapter of Mark, gave them that believe the power to take up serpents, to lay hands on the sick, etc. (Mark 16:17). It is a wonder that they have not made sacraments also of these things, for they have the same power and promise as the words of James. Therefore, this extreme—that is, this fictitious—unction is not a sacrament, but a counsel of James, which whoever will may use and it is derived from Mark 6, as I have shown. I do not believe it was a counsel given to all sick persons, for the Church's infirmity is her glory and death is gain (Rom. 5:3; Phil. 1:21), but it was given only to such as might bear their sickness impatiently and with little faith. These the Lord allowed to remain in the Church, in order that miracles and the power of faith might be manifest in them.

For this very contingency James provided with care and foresight by attaching the promise of healing and the forgiveness of sins not to the unction, but to the prayer of faith. For he says: "And the prayer of faith shall save the sick man, and the Lord shall raise him up, and if he be in sins, they shall be forgiven him." A sacrament does not demand prayer or faith on the part of the minister, since even a wicked person may baptize and consecrate without prayer; a sacrament depends solely on the promise and institution of God, and requires faith on the part of him who receives it. But where is the prayer of faith in our present use of extreme unction? Who prays over the sick one in such faith as not to doubt that he will recover? Such a prayer of faith James here describes, of which he said in the beginning of his epistle: "But let him ask in faith, nothing wavering" (Jas. 1:6). And Christ says of it: "Whatsoever you ask, believe that you shall receive, and it shall be done unto you" (Mark 11:24).

If such prayer were made, even today, over a sick man—that is, prayer made in full faith by older, grave, and saintly men—it is beyond all doubt that we could heal as many sick as we would. For what could not faith do? But we neglect this faith, which the authority of the apostle demands above all else. By presbyters—that is, men preeminent by reason of their age and their faith—we understand the common herd of priests. Moreover, we turn the daily or voluntary unction into an extreme unction, and finally, we not only do not effect the result promised by the apostle, namely, the healing of the sick, but we make it of none effect by striving after the very opposite. And yet we boast that our sacrament, nay, our figment is established and proved by this saying of the apostle, which is diametrically opposed to it. What theologians we are! Now I do not condemn this our sacrament of extreme unction, but I firmly deny that it is what the apostle James prescribes, for his unction agrees with ours neither in form, use, power, nor purpose. Nevertheless we shall number it among those sacraments which we have instituted, such as the blessing and sprinkling of salt and holy water. For we cannot deny that every creature is sanctified by the word and by prayer, as the apostle Paul teaches us (1 Tim. 4:4ff). We do not deny, therefore, that forgiveness of sins and peace are granted through extreme unction, not because it is a sacrament divinely instituted, but because he who receives it believes that these blessings are granted to him. For the faith of the recipient does not err, however much the minister may err. For one who baptizes or absolves in jest, that is, does not absolve so far as the minister is concerned, does yet truly absolve and baptize if the person he baptizes or absolves believe. How much more will one who administers extreme unction confer peace, even though he does not really confer peace, so far as his ministry is concerned, since there is no sacrament there. The faith of the one anointed receives even that which the minister either could not or did not intend to give; it is sufficient for him to hear and believe the Word. For whatever we believe we shall receive that we do really receive; it matters not what the minister may do or not do, or whether he dissemble or jest. The saying of Christ stands fast: "All things are possible to him that believeth" (Mark 9:23), and, "Be it unto thee even as thou hast believed" (Matt. 8:13). But in treating the sacraments our sophists say nothing at all of this faith, but only babble with all their might of the virtues of the sacraments themselves: "ever learning, and never attaining to the knowledge of the truth" (2 Tim. 3:7).

Still it was a good thing that this unction was made extreme unction, for, thanks to that, it has been disturbed and subjected least of all the sacraments by tyranny and greed. This one last mercy, forsooth, has been left to the dying: they may freely be anointed, even without confession and communion. If it had remained a practice of daily occurrence, especially if it had conferred health on the sick, even without taking away sins, how many worlds would not the pontiffs have under their control today? For through the one sacrament of penance and through the power of the keys, as well as through the sacrament of ordination, they have become such mighty emperors and princes. But now it is a fortunate thing that they despise the prayer of faith, and therefore do not heal any sick, and that they have made for themselves out of an ancient ceremony a brand-new sacrament.

Let this suffice now for these four sacraments. I know how it will displease those who believe that the number and use of the sacraments are to be learned not from the sacred Scriptures, but from the Roman See. As though the Roman See had given those sacraments and had not rather got them from the lecture halls of the universities, to which it is unquestionably indebted for whatever it has. The papal despotism would not have attained its present position had it not taken over so many things from the universities. For there was scarce another of the celebrated bishoprics that had so few learned pontiffs; only in violence, intrigue, and superstition has it hitherto surpassed the rest. For the men who occupied the Roman See a thousand years ago differ so vastly from those who have since come into power that one is compelled to refuse the name of Roman pontiff either to the former or to the latter.

There are yet a few other things it might seem possible to regard as sacraments, namely, all those to which a divine promise has been given, such as prayer, the Word, and the cross. Christ promised, in many places, that those who pray should be heard; especially in Luke 11, where He invites us in many parables to pray (v. 5ff). Of the Word He says: "Blessed are they that hear the word of God, and keep it" (v. 28). And who will tell how often He promises aid and glory to such as are afflicted, suffer, and are cast down? Nay, who will recount all the promises of God? The whole Scripture is concerned with provoking us to faith, now driving us with precepts and threats, now drawing us with promises and consolations. Indeed, whatever things are written are either precepts or promises: the precepts humble the proud with their demands, the promises exalt the humble with their forgiveness.

Nevertheless, it has seemed best to restrict the name of sacrament to such promises as have signs attached to them. The remainder, not being bound to signs, are bare promises. Hence there are, strictly speaking, but two sacraments in the Church of God: baptism and bread, for only in these two do we find both the divinely instituted sign and the promise of forgiveness of sins. The sacrament of penance, which I added to these two lacks the divinely instituted visible sign, and is, as I have said, nothing but a return to baptism. Nor can the scholastics say that their definition fits penance, for they too ascribe to the sacrament a visible sign, which is to impress upon the senses the form of that which it effects invisibly. But penance or absolution has no such sign; wherefore they are constrained by their own definition either to admit that penance is not a sacrament, and thus to reduce the number of sacraments, or else to bring forward another definition.

Baptism, however, which we have applied to the whole of life, will truly be a sufficient substitute for all the sacraments we might need as long as we live. And the bread is truly the sacrament of the dying, for in it we commemorate the passing of Christ out of this world, that we may imitate Him. Thus we may apportion these two sacraments as follows: baptism belongs to the beginning and the entire course of life, the bread belongs to the end and to death. And the Christian should use them both as long as he is in this poor body, until, fully baptized and strengthened, he passes out of this world and is born unto the new life of eternity, to eat with Christ in the Kingdom of His Father, as He promised at the Last Supper: "Amen I say to you, I will not drink from henceforth of this fruit of the vine, until it is fulfilled in the kingdom of God" (Matt. 26:29). Thus He seems clearly to have instituted the sacrament of the bread with a view to our entrance into the life to come. Then, when the meaning of both sacraments is fulfilled, baptism and bread will cease.

Herewith I conclude this prelude, and freely and gladly offer it to all pious souls who desire to know the genuine sense of the Scriptures and the proper use of the sacraments. For it is a gift of no mean importance to know the things that are given us, as it is said in 1 Corinthians 2:12, and what use we ought to make of them. Endowed with this spiritual judgment, we shall not mistakenly rely on that which does not belong here. These two things our theologians never taught us, nay, methinks they took particular pains to conceal them from us. If I have not taught them, I certainly did not conceal them, and have given occasion to others to think out something better. It has at least been my endeavor to set forth these two things. Nevertheless, not all can do all things. To the godless, on the other hand, and those who in obstinate tyranny force on us their own teachings instead of God's, I confidently and freely oppose these pages, utterly indifferent to their senseless fury. Yet I wish even them a sound mind, and do not despise their efforts, but only distinguish them from such as are sound and truly Christian.

I hear a rumor of new bulls and papal maledictions sent out against me, in which I am urged to recant or be declared a heretic. If that is true, I desire this book to be a portion of the recantation I shall make, so that these tyrants may not complain of having had their pains for nothing. The remainder I will publish ere long, and it will, please Christ, be such as the Roman See has hitherto neither seen nor heard. I shall give ample proof of my obedience. In the name of our Lord Jesus Christ. Amen.

> Why doth that impious Herod fear
> When told that Christ the King is near?
> He takes not earthly realms away,
> Who gives the realms that ne'er decay.[53]

---

53. The eighth stanza of Coehus Sedulius' Hymnus acrostichis totam vitam Christi continens (beginning, A solis ortus cardine), of the fifth century.

# ON THE FREEDOM
# OF THE CHRISTIAN

*Translated by W.A. Lambert*

# LETTER TO POPE LEO X

To Leo the Tenth, Pope at Rome: Martin Luther wishes thee salvation in Christ Jesus our Lord. Amen.

In the midst of the monsters of this age with whom I am now for the third year waging war, I am compelled at times to look up also to thee, Leo, most blessed Father, and to think of thee, nay, since thou art now and again regarded as the sole cause of my warfare, I cannot but think of thee always. And although the causeless raging of thy godless flatterers against me has compelled me to appeal from thy See to a future council, despite those most empty decrees of thy predecessors Pius and Julius, who with a foolish tyranny forbade such an appeal, yet I have never so estranged my mind from thy Blessedness as not with all my heart to wish thee and thy See every blessing, for which I have, as much as lay in me, besought God with earnest prayers. It is true, I have made bold almost to despise and to triumph over those who have tried to righten me with the majesty of thy name and authority. But there is one thing which I cannot despise, and that is my excuse for writing once more to thy Blessedness. I understand that I am accused of great rashness, and that this rashness is said to be my great fault, in which, they say, I have not spared even thy person.

For my part, I will openly confess that I know I have only spoken good and honorable things of thee whenever I have made mention of thy name. And if I had done otherwise, I myself could by no means approve of it, but would entirely approve the judgment others have formed of me, and do nothing more gladly than recant such rashness and impiety on my part. I have called thee a Daniel in Babylon, and everyone who reads knows with what zeal I defended thy notable innocence against thy dreamer, Sylvester Prierias. Indeed, thy reputation and the fame of thy blameless life, sung as they are throughout the world by the writings of so many great men, are too well known and too high to be assailed in any way by any one man, however great he may be. I am not so foolish as to attack him whom every one praises: it has rather been, and always will be, my endeavor not to attack even those whom public report decries, for I take no pleasure in the crimes of any man, since I am conscious enough of the great beam in my own eye (Matt. 7:3), nor could I be he that should cast the first stone at the adulteress (John 8:7).

I have indeed sharply inveighed against ungodly teachings in general, and I have not been slow to bite my adversaries, not because of their immorality, but because of their ungodliness. And of this I repent so little that I have determined to persevere in that fervent zeal, and to despise the judgment of men, following the example of Christ, who in His zeal called His adversaries a generation of vipers, blind, hypocrites, children of the devil (Matt. 23:13, 17, 33). And Paul arraigned the sorcerer as a child of the devil full of all subtilty and mischief (Acts 13:10), and brands others as dogs, deceivers, and adulterers (Phil. 3:2; 2 Cor. 11:13; 2 Cor. 2:17). If you will allow those delicate ears to judge, nothing would be more biting and more unrestrained than Paul. Who is more biting than the prophets? Nowadays, it is true, our ears are made so delicate by the mad crowds of flatterers that as soon as we meet with a disapproving voice we cry out that we are bitten, and when we cannot ward off the truth with any other pretext we put it to light by ascribing it to a fierce temper, impatience, and shamelessness. What is the good of salt if it does not bite? Or of the edge of the sword if it does not kill? Cursed be he that doeth the work of the Lord deceitfully (Jer. 48:10).

Wherefore, most excellent Leo, I pray thee, after I have by this letter vindicated myself, give me a hearing, and believe that I have never thought evil of thy person, but that I am a man who would wish thee all good things eternally, and that I have no quarrel with any man concerning his morality, but only concerning the Word of truth. In all things else I will yield to any man whatsoever: to give up or to deny the Word I have neither the power nor the will. If any man thinks otherwise of me, or has understood my words differently, he does not think aright, nor has he understood what I have really said.

But thy See, which is called the Roman Curia, and of which neither thou nor any man can deny that it is more corrupt than any Babylon or Sodom ever was, and which is as far as I can see characterized by a totally depraved, hopeless, and notorious wickedness—that See I have truly despised, and I have been incensed to think that in thy name and under the guise of the Roman Church the people of Christ are mocked. And so I have resisted and will resist that See, as long as the spirit of faith shall live in me. Not that I shall strive after the impossible or hope that by my lone efforts anything will be accomplished in that most disordered Babylon, where the rage of so many sycophants is turned against me, but I acknowledge myself a debtor to my brethren, whom it is my duty to warn, that fewer of them may be destroyed by the plagues of Rome, or at least that their destruction may be less cruel.

For as thou well knowest, these many years there has flowed forth from Rome, like a flood covering the world, nothing but a laying waste of men's bodies and souls and possessions, and the worst possible examples of the worst possible things. For all this is clearer than the day to all men, and the Roman Church, once the most holy of all, has become the most licentious den of thieves (Matt. 21:13), the most shameless of all brothels, the kingdom of sin, death, and Hell, so that even antichrist himself, should he come, could think of nothing to add to its wickedness.

Meanwhile thou, Leo, sittest as a lamb in the midst of wolves (Matt. 10:16), like Daniel in the midst of the lions (Dan. 6:16), and, with Ezekiel, thou dwellest among scorpions (Ezek. 2:6). What canst thou do single-handed against these monsters? Join to thyself three or four thoroughly learned and thoroughly good cardinals: what are even these among so many (John 6:9)? You would all be poisoned before you could undertake to make a single decree to help matters. There is no hope for the Roman Curia: the wrath of God is come upon it to the end (1 Thes. 2:16); it hates councils, it fears a reformation, it cannot reduce the raging of its wickedness, and is meriting the praise bestowed upon its mother, of whom it is written, "We have cured Babylon, but she is not healed: let us forsake her" (Jer. 51:9). It was thy duty, indeed, and that of thy cardinals, to remedy these evils, but that gout of theirs mocks the healing hand, and neither chariot nor horse heeds the guiding rein. Moved by such sympathy for thee, I have always grieved, most excellent Leo, that thou hast been made pope in these times, for thou wert worthy of better days. The Roman Curia has not deserved to have thee or men like thee, but rather Satan himself, and in truth it is he more than thou who rules in that Babylon.

O would that thou mightest lay aside what thy most mischievous enemies boast of as thy glory, and wert living on some small priestly income of thine own, or on thy family inheritance! To glory in that glory none are worthy save the Iscariots, the sons of perdition (John 17:12). For what dost thou accomplish in the Curia, my dear Leo? Only this: the more criminal and abominable a man is, the more successfully will he use thy name and authority to destroy the wealth and the souls of men, to increase crime, to suppress faith and truth and the whole Church of God. O truly, most unhappy Leo, thou sittest on a most dangerous throne: for I tell thee the truth, because I wish thee well. If Bernard pitied his Pope Eugene at a time when the Roman See, although even then most corrupt, yet ruled with better prospects, why should not we lament who have for three hundred years had so great an increase of corruption and worthlessness? Is it not true that under yon vast expanse of Heaven there is nothing more corrupt, more pestilential, more hateful than the Roman Curia? It surpasses the godlessness of the Turks beyond all comparison, so that in truth, whereas it was once a gate of Heaven, it is now an open mouth of Hell, and such a mouth as, because of the wrath of God, cannot be shut; there is only one thing that we can try to do, as I have said: perchance we may be able to call back a few from that yawning chasm of Rome and so save them.

Now thou seest, my Father Leo, how and why I have so violently attacked that pestilential See, for so far have I been from raging against thy person that I even hoped I might gain thy favor and save thee, if I should make a strong and sharp assault upon that prison, nay that Hell of thine. For thou and thy salvation and the salvation of many others with thee will be served by everything that men of ability can contribute to the confusion of this wicked Curia. They do thy work, who bring evil upon it; they glorify Christ, who in every way curse it. In short, they are Christians who are not Romans.

To go yet farther, I never intended to inveigh against the Roman Curia, or to raise any controversy concerning it. For when I saw that all efforts to save it were hopeless, I despised it and gave it a bill of divorcement (Deut. 24:1), and said to it, "He that is filthy, let him be filthy still, and he that is unclean, let him be unclean still" (Rev. 22:11). Then I gave myself to the quiet and peaceful study of holy Scripture, that I might thus be of benefit to my brethren about me. When I had made some progress in these studies, Satan opened his eyes and filled his servant John Eck, a notable enemy of Christ, with an insatiable lust for glory, and thereby stirred him up to drag me at unawares into a disputation, laying hold on me by one little word about the primacy of the Roman Church which I had incidentally let fall. Then that boasting braggart, frothing and gnashing his teeth, declared that he would venture all for the glory of God and the honor of the holy Apostolic See, and, puffed up with the hope of misusing thy power, he looked forward with perfect confidence to a victory over me. He sought not so much to establish the primacy of Peter as his own leadership among the theologians of our time, and to that end he thought it no small help if he should triumph over Luther. When that debate ended unhappily for the sophist, an incredible madness overcame the man, for he feels that he alone must bear the blame of all that I have brought forth to the shame of Rome.

But permit me, I pray thee, most excellent Leo, this once to plead my cause and to make charges against thy real enemies. Thou knowest, I believe, what dealings thy legate, Cardinal Cajetan of St. Sixtus, an unwise and unfortunate, or rather, unfaithful man, had with me. When because of reverence for thy name I had put myself and all my case in his hand, he did not try to establish peace, although with a single word he could easily have done so, since I at that time promised to keep silent and to end the controversy if my opponents were ordered to do the same. But as he was a man who sought glory, and was not content with that agreement, he began to justify my opponents, to give them full freedom and to order me to recant, a thing not included in his instructions. When the matter was in a fair way, his untimely arbitrariness brought it into a far worse condition. Therefore, for what followed later Luther is not to blame: all the blame is Cajetan's, who did not suffer me to keep silent and to rest, as I then most earnestly asked him to do. What more should I have done?

Next came Carl Miltitz, also a nuncio of thy Blessedness, who after great and varied efforts and constant going to and fro, although he omitted nothing that might help to restore that status of the question which Cajetan had rashly and haughtily disturbed, at last with the help of the most illustrious prince, Frederick the Elector, barely managed to arrange several private conferences with me. Again I yielded to your name, I was prepared to keep silent, and even accepted as arbiter either the archbishop of Treves or the bishop of Naumburg. So matters were arranged. But while this plan was being followed with good prospects of success, lo, that other and greater enemy of thine, Eck, broke in with the Leipzig Disputation which he had undertaken against Dr. Carlstadt. When a new question concerning the primacy of the pope was raised, he suddenly turned his weapons against me and quite overthrew that counsel of peace. Meanwhile Carl Miltitz waited: a disputation was held, judges were selected, but here also no decision was reached, and no wonder: through the lies, the tricks, the wiles of Eck everything was stirred up, aggravated, and confounded worse than ever, so that whatever decision might have been reached, a greater conflagration would have resulted. For he sought glory, not the truth. Here also I left nothing undone that I ought to have done.

I admit that on this occasion no small amount of corrupt Roman practices came to light, but whatever wrong was done was the fault of Eck, who undertook a task beyond his strength, and, while he strove madly for his own glory, revealed the shame of Rome to all the world. He is thy enemy, my dear Leo, or rather the enemy of thy Curia. From the example of this one man thou canst learn that there is no enemy more injurious than a flatterer. For what did he accomplish with his flattery but an evil which no king could have accomplished? Today the name of the Roman Curia is a stench throughout the world, and papal authority languishes, ignorance that was once held in honor is evil spoken of, and of all this we should have heard nothing if Eck had not upset the counsel of peace planned by Carl and myself, as he himself now clearly sees, and is angry, too late and to no purpose, that my books were published. This he should have thought of when, like a horse that whinnies on the picket-line, he was madly seeking only his own glory, and sought only his own gain through thee at the greatest peril to thee. The vainglorious man thought that I would stop and keep silent at the terror of thy name, for I do not believe that he trusted entirely to his talents and learning. Now, when he sees that I have more courage than that and have not been silenced, he repents him too late of his rashness and understands that there is One in Heaven who resists the proud and humbles the haughty (1 Pet. 5:5; Judith 6:15), if indeed he does understand it at last.

Since we gained nothing by this disputation except that we brought greater confusion to the cause of Rome, Carl Miltitz made a third attempt; he came to the fathers of the Augustinian Order assembled in their chapter, and asked counsel in settling the controversy which had now grown most confused and dangerous. Since, by the favor of God, they had no hope of being able to proceed against me with violence, some of the most famous of their number were sent to me, and asked me at least to show honor to the person of thy Blessedness, and in a humble letter to plead as my excuse thy innocence and mine; they said that the affair was not yet in the most desperate state if of his innate goodness Leo X would take a hand in it. As I have always both offered and desired peace that I might devote myself to quieter and more useful studies, and have stormed with so great fury merely for the purpose of overwhelming by volume and violence of words, no less than of intellect, those whom I knew to be very unequal foes, I not only gladly ceased, but also with joy and thankfulness considered it a most welcome kindness to me if our hope could be fulfilled.

So I come, most blessed Father, and, prostrate before thee, I pray, if it be possible do thou interpose and hold in check those flatterers, who are the enemies of peace while they pretend to keep peace. But that I will recant, most blessed Father, let no one imagine, unless he prefer to involve the whole question in greater turmoil. Furthermore, I will accept no rules for the interpretation of the Word of God, since the Word of God, which teaches the liberty of all things else, dare not be bound (2 Tim. 2:9). Grant me these two points, and there is nothing that I could not or would not most gladly do or endure. I hate disputations; I will draw out no one, but then I do not wish others to draw me out; if they do, as Christ is my Teacher, I will not be speechless. For when once this controversy has been cited before thee and settled, thy Blessedness will be able with a small and easy word to silence both parties and command them to keep the peace, and that is what I have always wished to hear.

Do not listen, therefore, my dear Leo, to those sirens who make thee out to be no mere man but a demigod, so that thou mayest command and require what thou wilt. It will not be done in that fashion, and thou wilt not succeed. Thou art a servant of servants, and beyond all other men in a most pitiable and most dangerous position. Be not deceived by those who pretend that thou art lord of the world and allow no one to be a Christian unless he accept thy authority, who prate that thou hast power over Heaven, Hell, and purgatory. These are thy enemies and seek thy soul to destroy it (1 Kings 19:10); as Isaiah says, "O my people, they that call thee blessed, the same deceive thee" (Is. 3:12; Vulgate rendering). They err who exalt thee above a council and above the Church universal. They err who ascribe to thee alone the right of interpreting Scripture or under cover of thy name they seek to establish all their own wickedness in the Church, and alas! through them Satan has already made much headway under thy predecessors. In short, believe none who exalt thee, believe those who humble thee. For this is the judgment of God; "He hath put down the mighty from their seat, and hath exalted the humble" (Luke 1:52). See, how unlike His successors is

Christ, although they all would be His vicars. And I fear that most of them have indeed been too literally His vicars. For a vicar is a vicar only when his lord is absent. And if the pope rules while Christ is absent and does not dwell in his heart, what else is he but a vicar of Christ? But what is such a Church except a Mass of people without Christ? And what is such a vicar else than antichrist and an idol? How much more correctly did the apostles call themselves servants of the present Christ, and not vicars of an absent Christ!

Perhaps I am impudent, in that I seem to instruct so great, so exalted a personage, from whom we ought all to learn, and from whom, as those plagues of thine boast, the thrones of judges receive their decisions. But I am following the example of St. Bernard in his book *De Consideratione ad Eugenium*, a book every pope should have by heart. For what I am doing I do not from an eagerness to teach, but as an evidence of that pure and faithful solicitude which constrains us to have regard for the things of our neighbors even when they are safe, and does not permit us to consider their dignity or lack of dignity, since it is intent only upon the danger they run for the advantage they may gain. For when I know that thy Blessedness is driven and tossed about at Rome, that is, that far out at sea thou art threatened on all sides with endless dangers, and art laboring hard in that miserable plight, so that thou dost need even the slightest help of the least of thy brethren, I do not think it is absurd of me, if for the time I forget thy high office and do what brotherly love demands. I have no desire to flatter in so serious and dangerous a matter, but if men do not understand that I am thy friend and thy most humble subject, there is One that understandeth and judgeth (John 8:50).

Finally, that I may not approach thee empty-handed, blessed Father, I bring with me this little treatise published under thy name as an omen of peace and of good hope. From this book thou mayest judge with what studies I would prefer to be more profitably engaged, as I could be if your godless flatterers would permit me, and had hitherto permitted me. It is a small thing if thou regard its bulk, but unless I am deceived it is the whole of Christian living in brief form, if thou wilt grasp its meaning. I am a poor man, and have no other gift to offer, and thou hast no need to be made rich by any other than a spiritual gift. With this I commend myself to thy Fatherhood and Blessedness. May the Lord Jesus preserve thee forever. Amen.

Wittenberg, September 6, 1520.

# THE FREEDOM OF A CHRISTIAN

Many have thought Christian faith to be an easy thing, and not a few have given it a place among the virtues. This they do because they have had no experience of it, and have never tasted what great virtue there is in faith. For it is impossible that anyone should write well of it or well understand what is correctly written of it, unless he has at some time tasted the courage faith gives a man when trials oppress him. But he who has had even a faint taste of it can never write, speak, meditate, or hear enough concerning it. For it is a living fountain springing up into life everlasting, as Christ calls it in John 4:14. For my part, although I have no wealth of faith to boast of and know how scant my store is, yet I hope that, driven about by great and various temptations, I have attained to a little faith, and that I can speak of it, if not more elegantly, certainly more to the point than those literalists and all too subtile disputants have hitherto done, who have not even understood what they have written.

That I may make the way easier for the unlearned—for only such do I serve—I set down first these two propositions concerning the liberty and the bondage of the spirit:

A Christian man is a perfectly free lord of all, subject to none.

A Christian man is a perfectly dutiful servant of all, subject to all.

Although these two theses seem to contradict each other, yet, if they should be found to fit together they would serve our purpose beautifully. For they are both Paul's own, who says, in 1 Corinthians 9, "Whereas I was free, I made myself the servant of all" (v. 19), and, Rom. 13, "Owe no man anything, but to love one another" (v. 8). Now love by its very nature is ready to serve and to be subject to him who is loved. So Christ, although Lord of all, was made of a woman, made under the law (Gal. 4:4), and hence was at the same time free and a servant, at the same time in the form of God and in the form of a servant (Phil. 2:6ff).

Let us start, however, with something more remote from our subject, but more obvious. Man has a twofold nature, a spiritual and a bodily. According to the spiritual nature, which men call the soul, he is called a spiritual, or inner, or new man, according to the bodily nature, which men call the flesh, he is called a carnal, or outward, or old man, of whom the apostle writes in 2 Corinthians 4, "Though our outward man is corrupted, yet the inward man is renewed day by day" (v. 16). Because of this diversity of nature the Scriptures assert contradictory things of the same man, since these two men in the same man contradict each other, since the flesh lusteth against the spirit and the spirit against the flesh (Gal. 5:17).

First, let us contemplate the inward man, to see how a righteous, free, and truly Christian man, that is, a new, spiritual, inward man comes into being. It is evident that no external thing, whatsoever it be, has any influence whatever in producing Christian righteousness or liberty, nor in producing unrighteousness or bondage. A simple argument will furnish the proof. What can it profit the soul if the body is well, be free and active, eat, drink, and do as it pleases? For in these things even the most godless slaves of all the vices are well. On the other hand, how will ill health or imprisonment or hunger or thirst or any other external misfortune hurt the soul? With these things even the most godly men are afflicted, and those who because of a clear conscience are most free. None of these things touch either the liberty or the bondage of the soul. The soul receives no benefit if the body is adorned with the sacred robes of the priesthood, or dwells in sacred places, or is occupied with sacred duties, or prays, fasts, abstains from certain kinds of food or does any work whatsoever that can be done by the body and in the body. The righteousness and the freedom of the soul demand something far different, since the things which have been mentioned could be done by any wicked man, and such works produce nothing but hypocrites. On the other hand, it will not hurt the soul if the body is clothed in secular dress, dwells in unconsecrated places, eats and drinks as others do, does not pray aloud, and neglects to do all the things mentioned above, which hypocrites can do.

Further, to put aside all manner of works, even contemplation, meditation, and all that the soul can do avail nothing. One thing and one only is necessary for Christian life, righteousness, and liberty. That one thing is the most holy Word of God, the Gospel of Christ, as He says, John 11, "I am the resurrection and the life: he that believeth in me, shall not die forever" (v. 25); and John 8, "If the Son shall make you free, you shall be free indeed" (v. 26); and Matthew 4, "Not in bread alone doth man live, but in every word that proceedeth from the mouth of God" (v. 4). Let us then consider it certain and conclusively established that the soul can do without all things except the Word of God, and that where this is not there is no help for the soul in anything else whatever. But if it has the Word it is rich and lacks nothing, since this Word is the Word of life, of truth, of light, of peace, of righteousness, of salvation, of joy, of liberty, of wisdom, of power, of grace, of glory, and of every blessing beyond our power to estimate. This is why the prophet in the entire 119th Psalm, and in many other places of Scripture, with so many sighs yearns after the Word of God and applies so many names to it. On the other hand, there is no more terrible plague with which the wrath of God can smite men than a famine of the hearing of His Word, as He says in Amos, just as there is no greater mercy than when He sends forth His Word (Amos 8:11ff), as we read in Psalm 107, "He sent His word and healed them, and delivered them from their destructions" (v. 20). Nor was Christ sent into the world for any other ministry but that of the Word, and the whole spiritual estate, apostles, bishops, and all the priests, has been called and instituted only for the ministry of the Word.

You ask, "What then is this Word of God, and how shall it be used, since there are so many words of God?" I answer, the apostle explains that in Romans 1: the Word is the Gospel of God concerning His Son, who was made flesh, suffered, rose from the dead, and was glorified through the Spirit who sanctifies. For to preach Christ means to feed the soul, to make it righteous, to set it free and to save it, if it believe the preaching. For faith alone is the saving and efficacious use of the Word of God, "If thou confess with thy mouth that Jesus is Lord, and believe with thy heart that God hath raised Him up from the dead, thou shalt be saved" (Rom. 10:9), and again, "The end of the law is Christ, unto righteousness to every one that believeth" (Rom. 10:4), and, "The just shall live by his faith" (Rom. 1:17). The Word of God cannot be received and cherished by any works whatever, but only by faith (Hab. 2:4). Hence it is clear that, as the soul needs only the Word for its life and righteousness, so it is justified by faith alone and not by any works, for if it could be justified by anything else, it would not need the Word, and therefore it would not need faith. But this faith cannot at all exist in connection with works, that is to say, if you at the same time claim to be justified by works, whatever their character, for that would be to halt between two sides: to worship Baal and to kiss the hand (1 Kings 18:21), which, as Job says, is a very great iniquity (Job 31:27ff). Therefore the moment you begin to believe, you learn that all things in you are altogether blameworthy, sinful and damnable, as Romans 3 says, "For all have sinned and lack the glory of God" (v. 23); and again, "There is none just, there is none that doeth good, all have turned out of the way: they are become unprofitable together" (v. 10ff). When you have learned this, you will know that you need Christ, who suffered and rose again for you, that, believing in Him, you may through this faith become a new man, in that all your sins are forgiven, and you are justified by the merits of another, namely, of Christ alone.

Since, therefore, this faith can rule only in the inward man, as Romans 10:10 says, "With the heart we believe unto righteousness," and since faith alone justifies, it is clear that the inward man cannot be justified, made free and be saved by any outward work or dealing whatsoever, and that works, whatever their character, have nothing to do with this inward man. On the other hand, only ungodliness and unbelief of heart, and no outward work, make him guilty and a damnable servant of sin. Wherefore it ought to be the first concern of every Christian to lay aside all trust in works, and more and more to strengthen faith alone, and through faith to grow in the knowledge, not of works, but of Christ Jesus, who suffered and rose for him, as Peter teaches in the last chapter of his first epistle (1 Pet. 5:10), since no other work makes a Christian. Thus when the Jews asked Christ (John 6:28ff) what they should do that they might work the works of God, He brushed aside the multitude of works in which He saw that they abounded (John 6:27), and enjoined upon them a single work, saying, "This is the work of God, that you believe in Him whom He hath sent. For Him hath God the Father sealed" (John 6:29).

Hence true faith in Christ is a treasure beyond comparison, which brings with it all salvation and saves from every evil, as Christ says in the last chapter of Mark: "He that believeth and is baptized shall be saved, but he that believeth not shall be condemned" (Mark 16:16). This treasure Isaiah beheld and foretold in chapter 10: "The Lord shall make an abridged and consuming word upon the land, and the consumption abridged shall overflow with righteousness" (v. 22), as if he said, "Faith, which is a brief and perfect fulfillment of the law, shall fill believers with so great righteousness that they shall need nothing more for their righteousness." So also Paul says, "With the heart we believe unto righteousness" (Rom. 10:10).

Should you ask how it comes that faith alone justifies without works offers us such a treasury of great benefits, when so many works, ceremonies, and laws are prescribed in the Scriptures, I answer: first of all, remember what has been said: faith alone, without works, justifies, makes free and saves, as we shall later make still more clear. Here we must point out that all the Scriptures of God are divided into two parts—commands and promises. The commands indeed teach things that are good, but the things taught are not done as soon as taught, for the commands show us what we ought to do, but do not give us the power to do it; they are intended to teach a man to know himself, that through them he may recognize his inability to do good and may despair of his powers. That is why they are called and are the Old Testament. For example: "Thou shalt not covet" (Exod. 20:17) is a command which convicts us all of being sinners, since no one is able to avoid coveting, however much he may struggle against it. Therefore, in order not to covet and to fulfill the command, a man is compelled to despair of himself, and to seek elsewhere and from someone else the help which he does not find in himself, as is said in Hosea, "Destruction is thy own, O Israel: thy help is only in Me" (13:9). And as we are with this one command, so we are with all, for it is equally impossible for us to keep any one of them.

But when a man through the commands has learned to know his weakness, and has become troubled as to how he may satisfy the law, since the law must be fulfilled so that not a jot or tittle shall perish, otherwise man will be condemned without hope; then, being truly humbled and reduced to nothing in his own eyes, he finds in himself no means of justification and salvation. Here the second part of the Scriptures stands ready: the promises of God, which declare the glory of God and say, "If you wish to fulfill the law, and not to covet, as the law demands, come, believe in Christ, in whom grace, righteousness, peace, liberty, and all things are promised you; if you believe you shall have all, if you believe not you shall lack all." For what is impossible for you in all the works of the law, many as they are, but all useless, you will accomplish in a short and easy way through faith. For God our Father has made all things depend on faith, so that whoever has faith shall have all, and whoever has it not shall have nothing. "For He has concluded all under unbelief, that He might have mercy on all" (Rom. 11:32). Thus the promises of God give what the commands of God ask, and fulfill what the law prescribes, that all things may be of God alone, both the commands and the fulfilling of the commands. He alone commands. He also alone fulfills. Therefore the promises of God belong to the New Testament, nay, they are the New Testament.

And since these promises of God are holy, true, righteous, free, and peaceful words, full of all goodness, it comes to pass that the soul which clings to them with a firm faith is so united with them, nay, altogether taken up into them, that it not only shares in all their power, but is saturated and made drunken with it. For if a touch of Christ healed, how much more will this most tender touch in the Spirit, rather this absorbing of the Word, communicate to the soul all things that are the Word's. This then is how through faith alone without works the soul is justified by the Word of God, sanctified, made true and peaceful and free, filled with every blessing, and made truly a child of God, as John 1 says, "To them gave He power to become the sons of God, even to them that believe on His Name" (v. 12).

From what has been said it is easily seen whence faith has such great power, and why no good work nor all good works together can equal it: no work can cling to the Word of God nor be in the soul;

in the soul faith alone and the Word have sway. As the Word is, so it makes the soul, as heated iron glows like fire because of the union of fire with it. It is clear then that a Christian man has in his faith all that he needs, and needs no works to justify him. And if he has no need of works, neither does he need the law, and if he has no need of the law, surely he is free from the law, and it is true, "the law is not made for a righteous man" (1 Tim. 1:9). And this is that Christian liberty, even our faith, which does not indeed cause us to live in idleness or in wickedness, but makes the law and works unnecessary for any man's righteousness and salvation.

This is the first power of faith. Let us now examine the second also. For it is a further function of faith, that whom it trusts it also honors with the most reverent and high regard, since it considers him truthful and trustworthy. For there is no other honor equal to the estimate of truthfulness and righteousness with which we honor him whom we trust. Or could we ascribe to a man anything greater than truthfulness, and righteousness, and perfect goodness? On the other hand, there is no way in which we can show greater contempt for a man than to regard him as false and wicked and to suspect him, as we do when we do not trust him. So when the soul firmly trusts God's promises, it regards Him as truthful and righteous, than which nothing more excellent can be ascribed to God. This is the very highest worship of God, that we ascribe to Him truthfulness, righteousness, and whatever else ought to be ascribed to one who is trusted. Then the soul consents to all His will, then it hallows His name and suffers itself to be dealt with according to God's good pleasure, because, clinging to God's promises, it does not doubt that He who is true, just, and wise will do, dispose, and provide all things well. And is not such a soul by this faith in all things most obedient to God? What commandment is there that such obedience has not abundantly fulfilled? What more complete fulfillment is there than obedience in all things? But this obedience is not rendered by works, but by faith alone. On the other hand, what greater rebellion against God, what greater wickedness, what greater contempt of God is there than not believing His promises? For what is this but to make God a liar or to doubt that He is truthful?—that is, to ascribe truthfulness to one's self, but to God lying and vanity? Does not a man who does this deny God and in his heart set up himself as his own idol? Then of what avail are works done in such wickedness, even if they were the works of angels and apostles (Rom. 11:32)? Rightly, therefore, has God concluded all—not in anger or lust, but in unbelief, so that they who imagine that they are fulfilling the law by doing the works of chastity and mercy required by the law (the civil and human virtues), might not be confident that they will be saved; they are included under the sin of unbelief, and must either seek mercy or be justly condemned.

But when God sees that we count Him to be true, and by the faith of our heart pay Him the great honor which is due Him, He in turn does us the great honor of counting us true and righteous for our faith's sake. For faith works truth and righteousness by giving to God what belongs to Him; therefore, God in turn gives glory to our righteousness. It is true and just that God is truthful and just, and to count Him and confess Him, so is to be truthful and just. So in 1 Samuel 2, he says, "Them that honor Me, I will honor, and they that despise Me, shall be lightly esteemed" (v. 30). So Paul says in Romans 4 that Abraham's faith was counted unto him for righteousness, because by it he most perfectly gave glory to God, and that for the same reason our faith shall be counted unto us for righteousness if we believe (v. 3).

The third incomparable benefit of faith is this: that it unites the soul with Christ as a bride is united with her bridegroom. And by this mystery, as the apostle teaches, Christ and the soul become one flesh (Eph. 5:31ff). And if they are one flesh and there is between them a true marriage, nay, by far the most perfect of all marriages, since human marriages are but frail types of this one true marriage, it follows that all they have they have in common, the good as well as the evil, so that the believing soul can boast of and glory in whatever Christ has as if it were its own, and whatever the soul has Christ claims as His own. Let us compare these and we shall see things that cannot be estimated. Christ is full of grace, life, and salvation; the soul is full of sins, death, and condemnation. Now let faith come between them, and it shall come to pass that sins, death, and Hell are Christ's, and grace, life, and salvation are the soul's. For it behooves Him, if He is a bridegroom, to take upon Himself the things which are His bride's, and to bestow upon her the things that are His. For if He gives her His body and His very self, how shall He not give her all that is His? And if He takes the body of the bride, how shall He not take all that is hers?

Lo! here we have a pleasant vision not only of communion, but of a blessed strife and victory and salvation and redemption. For Christ is God and man in one person, who has neither sinned nor died, and is not condemned, and who cannot sin, die, or be condemned; His righteousness, life and salvation are unconquerable, eternal, omnipotent, and He by the wedding-ring of faith shares in the sins, death, and pains of Hell which are His bride's, nay, makes them His own, and acts as if they were His own, and as if He Himself had sinned; He suffered, died, and descended into Hell that He might overcome them all. Now since it was such a one who did all this, and death and Hell could not swallow Him up, they were of necessity swallowed up of Him in a mighty duel. For His righteousness is greater than the sins of all men, His life stronger than death, His salvation more invincible than Hell. Thus the believing soul by the pledge of its faith is free in Christ, its Bridegroom, from all sins, secure against death and against Hell, and is endowed with the eternal righteousness, life, and salvation of Christ, its Bridegroom. So He presents to Himself a glorious bride, without spot or wrinkle (Eph. 5:27), cleansing her with the washing in the Word of life, that is, by faith in the Word of life, of righteousness, and of salvation. Thus He marries her to Himself in faith, in loving kindness, and in mercies, in righteousness and in judgment, as Hosea 2 says (v. 19ff).

Who then can fully appreciate what this royal marriage means? Who can understand the riches of the glory of this grace? Here this rich and godly Bridegroom Christ marries this poor, wicked harlot, redeems her from all her evil and adorns her with all His good. It is now impossible that her sins should destroy her, since they are laid upon Christ and swallowed up in Him, and she has that righteousness in Christ her husband of which she may boast as of her own, and which she can confidently set against all her sins in the face of death and Hell, and say, "If I have sinned, yet my Christ in whom I believe has not sinned, and all His is mine, and all mine is His," as the bride in the Song of Solomon says, "My beloved is mine, and I am his" (Song 2:16). This is what Paul means when he says, in 1 Cor. 15, "Thanks be to God, which giveth us the victory through our Lord Jesus Christ"(v. 57), that is, the victory over sin and death, as he there says, "the sting of death is sin, and the strength of sin is the law" (1 Cor. 15:36).

From this you see once more why so much is ascribed to faith, that it alone may fulfill the law and justify, without the Law, works. You see that the First Commandment, which says, "Thou shalt worship one God," is fulfilled by faith alone. For though you were nothing but good works from the sole of your foot to the crown of your head, yet you would not be righteous, nor worship God, nor fulfill the First Commandment, since God cannot be worshiped unless you ascribe to Him the glory of truthfulness and of all goodness, which is due Him. And this cannot be done by works, but only by the faith of the heart. For not by the doing of works, but by believing do we glorify God and acknowledge that He is truthful. Therefore, faith alone is the righteousness of a Christian man and the fulfilling of all the commandments. For he who fulfills the First has no difficulty in fulfilling all the rest. But works, being insensate things, cannot glorify God, although they can, if faith be present, be done to the glory of God. At present, however, we are not inquiring what works and what sort of works are done, but who it is that does them, who glorifies God and brings forth the works. This is faith which dwells in the heart, and is the head and substance of all our righteousness. Hence, it is a blind and dangerous doctrine which teaches that the commandments must be fulfilled by works. The commandments must be fulfilled before any works can be done, and the works proceed from the fulfillment of the commandments (Rom. 13:10), as we shall hear.

But that we may look more deeply into that grace which our inward man has in Christ, we must consider that in the Old Testament God sanctified to Himself every firstborn male, and the birthright was highly prized, having a two-fold honor, that of priesthood and that of kingship. For the firstborn brother was priest and lord over all the others, and was a type of Christ, the true and only Firstborn of God the Father and of the virgin Mary, and true King and Priest, not after the fashion of the flesh and of the world. For His kingdom is not of this world (John 18:36). He reigns in Heavenly and spiritual things and consecrates them—such as righteousness, truth, wisdom, peace, salvation, etc. Not as if all things on earth and in Hell were not also subject to Him—else how could He protect and save us from them?—but His kingdom consists neither in them nor of them. Nor does His priesthood consist in the outward splendor of robes and postures, like that human priesthood of Aaron and of our present-day Church, but it consists in spiritual things, through which He by an unseen service intercedes for us in Heaven before God, there offers Himself as a sacrifice and does all things a priest should do, as Paul in the epistle to the Hebrews describes Him under the type of Melchizedek (Heb. 6ff). Nor does He only pray and intercede for us, but within our soul He teaches us through the living teaching of His

Spirit, thus performing the two real unctions of a priest, of which the prayers and the preaching of human priests are visible types.

Now, just as Christ by His birthright obtained these two prerogatives, so He imparts them to and shares them with everyone who believes in Him according to the law of the aforesaid marriage, by which the wife owns whatever belongs to the husband. Hence we are all priests and kings in Christ, as many as believe on Christ, as 1 Peter 2 says, "Ye are a chosen generation, a peculiar people, a royal priesthood and priestly kingdom, that ye should show forth the virtues of Him who hath called you out of darkness into His marvelous light" (v. 9).

This priesthood and kingship we explain as follows: first, as to the kingship, every Christian is by faith so exalted above all things that by a spiritual power he is lord of all things without exception, so that nothing can do him any harm whatever, nay, all things are made subject to him and compelled to serve him to his salvation. Thus Paul says in Romans 8, "All things work together for good to them who are called" (v. 28). And, in 1 Corinthians 3, "All things are yours, whether life or death, or things present or things to come, and ye are Christ's" (3:22ff). Not as if every Christian were set over all things, to possess and control them by physical power—a madness with which some churchmen are afflicted—for such power belongs to kings, princes, and men on earth. Our ordinary experience in life shows us that we are subjected to all, suffer many things, and even die; nay, the more Christian a man is, the more evils, sufferings, and deaths is he made subject to, as we see in Christ the firstborn Prince Himself, and in all His brethren the saints. The power of which we speak is spiritual; it rules in the midst of enemies, and is mighty in the midst of oppression, which means nothing else than that strength is made perfect in weakness (2 Cor. 12:9), and that in all things I can find profit unto salvation, so that the cross and death itself are compelled to serve me and to work together with me for my salvation (Rom. 8:28). This is a splendid prerogative and hard to attain, and a true omnipotent power, a spiritual dominion, in which there is nothing so good and nothing so evil, but that it shall work together for good to me, if only I believe. And yet, since faith alone suffices for salvation, I have need of nothing, except that faith exercise the power and dominion of its own liberty. Lo, this is the inestimable power and liberty of Christians.

Not only are we the freest of kings, we are also priests forever, which is far more excellent than being kings, because as priests we are worthy to appear before God to pray for others and to teach one another the things of God. For these are the functions of priests, and cannot be granted to any unbeliever. Thus Christ has obtained for us, if we believe on Him, that we are not only His brethren, co-heirs and fellow-kings with Him, but also fellow-priests with Him, who may boldly come into the presence of God in the spirit of faith and cry, "Abba, Father!" (Heb. 10:19, 22), pray for one another, and do all things which we see done and prefigured in the outward and visible works of priests. But he who does not believe is not served by anything, nor does anything work for good to him, but he himself is a servant of all, and all things become evils to him, because he wickedly uses them to his own profit and not to the glory of God. And so he is no priest, but a profane man, whose prayer becomes sin and never comes into the presence of God, because God does not hear sinners (John 9:31). Who then can comprehend the lofty dignity of the Christian? Through his kingly power he rules over all things, death, life, and sin, and through his priestly glory is all powerful with God, because God does the things which he asks and desires, as it is written, "He will fulfill the desire of them that fear Him; He also will hear their cry, and will save them" (Phil. 4:13). To this glory a man attains, surely not by any works of his, but by faith alone.

From this any one can clearly see how a Christian man is free from all things and over all things, so that he needs no works to make him righteous and to save him, since faith alone confers all these things abundantly. But should he grow so foolish as to presume to become righteous, free, saved, and a Christian by means of some good work, he would on the instant lose faith and all its benefits: a foolishness aptly illustrated in the fable of the dog who runs along a stream with a piece of meat in his mouth, and, deceived by the reflection of the meat in the water, opens his mouth to snap at it, and so loses both the meat and the reflection. You will ask, "If all who are in the Church are priests, how do those whom we now call priests differ from laymen?" I answer: Injustice is done those words, "priest," "cleric," "spiritual," "ecclesiastic," when they are transferred from all other Christians to those few who are now by a mischievous usage called "ecclesiastics." For Holy Scripture makes no distinction between them, except that it gives the name "ministers," "servants," "stewards," to those who are now proudly called popes, bishops, and lords and who should by the ministry of the Word serve others and teach them the faith of Christ and the liberty of believers. For although we are all equally priests, yet we cannot all publicly minister and teach, nor ought we if we could. Thus Paul writes in 1 Corinthians 4, "Let a man so account of us, as of the ministers of Christ, and stewards of the mysteries of God" (v. 1).

But that stewardship has now been developed into so great a pomp of power and so terrible a tyranny that no heathen empire or earthly power can be compared with it, just as if laymen were not also Christians. Through this perversion the knowledge of Christian grace, faith, liberty, and of Christ Himself has altogether perished, and its place has been taken by an unbearable bondage of human words and laws, until we have become, as the Lamentations of Jeremiah say, servants of the vilest men on earth, who abuse our misfortune to serve only their base and shameless will (Lam. 1:11).

To return to our purpose, I believe it has now become clear that it is not enough nor is it Christian, to preach the works, life and words of Christ as historical acts, as if the knowledge of these would suffice for the conduct of life, although this is the fashion of those who must today be regarded as our best preachers, and far less is it enough for Christian to say nothing at all about Christ and to teach instead the laws of men and the decrees of the Fathers. And now there are not a few who preach Christ and read about Him that they may move men's affections to sympathy with Christ, to anger against the Jews, and such like childish and womanish nonsense. Rather ought Christ to be preached to the end that faith in Him may be established, that He may not only be Christ, but be Christ for thee and for me, and that what is said of Him and what His Name denotes may be effectual in us. And such faith is produced and preserved in us by preaching why Christ came, what He brought and bestowed, what benefit it is to us to accept Him. This is done when that Christian liberty which He bestows is rightly taught, and we are told in what way we who are Christians are all kings and priests and so are lords of all, and may firmly believe that whatever we have done is pleasing and acceptable in the sight of God, as I have said.

What man is there whose heart, hearing these things, will not rejoice to its very core, and in receiving such comfort grow tender so as to love Christ, as he never could be made to love by any laws or works? Who would have power to harm such a heart or to make it afraid? If the knowledge of sin for the fear of death break in upon it is ready to hope in the Lord; it does not grow afraid when it hears tidings of evil, nor is it disturbed until it shall look down upon its enemies (Psalm 112:7ff). For it believes that the righteousness of Christ is its own, and that its sin is not its own, but Christ's, and that all sin is swallowed up by the righteousness of Christ is, as has been said above, a necessary consequence of faith in Christ. So the heart learns to scoff at death and sin, and to say with the apostle, "Where, O death, is thy victory? Where, O death, is thy sting? The sting of death is sin, and the strength of sin is the law. But thanks be to God, which giveth us the victory through our Lord Jesus Christ" (1 Cor. 15:55ff). For death is swallowed up not only in the victory of Christ, but also by our victory, because through faith His victory has become ours, and in that faith we also are conquerors.

Let this suffice concerning the inward man, his liberty and its source, the righteousness of faith, which needs neither laws nor good works, nay, is rather injured by them, if a man trusts that he is justified by them.

Now let us turn to the second part, to the outward man. Here we shall answer all those who, misled by the word "faith" and by all that has been said, now say: "If faith does all things and is alone sufficient unto righteousness, why then are good works commanded? We will take our ease and do no works, and be content with faith." I answer, not so, ye wicked men, not so. That would indeed be proper, if we were wholly inward and perfectly spiritual men, but such we shall be only at the last day, the day of the resurrection of the dead. As long as we live in the flesh we only begin and make some progress in that which shall be perfected in the future life. For this reason the apostle, in Romans 8, calls all that we attain in this "the firstfruits" of the spirit (v. 23), because, forsooth, we shall receive the greater portion, even the fullness of the spirit, in the future. This is the place for that which was said above, that a Christian man is the servant of all and made subject to all. For insofar as he is free he does no works, but insofar as he is a servant he does all manner of works. How this is possible, we shall see.

Although, as I have said, a man is abundantly justified by faith inwardly, in his spirit, and so has all that he ought to have, except insofar as this faith and riches must grow from day to day even unto the future, yet he remains in this mortal life on earth, and in this life he must needs govern his own body and have dealings with men. Here the works begin; here a man cannot take his ease; here he must, indeed, take care to discipline his body by fastings, watchings, labors, and other reasonable discipline, and to make it subject to the spirit so that it will obey and conform to the inward man and to faith, and not revolt against faith and hinder the inward man, as it is the body's nature to do if it be not held in check. For the inward man, who by faith is created in the likeness of God, is both joyful and happy because of Christ in whom so many benefits are conferred upon him, and therefore it is his one occupation to serve God joyfully and for naught, in love that is not constrained.

While he is doing this, lo, he meets a contrary will in his own flesh, which strives to serve the world and to seek its own advantage. This the spirit of faith cannot tolerate, and with joyful zeal it attempts to put the body under and to hold it in check, as Paul says in Romans 7, "I delight in the law of God after the inward man; but I see another law in my members, warring against the law of my mind, and bringing me into captivity to the law of sin" (v. 22ff); and, in another place, "I keep under my body, and bring it into subjection, lest by any means, when I have preached to others, I myself should be a castaway" (1 Cor. 9:27), and in Galatians, "They that are Christ's have crucified the flesh with its lusts" (5:24).

In doing these works, however, we must not think that a man is justified before God by them, for that erroneous opinion faith, which alone is righteousness before God, cannot endure; but we must think that these works reduce the body to subjection and purify it of its evil lusts, and our whole purpose is to be directed only toward the driving out of lusts. For since by faith the soul is cleansed and made a lover of God, it desires that all things, and especially its own body, shall be as pure as itself, so that all things may join with it in loving and praising God. Hence a man cannot be idle, because the need of his body drives him and he is compelled to do many good works to reduce it to subjection. Nevertheless the works themselves do not justify him before God, but he does the works out of spontaneous love in obedience to God, and considers nothing except the approval of God, whom he would in all things most scrupulously obey.

In this way everyone will easily be able to learn for himself the limit and discretion, as they say, of his bodily castigations, for he will fast, watch, and labor as much as he finds sufficient to repress the lasciviousness and lust of his body. But they who presume to be justified by works do not regard the mortifying of the lusts, but only the works themselves, and think that if only they have done as many and as great works as are possible, they have done well, and have become righteousness; at times they even addle their brains and destroy, or at least render useless, their natural strength with their works. This is the height of folly, and utter ignorance of Christian life and faith, that a man should seek to be justified and saved by works and without faith.

In order that what we have said may be more easily understood, we will explain it by analogies. We should think of the works of a Christian man who is justified and saved by faith because of the pure and free mercy of God, just as we would think of the works which Adam and Eve did in Paradise, and all their children would have done if they had not sinned. We read in Genesis 2, "God put the man whom He had formed into the garden of Eden to dress it and to keep it" (v. 15). Now Adam was created by God righteous and upright and without sin, so that he had no need of being justified and made upright through his dressing and keeping the garden, but, that he might not be idle, the Lord gave him a work to do: to cultivate and to protect the garden. These would truly have been the freest of works, done only to please God and not to obtain righteousness, which Adam already had in full measure, and which would have been the birthright of us all.

Such also are the works of a believer. Through his faith he has been restored to Paradise and created anew, has no need of works that he may become or be righteous, but that he may not be idle and may provide for and keep his body, he must do such works freely only to please God, only, since we are not wholly re-created, and our faith and love are not yet perfect, these are to be increased, not by external works, however, but within themselves.

Again, a bishop, when he consecrates a church, confirms children, or performs any other duty belonging to his office, is not made a bishop by these works; nay, if he had not first been made a bishop, none of these works would be valid. They would be foolish, childish, and a mere farce. So the Christian who is consecrated by his faith does good works, but the works do not make him more holy or more Christian, for that is the work of faith alone, and if a man were not first a believer and a Christian all his works would amount to nothing at all and would be truly wicked and damnable sins.

These two sayings, therefore, are true: "Good works do not make a good man, but a good man does good works; evil works do not make a wicked man, but a wicked man does evil works," so that it is always necessary that the "substance" or person itself be good before there can be any good works, and that good works follow and proceed from the good person, as Christ also says, "A corrupt tree does not bring forth good fruit, a good tree does not bring forth evil fruit" (Matt. 7:18). It is clear that the fruits do not bear the tree, nor does the tree grow on the fruits, but on the contrary the trees bear the fruits and the fruits grow on the trees. As it is necessary, therefore, that the trees must exist before their fruits, and the fruits do not make trees either good or corrupt, but rather as the trees are so are the fruits they bear, so the person of a man must needs first be good or wicked before he does a good or a wicked work, and his works do not make him good or wicked, but he himself makes his works either good or wicked.

Illustrations of the same truth can be seen in all trades: a good or a bad house does not make a good or a bad builder, but a good or a bad builder makes a bad or a good house. And in general, the work never makes the workman like itself, but the workman makes the work like himself. So it is also with the works of man: as the man is, whether believer or unbeliever, so also is his work—good, if it was done in faith; wicked, if it was done in unbelief. But the converse is not true, that the work makes the man either a believer or an unbeliever. For as works do not make a man a believer, so also they do not make him righteous. But as faith makes a man a believer and righteous, so faith also does good works. Since then works justify no one, and a man must be righteous before he does a good work, it is very evident that it is faith alone which, because of the pure mercy of God through Christ and in His Word, worthily and sufficiently justifies and saves the person, and a Christian man has no need of any work or of any law in order to be saved, since through faith he is free from every law and does all that he does out of pure liberty and freely, seeking neither benefit nor salvation, since he already abounds in all things and is saved through the grace of God because of his faith, and now seeks only to please God.

Furthermore, no good work helps an unbeliever so as to justify or save him. And, on the other hand, no evil work makes him wicked or damns him, but the unbelief which makes the person and the tree evil does the evil and damnable works. Hence when a man is made good or evil, this is effected not by the works, but by faith or unbelief, as the wise man says, "This is the beginning of sin, that a man falls away from God" (Sirach 10:14ff), which happens when he does not believe. And Paul, Hebrews 11, says, "He that cometh to God must believe" (v. 6). And Christ says the same: "Either make the tree good and his fruit good, or else make the tree corrupt and his fruit corrupt" (Matt. 12:33), as if He would say, let him who would have good fruit begin by planting a good tree. So let him who would do good works not begin with the doing of works, but with believing, which makes the person good. For nothing makes a man good except faith, nor evil except unbelief.

It is indeed true that in the sight of men a man is made good or evil by his works, but this being made good or evil is no more than that he who is good or evil is pointed out and known as such, as Christ says in Matthew 7, "By their fruits ye shall know them" (v. 20). But all this remains on the surface, and very many have been deceived by this outward appearance and have presumed to write and teach concerning good works by which we may be justified, without even mentioning faith; they go their way, always being deceived and deceiving, advancing, indeed, but into a worse state, blind leaders of the blind (2 Tim. 3:13), wearying themselves with many works, and yet never attaining to true righteousness (Matt. 15:14). Of such Paul says in 2 Timothy 3, "Having the form of godliness, but denying its power, always learning and never attaining to the knowledge of the truth" (vv. 5, 7).

He, therefore, who does not wish to go astray with those blind men, must look beyond works, and laws and doctrines about works; nay, turning his eyes from works, he must look upon the person and ask how that is justified. For the person is justified and saved not by works nor by laws, but by the Word of God, that is, by the promise of His grace (Tit. 3:5), and by faith, that the glory may remain God's, who saved us not by works of righteousness which we have done, but according to His mercy by the word of His grace, when we believed (1 Cor. 1:21).

From this it is easy to know in how far good works are to be rejected or not, and by what standard all the teachings of men concerning works are to be interpreted. If works are sought after as a means to righteousness, are burdened with this perverse leviathan, and are done under the false impression that through them you are justified, they are made necessary and freedom and faith are destroyed; and this addition to them makes them to be no longer good, but truly damnable works. For they are not free, and they blaspheme the grace of God, since to justify and to save by faith belongs to the grace of God alone. What the works have no power to do, they yet, by a godless presumption through this folly of ours pretend to do, and thus violently force themselves into the office and the glory of grace. We do not, therefore, reject good works; on the contrary, we cherish and teach them as much as possible. We do not condemn them for their own sake, but because of this godless addition to them and the perverse idea that righteousness is to be sought through them, for that makes them appear good outwardly, when in truth they are not good; they deceive men and lead men to deceive each other, like ravening wolves in sheep's clothing (Matt. 7:15).

But this leviathan and perverse notion concerning works is insuperable where sincere faith is wanting. Those work-saints cannot get rid of it unless faith, its destroyer, come and rule in their hearts. Nature of itself cannot drive it out, nor even recognize it, but rather regards it as a mark of the most holy will. And if the influence of custom be added and confirm this perverseness of nature, as wicked magisters have caused it to do, it becomes an incurable evil, and leads astray and destroys countless men beyond all hope of restoration. Therefore, although it is good to preach and write about penitence, confession, and satisfaction, if we stop with that and do not go on to teach about faith, our teaching is unquestionably deceitful and devilish.

Christ, like His forerunner John, not only said, "Repent ye" (Matt. 3:2), but added the word of faith, saying, "The kingdom of Heaven is at hand" (Matt. 4:17). And we are not to preach only one of these words of God, but both; we are to bring forth out of our treasure things new and old (Matt. 13:52), the voice of the law as well as the word of grace. We must bring forth the voice of the law that men may be made to fear and to come to a knowledge of their sins, and so be converted to repentance and a better life. But we must not stop with that. For that would be only to wound and not to bind up, to smite and not to heal, to kill and not to make alive, to lead down into Hell and not to bring back again, to humble and not to exalt. Therefore, we must also preach the word of grace and the promise of forgiveness, by which faith is taught and strengthened. Without this word of grace the works of the law, contrition, penitence, and all the rest are performed and taught in vain.

There remain even to our day preachers of repentance and grace, but they do not so explain God's law and promise that a man might learn from them the source of repentance and grace. For repentance proceeds from the law of God, but faith or grace from the promise of God, as Romans 10 says, "Faith cometh by hearing, and hearing by the word of Christ" (v. 17), so that a man is consoled and exalted by faith in the divine promise, after he has been humbled and led to a knowledge of himself by the threats and the fear of the divine law. So we read in Psalm 30, "Weeping may endure for a night, but joy cometh in the morning" (v. 6).

Let this suffice concerning works in general, and at the same time concerning the works which a Christian does for his own body. Lastly, we will also speak of the things which he does toward his neighbor. A man does not live for himself alone in this mortal body, so as to work for it alone, but he lives also for all men on earth, nay, rather, lives only for others and not for himself. And to this end he brings his body into subjection, that he may the more sincerely and freely serve others, as Paul says in Romans 14, "No one lives to himself, and no man dies to himself. For he that liveth, liveth unto the Lord, and he that dieth, dieth unto the Lord" (v. 7ff). Therefore, it is impossible that he should ever in this life be idle and without works toward his neighbors, for of necessity he will speak, deal with and converse with men, as Christ also, being made in the likeness of men, was found in form as a man, and conversed with men, as Baruch 3:38 says.

But none of these things does a man need for his righteousness and salvation. Therefore, in all his works he should be guided by this thought and look to this one thing alone, that he may serve and benefit others in all that he does, having regard to nothing except the need and the advantage of his neighbor. Thus, the apostle commands us to work with our hands that we may give to him who is in need, although he might have said that we should work to support ourselves;

he says, however, "that he may have to give to him that needeth" (Eph. 4:28). And this is what makes it a Christian work to care for the body, that through its health and comfort we may be able to work, to acquire and to lay by funds with which to aid those who are in need, that in this way the strong member may serve the weaker, and we may be sons of God, each caring for and working for the other, bearing one another's burdens, and so fulfilling the law of Christ (Gal. 6:2). Lo, this is a truly Christian life, here faith is truly out effectual through love (Gal. 5:6), that is, it issues in works of the freest service cheerfully and lovingly done, with which a man willingly serves another without hope of reward, and for himself is satisfied with the fullness and wealth of his faith.

So Paul after teaching the Philippians how rich they were made through faith in Christ, in which they obtained all things, proceeds immediately to teach them further, saying, "If there be any consolation in Christ, if any comfort of love, if any fellowship of the Spirit, fulfill ye my joy, that ye be likeminded, having the same love, being of one accord, thinking nothing through strife or vainglory, but in lowliness each esteeming the other better than themselves, looking not every man on his own things, but on the things of others" (Phil. 2:1ff). Here we see clearly that the apostle has prescribed this rule for the life of Christians, that we should devote all our works to the welfare of others, since each has such abundant riches in his faith, that all his other works and his whole life are a surplus with which he can by voluntary benevolence serve and do good to his neighbor.

As an example of such a life the apostle cites Christ, saying, "Let this mind be in you, which was also in Christ Jesus, who being in the form of God thought it not robbery to be equal with God, but made Himself of no reputation, and took upon Him the form of a servant, and was made in the likeness of men, and being found in fashion as a man He became obedient unto death" (Phil. 2:5ff). This salutary word of the apostle has been obscured for us by those who have not at all understood the apostle's words, "form of God," "form of a servant," "fashion," "likeness of men," and have applied them to the divine and the human nature. Paul means this: although Christ was filled with the form of God and rich in all good things, so that He needed no work and no suffering to make Him righteous and saved (for He had all this always from the beginning), yet He was not puffed up by them, nor did He lift Himself up above us and assume power over us, although He could rightly have done so, but on the contrary He so lived, labored, worked, suffered, and died that He might be like other men, and in fashion and in actions be nothing else than a man, just as if He had need of all these things and had nothing of the form of God. But He did all this for our sake, that He might serve us, and that all things He accomplished in this form of a servant might become ours.

So a Christian, like Christ, his Head, is filled and made rich by faith, and should be content with this form of God which he has obtained by faith, only, as I have said, he ought to increase this faith until it be made perfect. For this faith is his life, his righteousness and his salvation: it saves him and makes him acceptable and bestows upon him all things that are Christ's, as has been said above, and as Paul asserts in Galatians 2, when he says, "And the life which I now live in the flesh, I live by the faith of the Son of God" (v. 20). Although the Christian is thus free from all works, he ought in this liberty to empty himself, to take upon himself the form of a servant, to be made in the likeness of men, to be found in fashion as a man, and to serve, help, and in every way deal with his neighbor as he sees that God through Christ has dealt and still deals with himself. And this he should do freely, having regard to nothing except the divine approval. He ought to think, 'Though I am an unworthy and condemned man, my God has given me in Christ all the riches of righteousness and salvation without any merit on my part, out of pure, free mercy, so that henceforth I need nothing whatever except faith which believes that this is true. Why should I not therefore freely, joyfully, with all my heart, and with an eager will, do all things which I know are pleasing and acceptable to such a Father, Who has overwhelmed me with His inestimable riches? I will therefore give myself as a Christ to my neighbor, just as Christ offered Himself to me; I will do nothing in this life except what I see is necessary, profitable, and salutary to my neighbor, since through faith I have an abundance of all good things in Christ.'

Lo, thus from faith flow forth love and joy in the Lord, and from love a joyful, willing, and free mind that serves one's neighbor willingly and takes no account of gratitude or ingratitude, of praise or blame, of gain or loss. For a man does not serve that he may put men under obligations, he does not distinguish between friends and enemies, nor does he anticipate their thankfulness or unthankfulness, but most freely and most willingly he spends himself and all that he has, whether he waste all on the thankless or whether he gain a reward. For as his Father does, distributing all things to all men richly and freely, causing His sun to rise upon the good and upon the evil (Matt. 5:45), so also the son does all things and suffers all things with that freely bestowing joy which is his delight when through Christ he sees it in God, the dispenser of such great benefits.

Therefore, if we recognize the great and precious things which are given us, as Paul says (Rom. 5:5), there will be shed abroad in our hearts by the Holy Ghost the love which makes us free, joyful, almighty workers and conquerors over all tribulations, servants of our neighbors, and yet lords of all. But for those who do not recognize the gifts bestowed upon them through Christ, Christ has been born in vain; they go their way with their works, and shall never come to taste or to feel those things. Just as our neighbor is in need and lacks that in which we abound, so we also have been in need before God and have lacked His mercy. Hence, as our Heavenly Father has in Christ freely come to our help, we also ought freely to help our neighbor through our body and its works, and each should become as it were a Christ to the other, that we may be Christs to one another and Christ may be the same in all, that is, that we may be truly Christians.

Who then can comprehend the riches and the glory of the Christian life? It can do all things, and has all things, and lacks nothing; it is lord over sin, death, and Hell, and yet at the same time it serves, ministers to, and benefits all men. But, alas, in our day this life is unknown throughout the world; it is neither preached about nor sought after; we are altogether ignorant of our own name and do not know why we are Christians or bear the name of Christians. Surely we are so named after Christ, not because He is absent from us, but because He dwells in us, that is, because we believe on Him and are Christs one to another and do to our neighbors as Christ does to us. But in our day we are taught by the doctrine of men to seek naught but merits, rewards, and the things that are ours; of Christ we have made only a taskmaster far more harsh than Moses.

Of such faith we have a pre-eminent example in the blessed virgin. As is written in Luke 2, she was purified according to the law of Moses, after the custom of all women, although she was not bound by that law, and needed not to be purified. But out of free and willing love she submitted to the law, being made like other women, lest she should offend or despise them. She was not justified by this work, but being righteous she did it freely and willingly. So our works also should be done, not that we may be justified by them, since being justified beforehand by faith, we ought to do all things freely and joyfully for the sake of others.

St. Paul also circumcised his disciple Timothy, not because circumcision was necessary for his righteousness, but that he might not offend or despise the Jews who were weak in the faith and could not yet grasp the liberty of faith. But on the other hand, when they despised the liberty of faith and insisted that circumcision was necessary for righteousness, he withstood them and did not allow Titus to be circumcised (Gal. 2:3). For as he was unwilling to offend or to despise any man's weak faith, and yielded to their will for the time, so he was also unwilling that the liberty of faith should be offended against or despised by stubborn work-righteous men. He chose a middle way, sparing the weak for a time, but always withstanding the stubborn, that he might convert all to the liberty of faith. What we do should be done with the same zeal to sustain the weak in faith, as Romans 14 teaches; but we should firmly withstand the stubborn teachers of works. Of this we will say more later.

Christ also, in Matthew 17, when the tribute money was demanded of His disciples, argued with St. Peter whether the sons of the king were not free from the payment of tribute, and Peter affirmed that they were. Nonetheless Christ commanded Peter to go to the sea, and said, "Lest we should offend them, go, and take up the fish that first cometh up, and when thou hast opened his mouth, thou shalt find a piece of money: that take, and give unto them for me and thee" (Matt. 17:24ff). This incident fits beautifully to our subject, since Christ here calls Himself and those that are His, children and sons of the King, who need nothing, and yet He freely submits and pays the tribute. Just as necessary or helpful as this work was to Christ's righteousness or salvation, just so much do all other works of His or of His followers avail for righteousness, since they all follow after righteousness and are free, and are done only to serve others and to give them an example of good works.

Of the same nature are the precepts which Paul gives, in Romans 13:1ff and Titus 3:1, that Christians should be subject to the powers that be, and be ready to do every good work, not that they shall in this way be justified, since they already are righteous through faith, but that in the liberty of the Spirit they shall by so doing serve others and the powers themselves, and obey their will freely and out of love. Of this nature should be the works of all colleges, monasteries, and priests. Each one should do the works of his profession and position, not that by them he may strive after righteousness, but that through them he may keep under his body, be an example to others, who also need to keep under their bodies, and finally that by such works he may submit his will to that of others in the freedom of love. But very great care must always be taken that no man in a false confidence imagine that by such works he will be justified, or acquire merit, or be saved, for this is the work of faith alone, as I have repeatedly said.

Anyone knowing this could easily and without danger find his way among those numberless mandates and precepts of pope, bishops, monasteries, churches, princes, and magistrates, upon which some ignorant pastors insist as if they were necessary to righteousness and salvation, calling them "precepts of the Church," although they are nothing of the kind. For a Christian, as a free man, will say, 'I will fast, pray, do this and that as men command, not because it is necessary to my righteousness or salvation, but that I may show due respect to the pope, the bishop, the community, some magistrate, or my neighbor, and give them an example, I will do and suffer all things, just as Christ did and suffered far more for me, although He needed nothing of it all for Himself, and was made under the law for my sake, although He was not under the law.' And although tyrants do violence or injustice in making their demands, yet it will do no harm, so long as they demand nothing contrary to God.

From what has been said, everyone can pass a safe judgment on all works and laws and make a trustworthy distinction between them, and know who are the blind and ignorant pastors and who are the good and true. For any work that is not done solely for the purpose of keeping under the body or of serving one's neighbor, so long as he asks nothing contrary to God, is not good nor Christian. And for this reason I mightily fear that few or no colleges, monasteries, altars, and offices of the Church are really Christian in our day, no, nor the special fasts and prayers on certain saints' days either. I fear, I say, that in all these we seek only our own profit, thinking that through them our sins are purged away and that we find salvation in them. In this way Christian liberty perishes altogether. And this comes from our ignorance of Christian faith and of liberty.

This ignorance and suppression of liberty very many blind pastors take pains to encourage: they stir up and urge on their people in these practices by praising such works, puffing them up with their indulgences, and never teaching faith. But I would counsel you, if you wish to pray, fast, or establish some foundation in the Church, take heed not to do it in order to obtain some benefit, whether temporal or eternal. For you would do injury to your faith, which alone offers you all things. Your one care should be that faith may increase, whether it be trained by works or by sufferings. Give your gifts freely and for nothing, that others may profit by them and are well because of you and your goodness. In this way you shall be truly good and Christian. For of what benefit to you are the good works which you do not need for the keeping under of your body? Your faith is sufficient for you, through which God has given you all things.

See, according to this rule the good things we have from God should flow from one to the other and be common to all, so that every one should "put on" his neighbor, and so conduct himself toward him as if he himself were in the other's place. From Christ they have flowed and are flowing into us: He has so "put on" us and acted for us as if He had been what we are. From us they flow on to those who have need of them, so that I should lay before God my faith and my righteousness that they may cover and intercede for the sins of my neighbor, which I take upon myself and so labor and serve in them as if they were my very own. For that is what Christ did for us. This is true love and the genuine rule of a Christian life. The love is true and genuine where there is true and genuine faith. Hence, the apostle says of love in 1 Corinthians 13, that it seeketh not its own (v. 5).

We conclude, therefore, that a Christian man lives not in himself, but in Christ and in his neighbor. Otherwise he is not a Christian. He lives in Christ through faith, in his neighbor through love; by faith he is caught up beyond himself into God, by love he sinks down beneath himself into his neighbor, yet he always remains in God and in His love, as Christ says in John 1, "Verily, I say unto you, hereafter ye shall see Heaven open, and the angels of God ascending and descending upon the Son of man" (v. 51).

Enough now of liberty. As you see, it is a spiritual and true liberty, and makes our hearts free from all sins, laws and mandates, as Paul says, 1 Timothy 1, "The law is not made for a righteous man" (v. 9). It is more excellent than all other liberty which is external, as Heaven is more excellent than earth. This liberty may Christ grant us both to understand and to preserve, Amen.

Finally, something must be added for the sake of those for whom nothing can be so well said that they will not spoil it by misunderstanding it, though it is a question whether they will understand even what shall here be said. There are very many who, when they hear of this liberty of faith, immediately turn it into an occasion for the flesh, and think that now all things are allowed them. They want to show that they are free men and Christians only by despising and finding fault with ceremonies, traditions, and human laws; as if they were Christians because on stated days they do not fast or eat meat when others fast, or because they do not use the accustomed prayers, and with upturned nose scoff at the precepts of men, although they utterly disregard all else that pertains to the Christian religion. The extreme opposite of these are those who rely for their salvation solely on their reverent observance of ceremonies, as if they would be saved because on certain days they fast or abstain from meats, or pray certain prayers; these make a boast of the precepts of the Church and of the Fathers, and care not a fig for the things which are of the essence of our faith. Plainly both are in error, because they neglect the weightier things which are necessary to salvation, and quarrel so noisily about those trifling and unnecessary matters.

How much better is the teaching of the apostle Paul, who bids us take a middle course, and condemns both sides when he says, "Let not him that eateth despise him that eateth not; and let not him which eateth not judge him that eateth" (Rom. 14:3). Here you see that they who neglect and disparage ceremonies, not out of piety, but out of mere contempt, are reproved, since the apostle teaches us not to despise them. Such men are puffed up by knowledge. On the other hand, he teaches those who insist on the ceremonies not to judge the others, for neither party acts toward the other according to the love that edifies. Wherefore, we ought here to listen to the Scriptures, which teach that we should not go aside to the right nor to the left (Deut. 28:14), but follow the statutes of the Lord which are right, rejoicing the heart (Ps. 19:8). For as a man is not righteous because he keeps and clings to the works and forms of the ceremonies, so also will a man not be counted righteous merely because he neglects and despises them.

Our faith in Christ does not free us from works, but from false opinions concerning works, that is, from the foolish presumption that justification is acquired by works. For faith redeems, corrects, and preserves our consciences, so that we know that righteousness does not consist in works, although works neither can nor ought to be wanting, just as we cannot be without food and drink and all the works of this mortal body, yet our righteousness is not in them, but in faith; and yet those works of the body are not to be despised or neglected on that account. In this world we are bound by the needs of our bodily life, but we are not righteous because of them. "My kingdom is not of this world" (John 18:36), says Christ, but He does not say, "My kingdom is not here, that is, in this world." And Paul says, "Though we walk in the flesh, we do not war after the flesh" (2 Cor. 10:3), and in Galatians 2, "The life which I now live in the flesh, I live in the faith of the Son of God" (v. 20). Thus what we do, live, and are in works and in ceremonies, we do because of the necessities of this life and of the effort to rule our body; nevertheless we are righteous not in these, but in the faith of the Son of God.

Hence, the Christian must take a middle course and face those two classes of men. He will meet first the unyielding, stubborn ceremonialists, who like deaf adders (Ps. 58:4) are not willing to hear the truth of liberty, but having no faith boast of, prescribe, and insist upon their ceremonies as means of justification. Such were the Jews of old, who were unwilling to learn how to do good. These he must resist, do the very opposite, and offend them boldly, lest by their impious views they drag many with them into error. In the presence of such men it is good to eat meat, to break the fasts, and for the sake of the liberty of faith to do other things which they regard the greatest of sins. Of them we must say, "Let them alone, they are blind and leaders of the blind" (Matt. 15:14). For on this principle Paul would not circumcise Titus when the Jews insisted that he should (Gal. 2:3), and Christ excused the apostles when they plucked ears of corn on the sabbath (Matt. 12:1ff), and there are many similar instances. The other class of men whom a Christian will meet, are the simple-minded, ignorant men, weak in the faith, as the apostle calls them, who cannot yet grasp the liberty of faith, even if they were willing to do so. These he must take care not to offend; he must yield to their weakness until they are more fully instructed. For since these do and think as they do, not because they are stubbornly wicked, but only because their faith is weak, the fasts and other things which they think necessary must be observed to avoid giving them offence. For so love demands, which would harm no one, but would serve all men. It is not by their fault that they are weak, but their pastors have taken them captive with the snares of their traditions and have wickedly used these traditions as rods with which to beat them. From these pastors they should have been delivered by the teaching of faith and liberty. So the apostle teaches us, Romans 14, "If my meat cause my brother to offend, I will eat no flesh while the world standeth" and again, "I know that through Christ nothing is unclean, except to him who esteemeth anything to be unclean, but it is evil for the man who eats and is offended" (v. 14).

Wherefore, although we should boldly resist those teachers of traditions and sharply censure the laws of the popes by means of which they plunder the people of God, yet we must spare the timid multitude whom those impious tyrants hold captive by means of these laws, until they be set free. Fight strenuously therefore against the wolves, but for the sheep, and not also against the sheep. This you will do if you inveigh against the laws and the lawgivers, and at the same time observe the laws with the weak, so that they will not be offended, until they also recognize the tyranny and understand their liberty. But if you wish to use your liberty, do so in secret, as Paul says, "Hast thou the faith? Have it to thyself before God" (Rom. 14:22), but take care not to use your liberty in the sight of the weak. On the other hand, use your liberty constantly and consistently in the sight of the tyrants and the stubborn, in despite of them, that they also may learn that they are impious, that their laws are of no avail for righteousness, and that they had no right to set them up.

Now, since we cannot live our life without ceremonies and works, and the froward and untrained youth need to be restrained and saved from harm by such bonds, and since each one should keep his body under by means of such works, there is need that the minister of Christ be farseeing and faithful; he ought so to govern and teach the people of Christ in all these matters that their conscience and faith be not offended, and that there spring not up in them a suspicion and a root of bitterness, and many be defiled thereby (Heb. 12:15), as Paul admonishes the Hebrews, that is, that they may not lose faith and become defiled by the false estimate of the value of works, and think that they must be justified by works. This happens easily and defiles very many, unless faith is at the same time constantly taught; it is impossible to avoid it when faith is not mentioned and only the devisings of men are taught, as has been done until now through the pestilent, impious, soul-destroying traditions of our popes and the opinions of our theologians. By these snares numberless souls have been dragged down to Hell, so that you might see in this the work of antichrist.

In brief, as wealth is the test of poverty, business the test of faithfulness, honors the test of humility, feasts the test of temperance, pleasures the test of chastity, so ceremonies are the test of the righteousness of faith. "Can a man," says Solomon, "take fire in his bosom, and his clothes not be burned?" (Prov. 6:27). Yet, as a man must live in the midst of wealth, business, honors, pleasures, and feasts, so also must he live in the midst of ceremonies, that is, in the midst of dangers. Nay, as infant boys need beyond all else to be cherished in the bosoms and by the hands of maidens to keep them from perishing, and yet when they are grown up their salvation is endangered if they associate with maidens, so the inexperienced and froward youth need to be restrained and trained by the iron bars of ceremonies, lest their unchecked ardor rush headlong into vice after vice. Yet it would be death for them to be always held in bondage to ceremonies, thinking that these justify them. They are rather to be taught that they have been so imprisoned in ceremonies, not that they should be made righteous or gain great merit by them, but that they might thus be kept from doing evil, and might be more easily instructed unto the righteousness of faith. Such instruction they would not endure if the impulsiveness of their youth were not restrained. Hence ceremonies are to be given the same place in the life of a Christian as models and plans have among builders and artisans. They are prepared not as permanent structures, but because without them nothing could be built or made. When the structure is completed they are laid aside. You see, they are not despised, rather, they are greatly sought after, but what we despise is the false estimate of them, since no one holds them to be the real and permanent structure. If any man were so egregiously foolish as to care for nothing all his life long except the most costly, careful, and persistent preparation of plans and models, and never to think of the structure itself, and were satisfied with his work in producing such plans and mere aids to work, and boasted of it, would not all men pity his insanity, and estimate that with what he has wasted something great might have been built? Thus we do not despise ceremonies and works, nay, we set great store by them, but we despise the false estimate placed upon works, in order that no one may think that they are true righteousness, as those hypocrites believe who spend and lose their whole lives in zeal for works, and never reach that for the sake of which the works are to be done, as the apostle says, "ever learning and never able to come to the knowledge of the truth" (2 Tim. 3:7). For they seem to wish to build, they make their preparations, and yet they never build. Thus they remain caught in the form of godliness and do not attain unto its power (2 Tim. 3:5). Meanwhile they are pleased with their efforts, and even dare to judge all others whom they do not see shining with a like show of works. Yet with the gifts of God which they have spent and abused in vain they might, if they had been filled with faith, have accomplished great things to the salvation of themselves and of others.

But since human nature and natural reason, as it is called, are by nature superstitious and ready to imagine, when laws and works are prescribed, that righteousness must be obtained through them, and further, since they are trained and confirmed in this opinion by the practice of all earthly lawgivers, it is impossible that they should of themselves escape from the slavery of works and come to a knowledge of the liberty of faith. Therefore there is need of the prayer that the Lord may give us (John 6:45) and make us *theodidacti*, that is, "taught of God," and Himself, as He has promised, write His law in our hearts; otherwise there is no hope for us. For if He Himself do not teach our hearts this wisdom hidden in a mystery (1 Cor. 2:7), nature can only condemn it and judge it to be heretical, because nature is offended by it and regards it as foolishness. So we see that it happened in olden times, in the case of the apostles and prophets, and so godless and blind popes and their flatterers do to me and to those who are like me. May God at last be merciful to them and to us, and cause His face to shine upon us (Ps. 67:1ff), that we may know His way upon earth, His salvation among all nations, God, Who is blessed forever (2 Cor. 11:31). Amen.

Made in the USA
Columbia, SC
30 October 2023